Reading the
Corinthian Correspondence

An Introduction

by
Kevin Quast

PAULIST PRESS

New York, N.Y./Mahwah, N.J.

The Scripture quotations contained herein are from the New Revised Standard Version of the Bible, copyrighted 1989 by the Division of Christian Education of the National Council of Churches of Christ in the United States of America, and are used by permission. All rights reserved.

Library of Congress Cataloging-in-Publication Data

Quast, Kevin
     Reading the Corinthian correspondence : an introduction / by Kevin Quast
          p.   cm.
     Includes bibliographical references and index.
     ISBN 0-8091-3481-0 (pbk.)
     1. Bible. N.T. Corinthians--Criticism, interpretation, etc. 2. Paul, the Apostle, Saint. 3. Bible. N.T. Epistles of Paul--Criticism, interpretation, etc. I. Title.
BS2675.2.Q37 1994
227'.207--dc20   94-15074
                                                                                                          CIP

Published by Paulist Press
997 Macarthur Blvd.
Mahwah, N.J. 07430

Printed and bound in the United States of America

CONTENTS

GUIDE TO CHARTS AND MAPS

Acknowledgments

This book is dedicated to my parents, John and Olive Quast. I will always be grateful for their love, support, and Christian example.

I thank Larry Matthews, my friend and editor, for his kind but thorough work on these chapters. Thanks also go to those students at Ontario Theological Seminary who took my courses on the Corinthian correspondence; they have helped me sort out many issues. As always, Sandra, Kira, and Graham have shared their love and encouragement at home as I wrote.

Chapter 1

THE LIFE AND LETTERS OF PAUL

Introduction

The news from Corinth is disturbing. Paul must respond. Yet, a visit is out of the question: the apostle also has pressing concerns here in Ephesus. He calls his secretary: it's time to write another letter. Tomorrow he will send Stephanas across the Aegean Sea with counsel for the troubled church...

* * *

During his ministry, Paul used letters to minister to a few struggling churches in Asia Minor and Greece. While the letters addressed immediate specific local issues, their influence did not end there. The author would have been surprised to learn that they were collected, copied, and distributed to an audience that would eventually span continents, cultures, and centuries.

Paul gave the church its earliest and most extensive written interpretations of Christ's saving work. As the canon of the New Testament grew, his place at its center was firmly established. Within fifty years of signing his last letter, other Christians were citing him authoritatively:

> So also our beloved brother Paul wrote to you according to the wisdom given him, speaking of this as he does in all his letters. There are some things in them hard to understand, which the ignorant and unstable twist to their own destruction, as they do the other scriptures (2 Pet 3:15-16).

1

We can draw several conclusions from this statement. First, by the time 2 Peter was written the writer could assume his readers knew several of Paul's letters. Collections were likely circulating. Second, even Paul's opponents summoned support from his letters. Such a tacit acknowledgment from unfriendly witnesses provides evidence of the apostle's stature. Third, Paul's letters are named with the "*other* scriptures." Simply put, they already enjoyed the same authoritative status as the Old Testament.

Since then, generations have turned to Paul for theology, inspiration, ethics, pastoral guidance, and mission strategy. His teachings have stimulated many pivotal steps in the history of Christianity. Even today Paul speaks directly to readers.

However, Paul's letters carry an equally timeless interpretive danger. As 2 Peter 3:16 says: "There are some things in them hard to understand, which the ignorant and unstable twist to their own destruction."

Certainly there are perplexing comments in Paul's letters. The Corinthian letters offer many examples: Who are the "virgins" Paul speaks of in 1 Corinthians 7:25-38? What did he mean when he said that women should cover their heads "because of the angels" (1 Cor 11:10)? Did he condone "baptism on behalf of the dead" (1 Cor 15:29)? How are we to understand our ongoing transformation "from one degree of glory to another" (2 Cor 3:18)? What was Paul's "thorn in the flesh" (2 Cor 12:2-7)?

Improperly interpreted, Paul's letters obscure first century congregations and create distortions in the church today. Properly interpreted, those same letters open a door into the world of the earliest Christians and yield ageless principles by which to live.

For example, the venue changes from chapter to chapter in 1 and 2 Corinthians. Paul travels by dusty road and merchant ship. Through his eyes we observe worship in the synagogue, the pagan temple, and the Christian house group. He brings us from the marketplace into the courtroom. We follow him to the prison and the stadium. He sketches imagery from the farmer's field and the construction site. At home, he faces issues in the kitchen and the bedroom.

In every place, Paul finds Christ. Because Christ is present, Paul finds meaning. This book is designed to help discover that meaning and apply it to our circumstances. We will enter the world of Corinthian Christians, wrestle with their issues, and learn from them.

The Corinthian letters chronicle a lengthy and involved ministry, so throughout the book we will correlate much of 1 and 2 Corinthians with information about Paul and his churches found elsewhere. Chapter 1 will survey Paul's life, chapter 15 will compare the Corinthian letters to other letters in the New Testament, and chapter 16 will isolate the major themes of Paul's theology. Hopefully, further studies in Paul will beckon.

The Life of Paul

The more we know about the person Paul, the better we understand his message to Corinth. To learn about him, we have his letters and the book of Acts.

Sources

As primary source material, the letters must be our starting point. When examined for setting, each contributes a chapter to Paul's life story. Contextual questions are a productive starting point: What is happening in the church to which Paul writes? How did the apostle learn of these circumstances? Where is Paul as he writes? Who is with him? When was Paul's last visit? Has he sent them anyone else on his behalf? What are his travel plans?

For these questions, even incidental comments become valuable. By relating the historical setting of the letters to each other we can reconstruct a large part of the apostle's career. We can trace developments in the life and thought of Paul, his churches, and their societies.

However, the nature of the correspondence also limits its perspective. First, we are listening only to one side of the conversation. Second, we enter the dialogue at midpoint and see just occasional snapshots of constantly changing situations. Third, even considering all the information, we still cannot be certain we have ordered some letters in their proper sequence.

Also, a few of the letters traditionally attributed to Paul may not have come directly from him. Most scholars believe that someone else wrote Ephesians, 1 and 2 Timothy, Titus, and perhaps 2 Thessalonians. Although cases can be made for Pauline authorship, these letters may offer portraits of Paul as seen through the eyes of another. Regardless of their theological importance, we are advised to consider them secondary sources for a biography of Paul.

Unarguably a secondary source, the book of Acts nonetheless augments Paul's story in the letters. Besides the corroboration it offers for much in Paul's letters, Acts provides original information. For example, only Acts reports that Paul was from Tarsus (Acts 9:11; 11:25; 21:39; 22:3) and was born a Roman citizen (Acts 16:37-38; 22:25-28). Without the testimony of Acts, we would not know that Paul was a tentmaker (Acts 18:3). Perhaps most significant, Acts gives a fixed date around which a chronology of Paul's life can be built: Paul was in Corinth when Gallio presided as proconsul (Acts 18:12-16). Archeological evidence places Gallio at Corinth in A.D. 51.

However, for historical reconstructions of Paul's activities, we must use Acts with discernment. We cannot be certain that the author of Acts ever accompanied Paul on any of his journeys. Though four passages read as if the author were one of Paul's companions (Acts 16:10-17; 20:5-15; 21:1-18; 27:1–28:16), scholars do not agree on the significance of the use of the first person plural "we" here.

Assuming he is the same person who wrote the gospel of Luke, we know that the author of Acts consulted many other sources to write his account (Lk 1:1-4; cf. Acts 1:1). In other words, "Luke" depends on the recollections of others. What is more, he shapes his sources according to definite theological and apologetic purposes.

Acts begins with Jesus' parting words to the apostles: "... you will receive power when the Holy Spirit has come upon you; and you will be my witnesses in Jerusalem, in all Judea and Samaria, and to the ends of the earth" (Acts 1:8). With these words, Luke gives us the governing structure for his second book to Theophilus. He features the expansion of the good news of salvation to all people from the city of Jerusalem, north through Judea, into Samaria and beyond to Antioch of Syria (Acts 1–12).

Once the church has established its identity independent of Judaism, it reaches out to the rest of the world (Acts 13–28). Paul now takes over from Peter as the central apostolic hero. The gospel takes hold in Asia Minor, the Aegean coastlands and, finally, Rome.

Luke describes a church that is in transition not only geographically, but religiously and socially. Despite hardships, misunderstandings, internal strife, and persecution, it grows under the prayer-induced power of the Holy Spirit. It is an encouraging story designed to elicit and strengthen faith.

Luke also wrote to defend Christianity from the charge that it was a political threat to the Roman empire. He argues that, as a newborn in the cradle of Judaism, the church deserved its mother's status of *religio licita* (legal religion). Consequently, Jerusalem figures prominently in Luke's unfolding scenario. Tensions arise only because Christianity is outgrowing the household rules of Judaism. Like Jews, however, Christians were not subversive. According to Acts, wherever local unrest surfaces Paul and his Christians are not responsible. When Roman officials investigate they hand down favorable verdicts for Christians.

Because of his apologetic agendas, Luke omits many of Paul's whippings by Jews, beatings by Gentiles, imprisonments, and even a life-threatening contest "with wild animals at Ephesus" (1 Cor 15:32; 2 Cor 1:8; 11:24-25). The protracted battle Paul wages in his churches with opponents who insist on circumcision and the Jewish law (cf. esp. Gal 3–5; Phil 3:1-11; 2 Cor 11) also receives understandably scant notice in Acts. Even the differences between the description of the "apostolic council" in Galatians 2 and Acts 15 can be explained in light of Luke's apologetic.

Consequently, when biographical discrepancies between Paul's letters and Acts arise, the testimony of the letters must prevail. Always Luke's theological and apologetic purposes must be factored into our interpretation. When we do this, an exciting story of a remarkable man emerges.

Paul, the Roman Citizen

We do not know much about Paul's childhood. He was born of Jewish parents in Tarsus, Cilicia sometime before A.D. 10. Situated on a fertile plain along a river ten miles from the Mediterranean, Tarsus then had a population of more than 500,000. It enjoyed a reputation as "an important city" (Acts 21:39) — a prosperous intellectual center rivaling Athens and Alexandria.

Tarsus no doubt contributed to the familiarity with Hellenistic and Asian philosophy, religion, and literature that Paul displays in his letters. Evidently, Tarsus also helped make him a true urbanite. Throughout his life Paul gravitated toward large cities, using all the dynamics of the urban environment to build churches. Metaphors from city life abound in Paul's teachings.

Besides being a citizen of Tarsus, Paul was also born a citizen of Rome (Acts 16:37-38; 22:25-28), a testimony to the social stature of his parents. More than once his dual citizenship stood him in good stead as he faced harsh treatment at the hands of municipal authorities in Greece and Asia Minor. Anywhere in the empire, Roman citizens had the right to appeal directly to Rome when serious charges were laid against them.

In Tarsus Paul learned the trade of tentmaking. Likely his father trained him, as was the custom. For Paul, tentmaking would prove to be a secure occupation that would provide well for him and give flexibility for his ministry. Made of either textiles or leather, tents were home for many throughout the Mediterranean. Growing up in Cilicia, Paul may have worked particularly with cilicum, a goat's hair cloth woven in the district and favored by seamen and soldiers.

Paul, the Jew

Paul's father passed on something more fundamental than his citizenship and craft to the young Paul—he handed down his Jewish heritage. Paul gives us some of this background in Philippians 3:5: "circumcised on the eighth day, a member of the people of Israel, of the tribe of Benjamin, a Hebrew born of Hebrews..." (see also chapter 14, Figure 14-1).

Circumcised an ethnic Israelite at one week old in strict accordance with the law, Paul began life with sterling Jewish credentials. Besides his Greek name, he was given the Benjaminite name "Saul" after the noble tribe's famous king. Unlike so many Jews outside Palestine who spoke only Greek, Paul's parents also spoke Hebrew (Aramaic) with their son (cf. also 2 Cor 11:22). He was educated in the traditions of Judaism from the cradle.

With other boys, Paul entered Torah instruction at the local synagogue school. He tells us he soon distinguished himself: "I advanced in Judaism beyond many among my people of the same age, for I was far more zealous for the traditions of my ancestors" (Gal 1:14). As he matured, he underwent further study in the Jewish legal traditions. Eventually he became a rabbi, or recognized teacher, of the Pharisaic party.

Pharisees, or "separated ones," were influential sectarians at the center of synagogue life. They were dedicated to obeying the Mosaic law and the legal traditions that arose as they were applied to everyday life. Their meticulous observance of moral imperatives, ritual purification, food tithing, dietary laws, and sabbath-keeping distinguished them. Unlike the Sadducees, they believed in a bodily resurrection, life after death, eternal reward and punishment, and a coming messiah.

Luke tells us that Paul came from a family of Pharisees (Acts 23:6). Luke also reports that Paul took his rabbinic training in Jerusalem under Gamaliel (Acts 22:3), though it is hard to explain why Paul's letters never claim this when listing his Jewish credentials. Still, Paul likely spent some time at the rabbi's school in Jerusalem for he models Gamaliel's method of scriptural interpretation and rabbinic reasoning.

He may have boarded at his married sister's home in Jerusalem (Acts 23:16).

The rabbi Gamaliel was the leading Pharisee of Paul's time. Carrying on in the tradition of his famous ancestor Hillel, Gamaliel was known for his respect of the Torah, his sensitivity, his righteousness, and his wisdom. After the preaching of the apostles incensed the Jewish ruling council, Gamaliel advised the Sanhedrin to be patient. "If this plan or this undertaking is of human origin, it will fail," he noted, "but if it is of God, you will not be able to overthrow them" (Acts 5:27-39).

Paul shared Gamaliel's convictions about God's sovereignty and the central place of the law in the life of God's people. However, if Paul were indeed a student of Gamaliel, he did not adopt his teacher's tolerance. Soon after Gamaliel's counsel won the apostles' release, we read of Paul (Saul) standing by, approvingly, while Stephen was stoned (Acts 7:58–8:1). After this he waged a personal holy war against Christians (e.g. 1 Cor 15:9; Gal 1:13, 23; Phil 3:6; Acts 8:3; 9:1-2; 26:9-11). This avowed enemy of the church was in for the biggest shock of his life.

Paul, the Christian

Compared to his encounter with Christ on the road to Damascus, Paul's childhood in Tarsus and his rabbinic education are but minor factors in the making of the man. Several accounts of this pivotal event illuminate its impact.

As Paul describes it, while he "was violently persecuting the church . . . God, who had set me apart before I was born and called me through his grace, was pleased to reveal his Son to me, so that I might proclaim him among the Gentiles" (Gal 1:13, 15-16). The risen Christ confronted Paul and immediately reoriented his life (cf. also 1 Cor 9:1; 15:8-10; Phil 3:4-12).

Acts relates Paul's conversion and commission in three places (Acts 9, 22, 26; see Figure 1-1). The first is Luke's narration of the event, the other two are part of Paul's speeches in his own defense. Including the story three times testifies to Luke's opinion of its importance.

Though the three accounts cohere well, there are significant differences in several details (see Figure 1-1). These differences can be harmonized, but to stop at that would be to miss Luke's point in each case. Acts 9 stresses that, unlike his traveling companions, Paul has truly seen the risen Christ just as other apostles have. Acts 22 elevates Paul's experience above even that of the other apostles. He has met

Parallel Accounts of Paul's Conversion in Acts

Acts 9:3-9

Now as he was going along and approaching Damascus, suddenly a light from heaven flashed about him. *He fell to the ground and heard a voice* saying to him, "Saul, Saul, why do you persecute me?" He asked, "Who are you, Lord?" The reply came, "I am Jesus, whom you are persecuting. But get up and enter the city, and you will be told what you are to do." *The men who were traveling with him stood speechless because they heard the voice but saw no one.* Saul got up from the ground, and though his eyes were open, he could see nothing; so they led him by the hand and brought him into Damascus. For three days he was without sight, and neither ate nor drank.

Acts 22:6-11

"While I was on my way and approaching Damascus, about noon a great light from heaven shone about me. *I fell to the ground and heard a voice* saying to me, 'Saul, Saul, why are you persecuting me?' I answered, 'Who are you, Lord?' Then he said to me, 'I am Jesus of Nazareth, whom you are persecuting.' *Now those who were with me saw the light but did not hear the voice* of the one who was speaking to me. I asked, 'What am I to do, Lord?' The Lord said to me, 'Get up and go to Damascus; there you will be told everything that has been assigned to you to do.' Since I could not see because of the brightness of that light, those who were with me took my hand and led me to Damascus."

Acts 26:12-18

"With this in mind, I was traveling to Damascus with the authority and commission of the chief priests, when at midday along the road, your Excellency, I saw a light from heaven, brighter than the sun, *shine about me and my companions. When we had all fallen to the ground, I heard a voice* saying to me in the *Hebrew language*, 'Saul, Saul, why are you persecuting me? *It hurts you to kick against the goads.*' I asked, 'Who are you, Lord?' The Lord answered, 'I am Jesus whom you are persecuting. But get up and stand on your feet; *for I have appeared to you for this purpose, to appoint you to serve and testify to the things in which you have seen me and to those in which I will appear to you. I will rescue you from your people and from the Gentiles — to whom I am sending you to open their eyes so that they may turn from darkness to light and from the power of Satan to God, so that they may receive forgiveness of sins and a place among those who are sanctified by faith in me.'*"

Significant Differences Between Accounts

1. Paul falls to the ground; the others "stood speechless."	1. Paul falls to the ground.	1. All fall to the ground.
2. Paul sees the light; the others "saw no one."	2. All see the light.	2. The light shines around all.
3. All hear the voice.	3. Only Paul hears the voice.	3. Only Paul hears the voice, and now we are told it is in Hebrew. The Greek idiom "It hurts you to kick against the goads" is included, as is Paul's commission to be apostle to the Gentiles.

--- **FIGURE 1-1** ---

Christ exalted in glory. Those with him can testify to the manifestation of that glory although they cannot share in the personal nature of Paul's encounter.

Finally, Acts 26 recalls the initial visions in which Israel's prophets received their commissions (cf. Jer 1:4-19; Ez 1–4; Is 6). In this version, Paul's call to preach to the Gentiles is linked directly to his initial encounter with the Lord on the road.

Paul includes the words "...it hurts you to kick against the goads" (Acts 26:14) as he describes his confrontation with the Lord. Goads were pointed sticks used to prod animals in the right direction while they were under harness. The Greek idiom was used figuratively to refer to the futility of resisting the will of the gods. So, in the context of Paul's speech, the Roman hearers would understand that Paul was acting contrary to God's will and he had to change direction. Paul may be further suggesting that his audience stop resisting God's proddings.

Rather than understand the reference to the goads as evangelistic strategy, a few scholars see in these words a disillusioned Pharisee. They suggest that Paul was fighting the nagging possibility that he was resisting God's will in his legalistic campaign. On the Damascus road his anxious doubts get the better of him. Finally defeated, Paul breaks down in frustration and surrenders to God.

That interpretation is inconsistent with what we know of Judaism and Paul's retrospective comments about his pre-Christian experience. All indications are that Paul was content as a Jew and certain of his covenantal relationship with God. Grateful love, and not internalized frustration, fueled Paul's zeal. In other words, he was a most unlikely candidate for conversion.

God presented the solution before Paul realized there was a problem. Now, however, the startled Paul recognized that he had been living contrary to God's will. This encounter gave Paul a radically different understanding of God's ways.

One conclusion was inescapable: Jesus was alive. What is more, Jesus, now exalted in glory, was somehow united with both the Lord whom Paul worshiped and the Christians he persecuted. Paul's reverent question "Who are you, Lord?" and the Lord's answer "I am Jesus, whom you are persecuting" united God the Father, Jesus the Son, and the church his body. Now Paul found himself part of this body—he was "in Christ."

These realizations were the foundation for the rest of Paul's ministry. Most scholars speak of Paul's theology being built on a "functional christology"—his understanding of God and his will for humanity began with what the apostle knew of Jesus Christ. Whenever Paul confronted a theological or pastoral question, he turned to his relationship with Christ for an answer.

Paul eventually saw Christ as the Lord of all creation. As in Adam all died, so in Christ all could live. Christ alone was victorious over the powers of sin and death. The Mosaic law's function was to lead to faith in Christ. By faith people were incorporated into Christ; he was the head of a mysterious, interdependent body that transcended geographical, racial, social, and sexual barriers. Those in Christ now lived by the "law of Christ" written in their hearts. Christ, the resurrected one, would be the resurrecter for those who died in him. That hope, and all others, would be realized when Jesus the messiah returned in glory to establish completely his reign.

At his conversion, God not only gave Paul a christological center around which to build a new life. He also gave him a special commissioning to be apostle to the Gentiles. Paul is particularly adamant in Galatians 1–2. He identifies himself as "an apostle — sent neither by human commission nor from human authorities, but through Jesus Christ" (Gal 1:1). He goes on to claim: "the gospel that was proclaimed to me is not of human origin; for I did not receive it from a human source, nor was I taught it, but I received it from a revelation of Jesus Christ" (Gal 1:11-12; cf. also 1:16-17).

Paul's distinctive understanding of the gospel, particularly as it relates to Gentiles and the Jewish law, did not arise from any human counsel. No church council in Jerusalem was convened; no other apostles nominated or initiated him. Still, the Jerusalem apostles did eventually approve of "Paul's gospel" and he did learn about the historical Jesus from other Christians. Paul invokes the support of these other "acknowledged leaders" for his gospel (Gal 2:2-10) and occasionally he passes on what others have taught him about Jesus (e.g. Rom 8:15; 1 Cor 7:10; 11:2, 23; 15:1-5).

While relations between Paul and the Jerusalem apostles were sometimes strained, he maintained a working arrangement with them and other Christian missionaries. He would not compromise on his understanding of the gospel but he preferred to work with a team. Above all, he was determined to fulfill his calling to spread the good news of Jesus Christ in the Gentile world.

A Basic Pauline Chronology

Most general introductions to the New Testament offer maps that trace Paul's "three missionary journeys." Gleaned from Acts, the itineraries all begin and end at Antioch. Paul visits Jerusalem before and after each expedition. The first journey ranges through Syria, Cyprus, southern Galatia and Cilicia. The second and third expand into Asia Minor and Greece.

These outlines may be convenient in organizing an outline of Paul's life. However, they impose an artificial structure on the chain of events. While the strategic place of Antioch and the repeated link to Jerusalem fit its agenda, the book of Acts does not clearly demarcate three distinct missions. More important, Paul's letters show he responded to immediate opportunities, traveling as needs arose, instead of planning a campaign from start to finish. He found himself returning to Corinth and Ephesus more often than the supposed "headquarters" in Jerusalem.

A basic outline of Paul's ministry can be drawn from his letters and corroborated from Acts, as Figure 1-2 shows. While scholars disagree on many details, we can see the important directions of Paul's travels as his apostolic ministry unfolded.

Dates are notoriously difficult to fix for most of Paul's career because there are few allusions in Paul's letters to events in the contemporary political world. Still, we can date Paul's arrival in Corinth in A.D. 49. A year and a half later he appeared before the Corinthian proconsul Gallio and then left Corinth (Acts 18:12). An inscription discovered at Delphi dates Gallio's short tenure in A.D. 51.

Different chronologies of Paul's life often vary by at least three years. This is because scholars are not sure whether the "three years" Paul mentions in Galatians 1:18 are to be added to, or included in, the "fourteen years" he cites in Galatians 2:1. More important than actual dates, however, is the *sequence* of events in Paul's life. Fortunately, this sequence is quite clear except for identifying how often Paul traveled to Jerusalem and the placement of the letter to the Galatians.

Paul may have written to the non-Galatian residents of the southern area of the Roman province of Galatia early, even before he wrote to the Thessalonians. Or he may have written the letter later to ethnic Galatians in the northern reaches of the province. If he wrote to the northern Galatians, as suggested in Figure 1-2, then we must take him at face value about making *only* two trips to Jerusalem when he wrote to Galatia. Luke, then, has described the same Jerusalem visit more than once (Acts 11 and 15).

In addition, we are not sure that we have all of Paul's letters, nor can we be certain of their exact setting and sequence. Their present canonical order, apparently based on letter length, does not represent their original chronology and form.

An Outline of Paul's Apostolic Career

	Date	Major Events	Letters Written
	34	Paul meets the risen Christ on the road to Damascus. He visits disciples in the city and receives confirmation of his apostolic calling (Gal 1:15-17; Acts 9:1-22; 22:4-16; 26:9-18).	
The Early Period	34-37	Leaving Damascus, Paul withdraws to Arabia for three years. Nothing is known of the nature of his activity here (Gal 1:17-18a).	
ca. A.D. 34-37	37	Upon returning to Damascus, Paul is threatened by the local governor at Jewish instigation. He escapes by night over the city wall (2 Cor 11:32-33; Acts 9:23-25).	
(All dates are approximate)	37	Now three years after his conversion, Paul makes his "acquaintance visit" to Jerusalem. He stays fifteen days, meeting only Peter and James (Gal 1:18-19; Acts 9:26-30).	
┌ – – – – ⁱ Journey 1	38	From Antioch, Paul begins missionary work in Syria and Cilicia (Gal 1:21-22; Acts 11:26).	
└ – – – –		[*Acts reports a "famine visit" to Jerusalem where Paul agreed to a collection for relief in Judea. After this Luke describes missionary work in Cyprus and southern Galatia (Acts 11:29-30). Paul makes no mention of this visit in a discussion where it would be crucial to acknowledge it (i.e. Gal 1–2).*]	
Initial Missionary Activity	48	"After fourteen years" Paul makes the "council visit" to Jerusalem (Gal 2:1-10; Acts 15:1-12). According to Paul, this is when he agreed to the collection (Gal 2:10).	
ca. A.D. 38-52 ┌ – – – –	48	Visiting Antioch, Paul confronts Peter's hypocritical disassociation from Gentile Christians (Gal 2:11-14).	
		Paul carries out evangelistic activity in north Galatia. Apparently, he had to stop there because of illness (Gal 4:13-14; Acts 16:6-12).	
Journey 2	49	Paul moves west to work in Macedonia. He begins in the north and moves south (Philippi, Thessalonica, Berea—1 Thes 2:2; Phil 4:15-16; Acts 16:12–7:14).	2 Thessalonians
└ – – – –	49-51	Still further south, Paul evangelizes Achaia (Athens, Corinth). He remains in Corinth for eighteen months (2 Cor 11:7-9; Acts 18:1-18).	1 Thessalonians

FIGURE 1-2

	Date	Major Events	Letters Written
Collection and Pastoral Visits (Journey 3) ca. A.D. 52-56	52-55	[*Acts narrates a voyage to Caesarea. From there, Paul travels to Jerusalem, up to Antioch, through Galatia, and on to Ephesus (Acts 18:18b–19:1). Paul reports none of this in his letters.*]	Previous letter to Corinth (cf. 1 Cor 5:9)
	52-55	In Ephesus for two to three years, Paul probably experienced a lengthy and life-threatening imprisonment. During this time, he received and responded to written and oral communications from Corinth, Philippi, and Galatia (1 Cor 15:12; 2 Cor 1:8-10; Phil 1:12-14; Acts 19:1–20:1).	1 Corinthians Galatians Philippians
	56	After sending Timothy to Corinth, Paul himself makes a "painful" visit. Returning to Ephesus disappointed (2 Cor 2:1; 13:2), he writes a "severe letter" (2 Cor 2:3-4; 7:8-12. Was the "severe letter" 2 Cor 10-13?). Paul sends Titus to follow up (2 Cor 7:6-7, 13-14).	"Severe Letter" to Corinth 2 Corinthians
	56	Anxious to reconcile with the Corinthians, Paul travels by land via Troas and Macedonia, where he meets Titus. He then arrives in Corinth for his third visit (1 Cor 16:1-6; 2 Cor 13:1; Acts 20:2-3).	Romans
Arrest and Imprisonments ca. A.D. 57-62	57	With a delegation from the Gentile churches, Paul visits Jerusalem to deliver the collection (1 Cor 16:3-8; 2 Cor 1:15-16).	
	57	In Jerusalem, Paul is arrested and imprisoned (Acts 21:17–23:30).	
	57-59	Because of threats from Jewish opponents, Paul is transferred to Caesarea and remains there in custody for two years (Acts 23:31–24:27).	
	59	Felix, the new Roman procurator of Judea, hears Paul's case in Caesarea. Paul appeals for a trial before the emperor and is sent to Rome (Acts 25:1–28:14).	
	60-62	In Rome, Paul remains under house arrest for at least two years. During this time he manages to continue preaching the gospel "without hindrance" (Acts 28:15-31).	Colossians Philemon Ephesians

[*Many scholars do not think Paul wrote the pastoral epistles (1 and 2 Timothy and Titus) since these letters do not fit well in the contexts of Paul's acknowledged letters or Acts. If the pastorals were written by Paul, however, then Acts 28 does not mark the end of Paul's career. Freed in Rome, Paul resumed his apostolic activity.*]

Continued on next page

FIGURE 1-2

	Date	Major Events	Letters Written
	An Outline of Paul's Apostolic Career (cont'd)		

	Date	Major Events	Letters Written
Final Aegean Ministry; Arrest; Second Roman Imprisonment	62	After an apparent release in Rome, Paul returns to the Aegean area. He, Timothy, and Titus evangelize the island of Crete, and Titus is left there to establish the young churches (Tit 1:5).	Titus
	63	Paul and Timothy travel through Asia Minor on their way to winter in Nicopolis (Titus 3:12). Stopping over in Ephesus, they discover the church in turmoil. Paul excommunicates two offending elders and leaves Timothy in Ephesus to restore order (1 Tim 1:3, 18-20).	
ca. A.D. 62-65		Paul continues north and is arrested in Troas. With no time to gather his belongings, he is again transported to Rome. Alone and depressed, he writes Timothy, asking him to come (2 Tim 4:9-22).	1 Timothy
	65		2 Timothy

―――――――――― **FIGURE 1-2** ――――――――――

The suggested outline of the Thessalonian correspondence in Figure 1-2 best accounts for historical allusions and theological development, but is by no means beyond argument.

In 1 Corinthians 5:9, Paul refers to an earlier letter he sent them concerning "immorality." This "previous letter," as scholars call it, is either totally lost or partially preserved in 2 Corinthians 6:14–7:1. Another letter to Corinth, the "severe letter" (2 Cor 2:3-4; 7:8-12) is also "missing." Most scholars believe that this severe letter is preserved as 2 Corinthians 10–13. If so, then 2 Corinthians is a composite letter comprised of sections from at least two, if not three, letters of Paul to Corinth. We will examine these possibilities in chapter 9.

As represented in Figure 1-2, Paul probably wrote Philippians at the mid-point of his ministry while imprisoned in Ephesus. Most scholars today work from this perspective. Traditionally, however, Philippians has been placed near the end of Paul's life, written from a Roman prison with Philemon, Colossians and Ephesians.

The letter to the Ephesians may not have been destined for Ephesus at all. Textual criticism reveals that originally the address specified no locale: it simply read "to the saints who are faithful" (Eph 1:1). This observation is coupled with Paul's reference to a letter to Laodicea in the accompanying Colossian letter (Col 4:16). Many scholars then conclude that "Ephesians" is Paul's letter to the Laodicean church.

Conclusion

In light of the full ministry Paul conducted over thirty years, it would be naive to propose that we can accurately reconstruct every chapter of his life story based on the limited records preserved for us. Still, we can be confident that we can know Paul and his message.

Even more fortunate for our immediate purposes, Paul's lengthy ministry with the church at Corinth is exceptionally well documented. As we narrow our focus to the Corinthian correspondence, many stages of interaction between Paul and Corinth will surface. We will become well acquainted with Paul, his ministry team, the Corinthian Christians, and their daily lives. We will learn from their relationships with Christ and with each other.

STUDY QUESTIONS

1. Why have you chosen to study 1 and 2 Corinthians?

2. Read 2 Peter 3:15-16. What are three observations you can make about Paul's letters in this passage?

3. Within the New Testament we find a variety of primary and secondary sources for a study of Paul's life. What is the main difference between primary and secondary sources? How does that difference affect how you interpret them?

4. What was Luke's main reason for writing the book of Acts?

5. Describe the relationship Luke portrays between Christianity and Judaism. How does this portrayal relate to the Roman government?

6. What is one fixed date from which we can construct a chronology of Paul's life?

7. What languages did Paul speak?

8. Paul's Jewishness is reflected in his ancestry, early education, and rabbinic career. List at least five of his Jewish "credentials."

9. Discuss the significance and ramifications of the words spoken to Paul: "I am Jesus, whom you are persecuting."

10. Who commissioned Paul to be an apostle to the Gentiles? When?

11. Judging by Paul's letters, what relationship did the Jerusalem apostles have with Paul and his ministry?

12. Summarize at least two problems we encounter when relating the chronology of Paul's life in Acts to that implied in his letters.

Chapter 2

PAUL AND CORINTH

Introduction

Any congregation is affected by its locale. It will either repudiate or assimilate characteristics of its surroundings. The church in Corinth embraced more than it rejected. As was the city, so too the church: energetic and immature; rich and indulgent; ambitious and status-conscious; confident and self-centered; diverse and divided.

Like the city, the church quickly realized some of its great potential. Paul's ongoing task was to harness and direct that potential in the right direction. A look at the city will reveal why he accepted the challenge, albeit with trepidation.

The City and the Church

Situated on a narrow isthmus uniting southern Achaia with the rest of Greece, Corinth was a geographical focal point (see map). All traffic—whether by land or sea; east, west, north, or southbound—passed through the city. Seafarers preferred the six kilometer portage to the dangerous three hundred kilometer trip by sail around the rocky southern shores of Greece. All but the largest ships were wheeled across the isthmus on wooden rollers. Beginning in the time of Nero, many attempts were made to build a canal but the deep channel through hard rock was not completed until 1893.

The early church depended on travel for both its establishment and its maintenance. Christian travelers carried documents, relayed greetings, exchanged congregational news, sent gifts, and shared hospitality

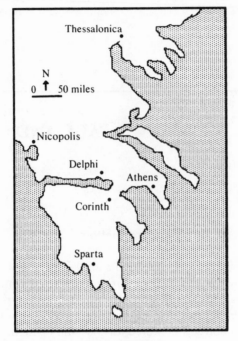

MAP OF GREECE

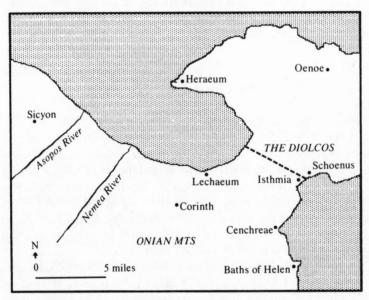

THE CORINTHIAN AREA

with one another. Given Corinth's pivotal position, a church there could play a crucial role in the growth and unity of the church universal.

Corinth itself provided many opportunities for church growth. The city was rebuilding after a desolate century. In 146 B.C. Rome razed Corinth and either killed its citizens or sold them into slavery when they defied Roman expansion. Then in 46 B.C. it was refounded as a Roman colony and repopulated with freedmen from the empire's capital.

Greeks and Asians seeking new opportunities joined the ex-slaves from Rome. During Paul's time, the city had a population of over 200,000. As a young colony, Corinth enjoyed relative autonomy in its civic and commercial administration.

Erastus, a Christian associate of Paul, was Corinth's "city treasurer" (Rom 16:23). If he is the Erastus of a first century inscription in Corinth, then he personally financed the paving of a street in return for his election as a city magistrate (*aedile*). Erastus was fortunate. For every freedman who made it rich in Corinth, there were scores who were still struggling, and the church reflected the disparity (cf. 1 Cor 1:26; 11:21-22).

More than other seaports, Corinth prospered. Transit taxes alone would make it rich. Mining and the manufacture of bronzeware contributed to the local economy. Archeological evidence from the first century reveals the empire's largest marketplace, bordered by rows of shops for various merchants and artisans. Paul likely made tents with Priscilla and Aquila in such a shop (Acts 18:1-3). The team also used the workplace as a center for evangelism and discipleship.

Customarily, citizens with a common occupation formed trade clubs. These voluntary associations provided a forum to meet the professional and social needs of members. Their activities included monthly meetings, special celebrations honoring generous members, common meals, weddings, funerals, and drinking parties. The clubs collected dues from their members and sponsored projects for the benefit of the profession and the city.

Other voluntary associations existed for those who did not have a trade. Some among the wealthier classes were simply social leagues. Even the poor formed burial societies to ensure a decent funeral. With modest fees they could conduct social meetings that brightened what could otherwise be a dreary month.

All voluntary associations chose a god or goddess to oversee their business and they sacrificed accordingly at their banquets. Because of these religious connections, Christians, like Jews, withdrew and incorporated their own fellowships. Unlike other associations, however, Christian trade clubs, burial services, and social outlets were all part of

a greater whole: the church. It transcended social barriers and evange-
listically promoted a faith in Christ that guided all aspects of daily life.

Corinthians worshiped their gods and goddesses beyond the context of the club banquet, of course. Devotees built many temples within
the city walls to honor their various patron deities (see Figure 2-1). One
temple dominated them: just south of the city, atop a five hundred
meter hill called the Acrocorinth, stood the temple of Aphrodite.

The goddess of love, fertility, and reproduction, Aphrodite drew
men and women in search of her blessing on their families, livestock,
and crops. Many modern commentators perpetuate a popular miscon-
ception introduced by Strabo around 7 B.C. that more than a thousand
temple prostitutes welcomed eager worshipers on the Acrocorinth.
While sexuality was doubtless associated with Aphrodite, we have no
solid evidence of temple prostitution here or anywhere in Greece. The
practice appears to have been limited to the east in Asia Minor.

Still, Corinth had a widespread reputation for sexual immorality
outside the temples. Sayings like "not for every man is the voyage to
Corinth" were repeated as far away as Rome. A verb was coined from
the city's name — *korinthiazesthai* — to refer to promiscuous living.
Plato called prostitutes "Corinthian girls" (*Republic*, 404D). As in all
transient urban populations, licentiousness flourished in Corinth.

Corinth offered additional diversions. During Paul's time, the
Corinthian theater held an audience of 14,000 that would gather for
music, drama, and oratory. Every two years, the stadium hosted the
Isthmian games in honor of Poseidon. Second in importance only to the
Olympics, these games attracted enormous crowds from throughout
the Mediterranean. Paul himself may have been a fan, witnessing them
in either A.D. 49 or 51. He draws from their imagery for his letters (cf.
esp. 1 Cor 9:24-27; Phil 3:12-16) and likely used the opportunity the
games provided to spread the gospel.

The entire Roman empire admired the Greeks for their philosophical and rhetorical schools. Platonists, Stoics, Epicureans, Pythagoreans,
Sophists, and Cynics all competed for disciples. Corinth, however, was
never a major arena for philosophical debate. That honor belonged to
its neighbor, Athens. Paul's words about striving after worldly wisdom
in 1 Corinthians 1–4 are probably to be read in light of a Corinthian
desire to gain respect in the shadow of Athens.

Though even less prominent than the philosophical schools of
Corinth, the synagogue still served as a focal point for Paul's initial missionary activity in the city. Limited archeological evidence testifies to
the existence of a Jewish colony in Corinth. Archeologists have excavat-
ed a doorframe inscribed with the words "Synagogue of the Hebrews,"

Corinth, like any other Greek city of Paul's time, honored its share of gods and goddesses. Writing in the second century A.D., the historian Pausanias narrates his visit to Corinth in his *Description of Greece*. He describes at least twenty-six sites built in honor of various deities from Greek, Asian, Roman, and Egyptian backgrounds. We may note some of the more important Greek ones that were worshiped in Corinth at Paul's time:

Aphrodite: The goddess of love and beauty. Her name is derived from the Greek word for "foam" (*aphros*): she was born out of the foam of the sea as the daughter of *Zeus* and *Dione*, who also had temples in Corinth. Aphrodite has pre-Greek origins and is identified as Venus in the Roman pantheon. Associated with the dove, hers was the largest temple in Corinth.

Eros: Son and companion of Aphrodite, Eros was the god of passion. Along with the sun god *Helius*, a statue of the youthful Eros is found in Aphrodite's temple on the Acrocorinth. Eros is identified with Cupid in the Roman pantheon.

Artemis: The goddess of hunting, she is the queen of wild beasts. Her twin brother is *Apollo*; together they are seen to bring death with their arrows. Although a virgin, Artemis was also the goddess of fertility and birth. Women turned to her for help in conception, pregnancy, labor, and delivery. Overlapping with other goddess imagery, Artemis became identified with the Great Mother goddess and was associated with the moon. She went by many names in various cultures. In Rome she was called Diana.

Apollo: Statues of this handsome god were erected throughout Corinth. The son of Zeus and twin to Artemis, Apollo was a huntsman, healer, musician, shepherd, and prophet. His son Asclepius became the god of healing.

Asclepius: He took over the role of divine healer from his father, Apollo. Perhaps originally a snake-god, he appears as a bearded man with a staff entwined by a snake. He had a gentle, peaceful, and wise character and was the patron god of physicians. According to varying myths, the goddess of health, *Hygieia*, is either Asclepius' wife or daughter. She also was worshiped in her temple in Corinth.

Poseidon: One would expect the god of the sea, Poseidon, to be a central figure in a seaport city like Corinth. The Isthmian games were held in his honor. A powerful god, Poseidon could either bring on storms and earthquakes or allow a peaceful journey. Like his Roman counterpart, Neptune, he is pictured as a muscular figure who carries a trident.

Melicertes: The son of Poseidon, Melicertes is also connected with the sea. As the patron deity of sailors, he is often depicted riding a sea-horse. The ports of Corinth had shrines in honor of Melicertes where sailors would pay their vows for safe voyages.

FIGURE 2-1

but its date is uncertain. The book of Acts provides us with the most information about the Corinthian Jewish community (Acts 18:4-17). It was large and influential enough to influence the city's tribunal to hear a case against Paul.

People's households were also crucial in the life of the church. Once Paul had made his initial contacts, he needed a gathering place in which to nurture the believing community. As members of an unestablished, unofficial religion, Christians would not have access to public meeting places. The only available setting would be the family dwelling.

Corinthian homes of the Roman period varied from seasonal tents, to the cramped workshop quarters of artisans at the city's center, to more spacious villas in outlying areas. These larger homes were the only ones in which a congregation could meet. Even these residences would not have a room that exceeded fifty square meters.

Besides the kitchen and bedrooms, the typical home of a wealthy citizen had a dining room (*triclinium*) and an outer courtyard (*atrium*). At most, the dining room could comfortably fit about ten people. Up to fifty guests could assemble in the larger court. Given that most households included spouses, children, slaves, and relations, it would not take many families to overcrowd the home of even the wealthiest patron.

Several Corinthian Christians sponsored house churches: Gaius (Rom 16:23; 1 Cor 14:23), Titus Justus (Acts 18:7), and perhaps Stephanas (1 Cor 16:15). As well, Priscilla and Aquila may have hosted a church as they did in Ephesus (1 Cor 16:19) and Rome (Rom 16:5). Paul also speaks of "Chloe's people" in 1 Corinthians 1:11: either Chloe led a house group or "Chloe's people" were members of her household who became Christians and met with another group.

Rarely would the whole church in Corinth gather at one time, although this happened on occasion (Rom 16:23). Some divisions that arose among Corinthian Christians may have run *along* household lines (cf. 1 Cor 1:10-17). Even *within* the house churches unity was elusive (1 Cor 11:18-19). Socio-economic tensions arose when Corinthian Christians gathered for a communal meal and the Lord's supper (1 Cor 11:17-34). Closer friends of the patron would gather early in the dining room for the choice food and wine. The poorer members would arrive later, gather in the courtyard, and receive the left-overs. 1 Corinthians 11:17-34 contains Paul's stern correction of such disparity at the Lord's table.

From the marketplace to the home; from the pagan temples to the synagogue; from the ports to the stadium — Corinth was a young city quickly realizing its potential. As Paul saw, though, that potential was not all positive. Personally and strategically, he was drawn to the cities.

Yet he states that he arrived at Corinth "in fear and much trembling" (1 Cor 2:3). Had he some idea of the nature and extent of the problems that would arise in this notorious center? The struggles he had just endured in Philippi, Thessalonica, and Athens did not bode well for a campaign in Corinth.

In Acts 18:1-18 we read the story of the founding of the church. Paul began in Corinth as he did elsewhere: he set up a tentmaking shop. Earning his own living in Corinth would prove to be wise as questions later arose regarding the collection for Jerusalem and Paul's financial integrity (cf. 1 Cor 4:1-5; 9:3-23; 16:1-4; 2 Cor 8–9; 11:7-11).

Teaming up with Priscilla and Aquila meant that he would have a certain amount of flexibility and moral support as he made inroads at the synagogue. Significantly, it does not appear that Paul limited the role of women in his church-planting endeavors. From all accounts, Priscilla, whom Paul regularly calls "Prisca," played a leading role alongside the men (Acts 18:2, 18, 26; Rom 16:3; 1 Cor 16:19; 2 Tim 4:19). Perhaps indicating greater influence, her name most often appears before her husband's when either Luke or Paul names them.

Silas and Timothy joined the team when they arrived from Macedonia, where Paul had left them to escape the wrath of some Thessalonian Jews (Acts 17:13-14). The five missionaries initially concentrated on the Jewish community. Yet, as usual, they soon wore out their welcome at the synagogue.

Rejection by the Jews provoked a turning to the Gentiles. Titus Justus, a Gentile attracted to Judaism, invited Paul to preach from his home next door to the synagogue. Presumably, this man had become a Christian. Some scholars understand Titus Justus to be Gaius, one of Paul's first baptismal candidates (1 Cor 1:14) and host of the church in his home (Rom 16:23). Roman citizens would often adopt a *praenomen* (personal name) to use with their formal names. For example, Gaius Julius Caesar is a better known "Gaius."

The identification of Titus Justus as Gaius is strengthened by his association with Crispus, the synagogue ruler. Both "Titus Justus" and Crispus converted in this early period of the Corinthian ministry (Acts 18:7-8) and Paul baptized both "Gaius" and Crispus then (1 Cor 1:14).

For his conversion to Christianity, Crispus was unseated as synagogue ruler. Luke describes the mobbing of another synagogue ruler, Sosthenes, eighteen months later when Gallio refused to get involved in a Jewish-Christian dispute (Acts 18:17). There is some question whether anti-semitic Greeks or anti-Pauline Jews beat Sosthenes. In either case, Luke makes his point: a respected Roman authority has treated Christianity as a *religio licita*. If the mob's victim is the same

Sosthenes of 1 Corinthians 1:1, then he was the *second* synagogue ruler of Corinth to become a Christian under Paul's persuasive preaching.

Paul stayed in Corinth for a year and a half. He left behind a large, vibrant, and diverse church. His pastoral ministry at Corinth, however, was only beginning. With ensuing events both in Corinth and Paul's wider ministry, there would be much for the apostle and the church to discuss.

Oral and Written Communications

After his founding visit, Paul did not return to Corinth for several years. Meanwhile, he still maintained contact with the church. At least six other people traveled between the city and the apostle; some brought "official" communiqués, others let rumors slip. Letters were exchanged. Stages of communication can be reconstructed from comments in 1 and 2 Corinthians (see Figure 2-2).

In 1 Corinthians 5:9, Paul says: "I wrote to you in my letter not to associate with sexually immoral persons." He then goes on to explain what he meant in this previous letter. How did Paul know that he needed to clarify certain statements in his previous letter? The answer to this question is found in 1 Corinthians 7:1 where Paul continues to respond to the church: "Now concerning the matters about which you wrote...." Prompted by Paul's previous letter, the Corinthians have written to him with some questions.

In addition, Paul got a fuller picture of the situation in Corinth from the delegation that brought the letter. As well, Paul has heard some disturbing news from "Chloe's people" (1 Cor 1:11). Sosthenes also may have informed Paul (1 Cor 1:1).

In response to the questions and rumors, Paul writes 1 Corinthians. A careful reading of 1 Corinthians distinguishes between Corinthian questions about Paul's "previous letter" and aspects of their behavior that they would rather not bring before the apostle.

1 Corinthians as a Letter

An appreciation of Paul's typical letter-writing form is necessary for a full understanding of the message of any of his letters. So, chapter 15 of our book will examine the form and function of Paul's letters in light of Greek letter-writing conventions of the Roman period. At this point, however, we need only to outline the epistolary structure of 1 Corinthians (see Figure 2-3).

Stages of Communication Between Paul and the Corinthians

Stage One
Paul >>> Corinth

Paul arrives in Corinth. After eighteen months, he has founded a church of Jewish and Greek Christians and sails for Syria and Asia.

Stage Two
Paul >>> Corinth

Paul writes the "previous letter" to Corinth (cf. 1 Cor 5:9-11). Its topics include immorality, idolatry, spiritual gifts, resurrection, and the Jerusalem collection.

Stage Three
Corinth >>> Paul

The Corinthians respond with a letter of questions brought to Paul by Stephanus, Fortunatus, and Achaicus (cf. 1 Cor 7:1; 17:17-18). As well, Paul hears oral reports about aberrant attitudes and behavior in the church (cf. 1 Cor 1:11; 11:18).

Stage Four
Paul >>> Corinth

Paul responds to the letter from the church and the news he has heard by writing *1 Corinthians* and sends the delegation back.

Stage Five
Paul >>> Corinth

Still concerned about Corinthian attitudes, Paul sends Timothy to Corinth (1 Cor 4:17-19; 16:10-11).

Stage Six
Corinth >>> Paul

A dejected Timothy reports back to Paul: his visit has had little effect.

Stage Seven
Paul >>> Corinth

Paul travels from Ephesus to Corinth to settle matters himself. He finds it a disappointing visit and leaves with the issues unresolved (2 Cor 2:1).

Stage Eight
Paul >>> Corinth

Paul sends a "severe letter" with Titus (2 Cor 2:3-4). The letter produces repentance (2 Cor 7:8-13). Some suggest that *2 Corinthians 10–13* is this severe letter.

Stage Nine
Corinth >>> Paul

Paul is anxious for news, so he travels north to meet Titus in Macedonia. He hears of the Corinthian repentance and reconciliation (2 Cor 7:5-7, 13-16).

Stage Ten
Paul >>> Corinth

Paul writes *2 Corinthians* (1–9, at least). He sends Titus and others back to Corinth with instructions to complete the Corinthian collection for Jerusalem (2 Cor 8-9).

Stage Eleven
Paul >>> Corinth

Paul is planning a *third* visit to Corinth (2 Cor 12:14; 13:1).

FIGURE 2-2

The Structure of 1 Corinthians

Salutation
(1:1-3)

• names the senders and recipients
• relays greetings

Thanksgiving
(1:4-9)

• offers a prayer
of thanksgiving for the past
and hope for the future
• foreshadows concerns in the letter

Body
(1:10–16:12)

• Paul's responses to oral reports and written questions
from Corinth are arranged topically:

Striving after Wisdom (1:10–4:21)
Immorality (5:1–6:20)
Sexuality and Marriage (7:1-40)
Idolatry (8:1–11:1)
Worship (11:2–14:40)
• women and men (11:2-16)
• the Lord's supper (11:17-34)
• spiritual gifts (12:1–14:40)
Resurrection (15:1-58)
The Collection (16:1-4)
Travel Plans (16:5-12)

Conclusion
(16:13-24)

Final Exhortations (16:13-18)
Personal Greetings and Benediction (16:19-24)

FIGURE 2-3

While the opening and closing sections follow a pattern, the bodies of Paul's letters vary considerably. This is because the subject matter dictates form and no two letters were written to address the same situation. In the body of 1 Corinthians, there are two types of responses from Paul, depending on the source of the information from Corinth.

On the one hand, rumors provoke the apostle to a categorical condemnation of their attitude and behavior. He does not reason with his readers, he simply commands obedience. Differing viewpoints are not balanced with one another. There is no room for discussion on these matters.

On the other hand, written requests for clarification elicit a patient, sensitive response from Paul. The topic appears abruptly, often with the simple preface "Now concerning...." Paul does not censor earlier conduct; he provides guidance for future behavior. While making his case, he uses several supporting arguments. He will quote and then qualify "slogans" the Corinthians likely used themselves.

Judging by Paul's responses in 1 Corinthians, he has heard that there are congregational divisions caused by misplaced allegiance to human leaders. Some are saying "I belong to Paul," or "I belong to Apollos" or "I belong to Peter" or "I belong to Christ" (1 Cor 1:12).

Paul has also heard that a man is having sexual relations with his stepmother and the church was boasting of the relationship (1 Cor 5:1-2)! Members of the church are defrauding each other and then going to court to settle the matter (1 Cor 6:1-8). When gathering for worship, the church allows fervor to develop into thoughtless bedlam (1 Cor 12–14). The Lord's supper has degenerated into a class-conscious drinking party (1 Cor 11:17-33).

Considering their behavior, the Corinthian question about how to avoid immoral people seems out of place (1 Cor 5:9). However, the context of their other questions reveals an attitude that separated morality from spirituality. The Corinthian Christians asked how marriage could be compatible with the spiritual life (1 Cor 7). They wondered why it was wrong to eat idol meat now that they were free from domination by pagan gods (1 Cor 8–10). They asked Paul's opinion concerning spiritual gifts. Were not the spectacular gifts, like speaking in tongues, the greatest? Should not all Christians seek them?

Apparently Paul had earlier taught, perhaps in the previous letter, that there would be a resurrection of the dead. In their over-spiritualized faith some Corinthian Christians were now denying this, probably believing that the soul lived eternally independent of the old body. Paul is asked to explain how a decomposing corpse can be raised again (1 Cor 15).

Finally, in 1 Corinthians 16, Paul answers ordinary questions: How are they to collect money for the church in Jerusalem? Is Apollos going to come to visit them soon?

Conclusion

The church in Corinth suffered no serious external persecution. Yet, it suffered internal divisions.

These divisions developed along various lines and arose over time. Perhaps they were to be expected, given the diversity of the congregations in Corinth. Social and ethnic distinctions existed. Separate house groups contributed to divided loyalties. Some Corinthian Christians felt under no compulsion to dissociate themselves from a lifestyle that other Christians associated with paganism. Corinthian Christians wrestled with the relevance of their physical existence now that they were living "spiritual" lives. Judgmentalism grew. Individualism ran rampant. Responsibility to the church gave way to personal freedom.

The challenge before Paul was to bring orthodoxy and unity in Christ. Writing 1 Corinthians would be the next step.

STUDY QUESTIONS

1. List at least four settings for Paul's ministry in the city of Corinth.

2. Paul followed the same basic approach to church-planting in the cities of Asia and Greece. Outline the pattern.

3. What are some similarities between the Christian church and other voluntary associations that formed in Roman cities? What is the main difference?

4. Describe at least three causes for division within the church in Corinth.

5. Why do interpreters think that the man named Gaius in Paul's letters is the same person Luke calls Titus Justus?

6. Who was Crispus?...Sosthenes?...Stephanas?...Chloe?...Erastus?

7. What rumors did Paul hear about Corinth since his departure?

8. What questions did the Corinthians ask Paul in their letter to him?

Chapter 3

THE CHURCH AND ITS LEADERS: SEEKING TRUE WISDOM
(1 Corinthians 1–4)

Introduction

By making comparisons, the Corinthians divided their church. Individuals were concerned with their rank in the church and in society. Misguided Corinthians saw Christianity as a vehicle for social advancement and a source of urbane wisdom. They graded church leaders according to society's standards for eloquence among philosophers. Paul did not fare as well as others in the rhetorical arena. Loyalties were tested and arguments arose.

News about such comparisons in Corinth dismayed Paul. Judging by his response, he saw the rivalrous climate as the underlying cause of many church problems. Significantly, he begins his letter by realigning the Corinthians' estimate of themselves and their leaders before answering their questions.

Paul's Preliminaries
(1 Cor 1:1-17)

As today, letters in Paul's era followed a conventional form identifying the sender and recipient and relaying an obligatory greeting. With a glance readers noted the source and destination and proceeded quickly to the business at hand. Paul used a similar form, although he expanded his greetings to suit his pastoral purposes. Today, readers familiar with

Paul's writing tend too often mistakenly to only skim the opening on their way to the body of the letter.

Paul's salutation and thanksgiving prayer usually suggest his agenda for the letter. In 1 Corinthians, we immediately see a stress on unity of a church set apart from the world. After identifying himself in v. 1 as an apostle "by the will of God," and not by a popularity poll, he goes on to describe his readers. They are "sanctified in Christ Jesus, called to be saints, together with all those who in every place call on the name of our Lord Jesus Christ, both their Lord and ours..." (1 Cor 1:2).

Note the stress on "calling" in the salutation. Paul is called to be an apostle; the Corinthians are called to be saints; Christians everywhere call on the Lord. God has taken the initiative through Christ Jesus to call the Corinthians into his church. Christ's lordship unites the Corinthians with those in every place who profess faith. All share in grace and peace from God. Divided loyalties have no place in either the local church or the church universal of which the Corinthians are a part.

Before tackling the problem of divisions directly, Paul offers a prayer of thanksgiving for the church, as he does in each letter except Galatians. Typically, Paul begins with a reference to the past faithfulness of the congregation. He then expresses appreciation for their continued growth in discipleship. The thanksgivings usually end on an eschatological note confidently predicting the completion of Christ's work in the lives of his readers.

Epistolary studies have shown that Paul's thanksgivings function as a "table of contents" for the rest of the letter. In 1 Corinthians, the thanksgiving shows that Paul intends to address the issues of "speech," "knowledge," "spiritual gifts," and "the day of our Lord" (1 Cor 1:5-8; see Figure 3-1).

First on his agenda is the Corinthian enrichment in "speech and knowledge of every kind" (1 Cor 1:5). It is true: Christ has given them wisdom to proclaim. Yet, they have misunderstood that wisdom, as Paul shows when he begins to address their squabbling. "Now I appeal to you, brothers and sisters...that all of you be in agreement..." (1 Cor 1:10). This exhortation marks the formal turning point from the thanksgiving to the main body of the letter. Chloe's people have informed Paul that church members are quarreling among themselves, each claiming allegiance to a different leader (1 Cor 1:11-12). This is not the sort of information the church would volunteer to Paul in the hope of gaining some guidance from the apostle. Still, it reveals more about the church than its letter would disclose.

The discord in the Corinthian church is focused on personalities. Some remain loyal to Paul while others extol Apollos or Cephas. The

In all his letters except Galatians Paul offers a thanksgiving prayer for the church to which he writes. Typically, he begins with a reference to the past faithfulness of the congregation. He then expresses appreciation for their continued growth in discipleship. He ends on an eschatological note confidently predicting the completion of Christ's saving work in the lives of his readers.

The thanksgivings subtly announce the themes that Paul will deal with in the bodies of the letters. This pattern can be discerned in 1 Corinthians.

Thanksgiving (1 Cor 1:4-9)	Body of 1 Corinthians
"...in every way you have been enriched in him, in *speech* ..." (1 Cor 1:5).	In chapters 1–4, Paul corrects the Corinthian pursuit of philosophical eloquence.
"...you have been enriched in...*knowledge of every kind* ..." (1 Cor 1:5).	In chapters 8–10, Paul counters a self-centered "enlightened" attitude that is expressed in mottos like "All of us possess knowledge" (1 Cor 8:1).
"...you are not lacking in any *spiritual gift* ..." (1 Cor 1:7).	In chapters 12–14, Paul addresses the abuse of some spiritual gifts and the neglect of others in the corporate life of the church.
"...*as you wait for the revealing of our Lord Jesus Christ.* He will also strengthen you to the end, so that you may be blameless on the day of our Lord Jesus Christ" (1 Cor 1:7-8).	In chapter 15, Paul explains to his readers about their victory over death: "...the dead will be raised imperishable, and we will be changed" (1 Cor 15:52).

FIGURE 3-1

fourth slogan Paul cites "I bel͟   to Christ," may be Paul's correction
of the other three, but the ͟ammatical parallelism suggests that the
words come from a four͟ʟᴾ ᵗ ͟ in the church.

Other than their ͟ᵗ᷎ ͟cries, we know little about the four
groups. Paul makes no theological distinctions between them but
accuses them all of detracting from Christ's saving work. They do so in
at least two ways. First, they focus on who baptized them rather than
on the one who died on the cross for them (1 Cor 1:14-16). Second,
they value eloquent wisdom more than the unpretentious proclamation
of the gospel (1 Cor 1:17).

The opening paragraphs of 1 Corinthians point to one conclusion:
Paul considers the divisions to be an immediate threat to the welfare of
the church. The Corinthians are using Christianity for personal
glorification at each other's expense. They present themselves as wise and
draw from the prestige of one leader or another to bolster their own reputation. Paul must revise their view of Christian wisdom and leadership.

The Wisdom of God and the Wisdom of the World
(1 Cor 1:18–3:4)

The theme of wisdom dominates the first three chapters of 1
Corinthians. The Greek words for "wisdom" (*sophia*) and "wise"
(*sophos*) together occur twenty-six times in this section, comprising
forty percent of the total number of times they are found in the New
Testament. Add the frequent references to "knowing," "understanding," "speaking," and "discerning" and Paul's primary concern about the
church emerges. They are obsessed with the pursuit of wisdom yet they
do not understand its true nature.

All societies idealize wisdom in one form or another. Egypt developed wisdom schools as early as 2500 B.C. and many nations, including
Israel, followed suit. The sages of Israelite wisdom produced such
books as Proverbs, Job, Ecclesiastes, and the Wisdom of Solomon.
These writings promote a common-sense approach to life. They teach
how to cope in the created order. They cultivate respect and humility in
the face of Yahweh's unfathomable mysteries. Unfortunately, in the
minds of the pretentious, wisdom offered self-glorification and even the
opportunity to outmaneuver God.

According to Isaiah 28–33, the pursuit of self-centered "wisdom"
led to the kingdom of Judah's downfall. Paul picks up on this and compares the Corinthians with Judah, quoting from Isaiah 29:14:

For it is written,
> "I will destroy the wisdom of the wise,
> and the discernment of the discerning I will thwart."

Where is the one who is wise? Where is the scribe? Where is the debater of this age? Has not God made foolish the wisdom of the world? (1 Cor 1:19-20).

In these first three chapters, Paul alludes to the Old Testament six times to say that those who think they are wise cannot begin to comprehend God's wisdom (see Figure 3-2). From Paul's perspective, the Corinthian Christians have fallen into the same trap as some among earlier generations of God's people. They have presumed that God's wisdom will give them status by this world's standards.

For the Corinthians, "this world's standards" meant Greek philosophy and rhetoric. Platonism, stoicism, epicureanism, and cynicism all found various forms of expression in Corinth (see Figure 3-3). Besides philosophers, Corinth was host to orators who exploited eloquence as an end in itself.

In Paul's world, elements of "gnosticism" were already circulating, though this syncretistic religion would not produce its own literature until the second century. Gnostics taught that salvation came through secret knowledge (*gnosis*) available to a select group. A few scholars see Paul countering gnosticism by using its terminology in defense of *Christian* wisdom (cf. esp. 1 Cor 2:6-16).

Whatever the exact nature of the "wisdom" that attracted the Corinthians, it was not true wisdom from God. Paul sharply distinguishes between wisdom of the world and the wisdom of God. Typical responses to these two types of wisdom show that humanity consists of two types of people: the "spiritual" (*pneumatikos*) and the "natural" (*psychikos*). The "natural" person has not received the Spirit of God.

Paul gives a synopsis of his argument: "For Jews demand signs and Greeks desire wisdom, but we proclaim Christ crucified, a stumbling block to Jews and foolishness to Gentiles, but to those who are the called, both Jews and Greeks, Christ the power of God and the wisdom of God" (1 Cor 1:22-24).

The crucifixion of Christ reveals God's wisdom. For people enamored with manifestations of divine power, self-centered reasoning, or clever speech, Christ's suffering is incomprehensible. Jews regarded the cross as a sign of God's curse, not his blessing (cf. Deut 21:23). To the Greeks the proclamation of the saving power of the crucifixion was foolish, especially in comparison to the brilliance of their philosophies.

"I will destroy the wisdom of the wise
and the discernment of the discerning I will thwart."

— *1 Cor 1:19; cf. Is 29:14*

* * *

"Let him who boasts, boast in the Lord."
— *1 Cor 1:31; cf. Jer 9:23-24*

* * *

"What no eye has seen, nor ear heard,
nor the human heart conceived,
what God has prepared for those who love him" —
these things God has revealed to us. . . .

— *1 Cor 2:9; cf. Is 64:4*

* * *

"For who has known the mind of the Lord
so as to instruct him?"

— *1 Cor 2:16; cf. Is 40:13*

* * *

"He catches the wise in their craftiness."
— *1 Cor 3:19; cf. Job 5:13*

* * *

"The Lord knows the thoughts of the wise,
that they are futile."

— *1 Cor 3:20; cf. Ps 94:11*

FIGURE 3-2

Cynicism

Although a minor philosophy in New Testament times, Cynicism nevertheless had a long history in Corinth. As well, it gave Stoicism its foundational doctrines of virtue and austerity.

With self-sufficiency as the ideal, Cynics lived for the moment with no concern for public opinion, wealth, or culture. In short, they lived like homeless dogs of the street and were so named—the Greek word for dog is *kyne*.

Cynics believed that virtue was an end in itself and did not need to be organized into a coherent ethical, religious, or philosophical system. Cynics simply lived out their immediate convictions.

The best known Cynic, Diogenes of Sinope, pushed this lifestyle to its extreme, living in a barrel, performing all bodily functions on the street, and begging for the next meal. Diogenes is said to have died at Corinth in 325 B.C. Cynic philosophers continued to attract followers and produce pseudonymous letters into the third century A.D.

Stoicism

The dominant Greek philosophy of Paul's time, Stoicism took the cynic's commitment to unadorned morality and a simple life in a direction more acceptable to society. The pursuit of virtue was the highest good, and virtue was generally equated with reason or the "word" (*logos*). Reason, or the word, was described in material terms as a divine essence that held the universe together in a working order.

To live in harmony with reason meant that the Stoic had to discern the all-encompassing order of the cosmos and accept its cycles. Stoics argued that nothing could be done to change the laws that governed life; we could only control our reactions to them. The Stoic's goal was to live with a serene, fatalistic worldview detached from strong passions.

Epicureanism

This popular ethical philosophy taught that all things, including the mind and soul, were made up of variously shaped atoms bound together temporarily. Even the gods consisted of atoms and, as long as they existed in their own state of "blessedness," they had no interest in the affairs of humans.

According to the Epicureans, death was simply the rearrangement of our constituent atoms into new forms. We would not experience death or afterlife; we would no longer exist.

Continued on next page

FIGURE 3-3

Like the Stoics, Epicureans maintained that we could control nothing in life but our personal behavior. Hence, the goal of life was to be as private and comfortable as possible. Epicurean fellowships were known for their independence from society and strong ties of friendship.

Platonism

Unlike the Stoics and Epicureans, who described all existence in material terms, Platonists rooted ultimate reality in the spiritual realm. They argued that the material world of the other philosophical systems was a pale shadow of ideal realities.

According to the Platonists, reality was approximated by physical sensations. However, the ideals upon which the material approximations were based could more directly be discerned through the reasoning of the mind (or soul).

Platonists taught that the soul was an eternal part of the divine realm. When our bodies die, our souls are released from captivity. Souls that had already transcended the physical realm through rational reflection would remain free in the world of ultimate reality. Others that had yet to break their physical attachment would return to another body.

——————————————— FIGURE 3-3 ———————————————

God reversed the common view of wisdom that esteems human competence, reputation, and power. None too tactfully, Paul reminds the Corinthian Christians that, given their credentials, they should be grateful for this reversal (1 Cor 1:26)!

True wisdom is a gift from God. He takes the initiative to give it to those whom he chooses, thereby leveling our estimates of each other. Because the gift of God's saving wisdom is not based on human performance, no one should boast about receiving it (1 Cor 1:31; cf. also 4:7).

To underscore the point, Paul reminds the Corinthians of his "performance" in proclaiming God's wisdom (1 Cor 2:1-5). He was neither eloquent nor erudite. Instead, he spoke simply of the crucifixion of Jesus Christ. The power of the message lay not in the skill and style of the messenger but in the Spirit of God.

If Paul had not learned this lesson before, he certainly did at Athens. There he tried to engage Stoics and Epicureans in their game, evangelizing them with logic and rhetoric (Acts 17:16-34). For the most part, the philosophers ridiculed him. His next stop was Corinth. He arrived "in weakness and in fear and in much trembling" (1 Cor 2:3) that may have had as much to do with the Athenian encounters as Corinth's reputation.

From Paul's comments to this point, we might conclude that Christians are to avoid wisdom altogether. Yet Paul goes on to say that there is a true wisdom that only mature Christians can appreciate. This wisdom alone describes how God saves.

God's wisdom revolves around Christ. Foreshadowed by Israel's personification of wisdom (cf Prov 1:20-33; 3; 8; 9), Christ "became for us wisdom" (1 Cor 1:30). He is the source and meaning of life. As such, says Paul, Christ is "righteousness and sanctification and redemption" (1 Cor 1:30).

"Righteousness," a legal term, signifies that believers are acquitted, or declared "not guilty," because Christ has represented them before the judge. "Sanctification" is necessary because we can approach God only if we are holy or "set apart" from the world for God. Christ has become our holiness. "Redemption" refers to freedom bought by Christ.

Once Paul has realigned the Corinthians' perspective, he attracts them to God's wisdom with *their* gnosticizing language (1 Cor 2:6-13). Christian wisdom is "not of this age or of the rulers of this age"; it is "secret and hidden." God has now revealed the wisdom he had "decreed before the ages for our glory."

Not all can fathom the depths of God's wisdom. Paul says it is meant for "the mature" (1 Cor 2:6). At least three qualities identify such people: they focus on the cross (1 Cor 1:18-24), they depend on the Holy Spirit (1 Cor 2:10-13), and they are motivated by love (1 Cor 2:9). Mature Christians "have the mind of Christ" (1 Cor 2:16).

With the mind of Christ, the spiritual person can "discern all things," says Paul, including the wisdom of the unspiritual person. Yet the opposite is not true: the unspiritual cannot understand or accurately evaluate the wisdom of the Christian (1 Cor 2:15). The situation is comparable to parents and their children. Parents who remember their childhood can understand the world of both the adult and the child. The children, however, cannot comprehend their parents' perspective.

Developing the analogy, Paul likens the Corinthian Christians to babies (1 Cor 3:1-4). Contrary to their presumptions, the Corinthians are *not* displaying wise "spiritual" attitudes and behavior. As infants in Christ, they are unable to digest anything but the elementary principles of the gospel. Their distorted view of spiritual parents proves that they see life from a "natural" or "fleshly" perspective.

Servant Leadership for God's Church
(1 Cor 3:5–4:21)

Although Paul calls his readers immature, he does want to give them a full and proper sense of self-worth. They are the church of *God*, not the church of Paul, Apollos, or Peter. God established the church; he continues to nurture and protect it. He has appointed leaders to serve his church and he will call them to account for their work in its midst.

Paul describes the church as a cultivated field (1 Cor 3:5-9) and a building under construction (1 Cor 3:9-17). In both images, God has assigned workers for different tasks. Paul says that their individual responsibilities are interdependent and ultimately dependent on God.

"What then is Apollos? What is Paul? Servants through whom you came to believe, as the Lord assigned to each" (1 Cor 3:5). Although this statement could mean that God gives the opportunity for belief to the Corinthians, the context suggests that Paul is saying that God has given Apollos and him the opportunity for ministry.

A comparison of the preaching of Apollos (Acts 18:24-28) and Paul (1 Cor 2:1-5) shows why Apollos attracted some in Corinth who would not be attracted to Paul. Yet, Paul insists, each servant is being faithful to God's call. In the field, "as the Lord assigned to each," Paul planted, Apollos watered, and God gave the growth (1 Cor 3:5-6). At the construction site, "according to the grace of God given," Paul laid the foundation and "someone else" builds on it (1 Cor 3:10).

Servants of the church must exercise care, skill, and self-sacrifice in carrying out their responsibilities. They must work together with a common purpose. They must strive to be trustworthy "stewards of God's mysteries" (1 Cor 4:1).

The Corinthians have not properly evaluated these qualities in their leaders, being "puffed up in favor of one against another" (1 Cor 4:6). They have measured their leaders according to worldly ideals of wealth, power, wisdom, and honor. With pointed irony Paul concedes that apostles like him fail miserably by worldly standards (1 Cor 4:8-13). "We have become the rubbish of the world, the dregs of all things, to this very day" (1 Cor 4:13).

Paul puts little store in the Corinthian appraisals. "With me," he writes, "it is a very small thing that I should be judged by you or by any human court. I do not even judge myself" (1 Cor 4:3). Human opinions, including Paul's own, do not form the standard by which Christian service is judged.

God alone will judge. He will expose the quality (1 Cor 3:13) and motivation (1 Cor 4:5) of *all* who work in his church. For some, God's judgment will issue in an unspecified reward (1 Cor 3:8, 14; 4:5). Others will suffer loss and destruction (1 Cor 3:15, 17).

The metaphor of the church as a building ends on an ominous note. Paul has laid a foundation of faith in Christ. Others are building on that base. Some build with gold, silver, and precious stones. Others build with wood, hay, and straw. On "the day," fire will test each builder's work (1 Cor 3:13). "If the work is burned up, the builder will suffer loss; the builder will be saved, but only as through fire" (1 Cor 3:15).

What is more, Paul extends the imagery into talk of God's temple:

Do you not know that you are God's temple and that God's Spirit dwells in you? If anyone destroys God's temple, God will destroy that person. For God's temple is holy, and you are that temple (1 Cor 3:16-17).

The pronoun "you" in this passage is plural, indicating that Paul is speaking corporately; the Christian *community* is the temple. Just as the "glory of the Lord" filled the Old Testament temple (1 Kgs 8:11), the Holy Spirit abides in the New Testament church (1 Cor 3:16). As God's temple, the church in Corinth is "holy" (1 Cor 3:17).

These words both promise and warn. God cherishes his church and he has blessed it with his presence. However, those who work in the church must beware: he will protect it against desecration. Those who destroy the church will themselves be destroyed by God.

Some scholars hesitate to interpret literally the references to "destroying" in v. 17. After all, they reason, the church can never be destroyed. As well, 1 Corinthians 3:15 teaches that the careless builder will be saved even when his or her work burns. A few resolve their difficulties by interpreting "destroy" to mean "mar" or "ruin." Others propose that in v. 15 Paul is speaking of Christian workers while in v. 17 he targets non-Christian enemies of the church.

Paul, however, is more direct, outlining a straightforward principle: God will return in kind what people bring to the church. In particular, those who *lead* the church must account for their handling of it.

To conclude his section on church leadership, Paul returns to the relationship between parents and children (1 Cor 4:14-21; cf. 3:1-5). The Corinthian "children" may have "ten thousand guardians," but Paul is their only spiritual father (1 Cor 4:15). While the apostle's hyperbole does not deny the need for guardians, by it Paul makes an exclusive

Children and Parents

"And so, brothers and sisters, I could not speak to you as spiritual people but as people of the flesh, as infants in Christ. I fed you with milk, not solid food, for you were not yet ready for solid food. Even now you are still not ready…" (1 Cor 3:1-2).

"I am not writing this to make you ashamed, but to admonish you as my beloved children. For though you might have ten thousand guardians in Christ, you do not have many fathers. Indeed, in Christ Jesus I became your father through the gospel. I appeal to you, then, be imitators of me.… What would you prefer? Am I to come to you with a stick, or with love in a spirit of gentleness?" (1 Cor 4:14-21).

A Field and Farmers

"I planted, Apollos watered, but God gave the growth. So neither the one who plants nor the one who waters is anything, but only God who gives the growth. The one who plants and the one who waters have a common purpose, and each will receive wages according to the labor of each. For we are God's servants, working together; you are God's field…" (1 Cor 3:5-9).

A Building and Builders

"You are… God's building. According to the grace of God given to me, like a skilled master builder I laid a foundation, and someone else is building on it. Each builder must choose with care how to build on it. For no one can lay any foundation other than the one that has been laid; that foundation is Jesus Christ. Now if anyone builds on the foundation with gold, silver, precious stones, wood, hay, straw — the work of each builder will become visible, for the Day will disclose it, because it will be revealed with fire, and the fire will test what sort of work each had done. If what has been built on the foundation survives, the builder will receive a reward. If the work is burned up, the builder will suffer loss; the builder will be saved, but only as through fire" (1 Cor 3:9-15).

The Temple

"Do you not know that you are God's temple and that God's Spirit dwells in you? If anyone destroys God's temple, God will destroy that person. For God's temple is holy, and you are that temple" (1 Cor 3:16-17).

Kings and Outcasts

"Already you have all you want! Already you have become rich! Quite apart from us you have become kings! Indeed, I wish that you had become kings, so that we

FIGURE 3-4

might be kings with you! For I think that God has exhibited us apostles as last of all, as though sentenced to death, because we have become a spectacle to the world, to angels and to mortals. We are fools for the sake of Christ, but you are wise in Christ. We are weak, but you are strong. You are held in honor, but we in disrepute. To the present hour we are hungry and thirsty, we are poorly clothed, beaten and homeless, and we grow weary from the work of our own hands. When reviled, we bless; when persecuted, we endure; when slandered, we speak kindly. We have become like the rubbish of the world, the dregs of all things, to this very day" (1 Cor 4:8-13).

FIGURE 3-4
---

claim on the Corinthian Christians. Of the several images of the church and its leaders that Paul uses, this is the only one he makes that singles him out (see Figure 3-4).

Paul brought the gospel to the Corinthians and by that "fathered" their new life in Christ. As their father, Paul carries unique responsibility and authority. He has a parent's love for the Corinthian church (1 Cor 4:14, 17, 21). He is their prime example for the Christian life (1 Cor 4:16-17). When discipline is necessary, he can admonish (1 Cor 4:14) or even come "with a stick" (1 Cor 4:21).

Conclusion

From his opening words, Paul addresses the fundamental problem of the Corinthian church: a proud and divisive misunderstanding of wisdom. In 1 Corinthians 1–4, Paul teaches that wisdom from God centers on Christ. It is the message of salvation through the cross. Only mature Christians can recognize this as true wisdom.

A proper understanding of wisdom will result in a true perception of oneself, the church, and its leaders. God in Christ has saved the Corinthians, established his church, and appointed leaders to serve it. All this stems from God's grace and not human merit.

Only when the Corinthians realize these truths can their father in the faith offer them specific guidance for their various problems.

STUDY QUESTIONS

1. Judging by the greeting and thanksgiving sections of 1 Corinthians, what are Paul's main concerns as he writes?

2. What are the similarities and differences between the wisdom of the Old Testament and that of the New Testament? Contrast biblical wisdom and the wisdom that enamored the Corinthians.

3. List words used to describe the preaching of Apollos (Acts 18:24-28) and that of Paul (1 Cor 2:1-5). Is Apollos wiser than Paul? Would the Corinthians think he was? What does Paul think of Apollos?

4. What role does the Spirit play in a Christian's comprehension of wisdom?

5. Paul uses various images to describe the church (see Figure 3-4). What is the main point conveyed by each metaphor?

6. List all possible references in 1 Corinthians 3–4 to reward and punishment for work in the church. What, if anything, can be said about the nature of the reward and punishment?

7. Who was your spiritual parent? Have you had other guardians?

8. Have you ever "planted" or "laid a foundation"? Have you "watered" or "built on the foundation"?

Chapter 4

THE CHURCH AND ITS RELATIONSHIPS
(1 Corinthians 5–7)

Introduction

Because Corinthian Christians misunderstood what it means to be "spiritual," their sense of being "set apart" was also skewed. Instead of avoiding unrighteous behavior, they have separated their physical and spiritual lives. For some, this permits immoral living: what happens in the body lacks spiritual consequence. For others, the dichotomy requires an ascetic lifestyle: to experience fully the spiritual life, the physical must be stifled.

Both tendencies express themselves clearly in the area of sexuality. So, Paul deals with sexual ethics. Yet, failure to integrate faith with practice also distorts other relationships. Paul therefore addresses a range of ethical problems.

Immorality Within and Without
(1 Cor 5–6)

Relationships between church members should distinguish them from those outside the household of faith. God gives Christians the Spirit to live according to his will. Devoid of that power, unbelievers cannot enjoy the same quality of life.

The behavior of the Corinthian Christians, however, denied the difference between life inside the church and that outside. Some prided themselves in living by standards that even pagans deemed immoral. In personal conflicts, others resorted to worldly methods of appeasement.

In particular, Paul isolates two examples: incest (1 Cor 5:1-8) and litigation (6:1-8). For each case, Paul offers specific corrections followed by general exhortations against all immorality.

Proud About Incest (1 Cor 5:1-8)

Paul can hardly believe what he has heard: "It is actually reported that there is sexual immorality among you, and of a kind that is not found even among pagans; for a man is living with [lit. *is having*] his father's wife" (1 Cor 5:1)—that is, a church member is having regular sexual intercourse with his stepmother.

Both Jewish and Roman law specifically forbade such a relationship, as Paul alludes (cf. Lev 18:8; Deut 27:20; Cicero, *Pro Cluentia* 6.15; and Gaius, *Institutes*, 1.63). Yet, the response of the church disturbs Paul as much as the incest itself. Incredibly, the church boasts about the scandal, heralding his lifestyle as an example of Christian freedom (1 Cor 5:2, 6). "Should you not rather have mourned, so that he who has done this would have been removed from among you?" Paul asks (1 Cor 5:2). The church has lost its ethical discernment and abdicated its responsibility for corporate discipline.

From Ephesus Paul has already passed judgment. He now directs the church to effect the sentence. "You are to hand this man over to Satan for the destruction of the flesh, so that his spirit may be saved in the day of the Lord" (1 Cor 5:5).

"Handing over to Satan" means being cast out of the Christian fellowship and back into the world, the realm of Satan (cf. 1 Tim 1:20). Paul says the expulsion will result in "the destruction of the flesh." The word "flesh" can refer either to the man's physical body, as most scholars believe, or to his sinful nature.

Nowhere does the Bible teach that physical death might ensure spiritual salvation. If Paul envisages the death of the man, then it is because he is already saved. According to this view, Paul decides that it is now best for the church and its witness that the man's sinful earthly life end. If, however, the "destruction of the flesh" describes the eradication of the man's sinful nature, then this passage corresponds with Paul's teaching elsewhere. To live "in Christ" is to walk "in the Spirit" and not "according to the flesh" (e.g. 1 Cor 3:1-3; Gal 5:16-26; Rom 8:1-14). The goal of discipline is to restore—not destroy—life in its fullness (1 Cor 11:32).

Once ostracized, the incestuous man's entire existence would be challenged. Exposed to a fallen world without any religious and social benefits of the Christian circle, he would be compelled to re-evaluate his faith and lifestyle. Hopefully, repentance and return to the church would follow.

Excommunication also purifies the church. In 1 Corinthians 5:6-8, Paul mixes passover metaphors both to *warn* and to *affirm* the congregation. Just as passover preparations involved removing all yeast from one's house (Ex 12:15), the congregation must cleanse itself from immorality. Like yeast in dough, even a small amount of evil can permeate the entire community (cf. Gal 5:9). Paul reminds them that they "really are unleavened" because Christ the passover lamb has been sacrificed for them. Therefore, they should celebrate their purified status by living up to it.

Lawsuits Among Christians (1 Cor 6:1-8)

Living up to Christian standards also excludes launching a civil lawsuit against a fellow church member. Again Paul is astonished at their behavior, asking: "Do you dare take it [*a grievance*] to court before the unrighteous?" (1 Cor 6:1).

Paul's indignation shows the difference between his Jewish heritage and Greek culture. The rabbis instituted a court of arbitration for disagreements in the synagogue community; it defamed God to bring Jewish disputes before Gentile judges. By contrast, Hellenistic business life regularly entailed lawsuits; Greeks felt no shame in being frequent litigants.

Paul's view of Christ's return also militated against the church's use of the courts. Believers would join Christ in judging the world and angels. Meanwhile, it was absurd for Christians to submit to the world's judgments. Paul sarcastically asks, "If the world is to be judged by you, are you incompetent to try trivial cases?...Do you appoint as judges those who have no standing in the church?" (1 Cor 6:2, 4).

Further, when they are Christian, *both* sides in the courtroom lose even before a judgment is handed down. "To have lawsuits at all with one another is already a defeat for you," says Paul (1 Cor 6:7), offering two reasons.

First, to lay a case before unbelievers, the believer sacrifices the role and reputation of the church. Such a price is too high, suggests Paul. "Why not rather be wronged? Why not rather be defrauded?" (1 Cor 6:7; cf. Mt 5:39-40, Lk 6:29-30; 17:3-4). Second, defrauding someone, let alone a fellow Christian, shows that the malefactor has lost all personal integrity.

The public defeat can be avoided altogether while the church deals with the more fundamental problem of self-centeredness. Paul proposes that, as in the synagogue, the church should handle internally disputes among its members. This might involve the appointment of Christian judges to arbitrate between believers (1 Cor 6:5; cf. also Mt 18:15-17).

General Exhortations (1 Cor 5:9-13; 6:9-11)

Paul's specific directions for excommunication and internal arbitration are aimed at restoring the church's corporate integrity, but personal immorality is the underlying problem. So, in both cases the apostle follows up with ethical exhortations for individuals.

In 1 Corinthians 5:9-13 Paul still is responding to the report about the incestuous man, for he twice calls for expulsion (1 Cor 5:11, 13 quoting Deut 17:7). Still, that scandal alone has not by itself prompted this paragraph. Paul had previously instructed the church "not to associate with sexually immoral persons" (1 Cor 5:9). The Corinthians have distorted his command and likely have questioned it in their letter to Paul (cf. 1 Cor 7:1). He now clarifies his point.

Of course Christians cannot avoid all immoral people, argues Paul, "since you would then need to go out of the world" (1 Cor 5:10). Ultimately only God can stand in final judgment over the world, although he will then use the church (1 Cor 6:2). Meanwhile, the believing community should confront immorality *within* its membership. Specifically, Paul instructs the congregation not to associate with immoral *Christians*.

In both 1 Corinthians 5:9-11 and 6:9-10, Paul gives explicit examples of what he means by immorality in two lists:

... sexually immoral persons ... the immoral of this world ... the greedy and robbers ... idolaters ... revilers ... drunkards (1 Cor 5:9-11)	... wrongdoers ... fornicators, idolaters, adulterers, male prostitutes, sodomites, thieves, the greedy, drunkards, revilers, robbers ... (1 Cor 6:9-10)

Because Paul follows a traditional Hellenistic literary form, many scholars conclude that these vices are not specific to the Corinthian church. Rather, they are standard catchwords brought together to convey a total sense of reprobation (cf. Mk 7:21-23; Mt 5:19; Rom 1:29-31; 13:13; 2 Cor 12:20; Gal 5:19-21; Eph 5:3-5; Col 3:5-9; 1 Tim 1:9-10; 2 Tim 3:2-5). Yet, Paul imbues the Corinthian lists with unusual realism by reminding the congregation: "And this is what some of you used to be" (1 Cor 6:11).

Now, says Paul, they have a new life in Christ. "You *were washed*, you *were sanctified*, you *were justified* in the name of the Lord Jesus Christ and the Spirit of our God" (1 Cor 6:11). The three verbs are passive: the Corinthians did not change themselves; God through his Son and his Spirit cleansed them, set them apart as his holy people, and acquitted them.

Many scholars read the word "washed" as a reference to baptism. They note that the Greek verb also can be understood reflexively, meaning the Corinthians "washed themselves." In other words, they consented to baptism and were by that cleansed from sin. If Paul is alluding to baptism here, he does so indirectly and only under descriptions of *God's* saving work.

The Corinthian Christians have not realized the ethical implications of their salvation in Christ. Paul quotes their slogans: "All things are lawful for me" and "Food is meant for the stomach and the stomach for food" (1 Cor 6:12-13). These mottos in this context betray a belief that the body's sexual hunger could be fed as indiscriminately as its physical hunger. After all, they reasoned, whatever happened in the body had no eternal, spiritual consequence.

Paul utterly rejects this, affirming a view of the whole person that includes the physical body (1 Cor 6:13-20). He teaches that our physical bodies are now the Lord's forever. As Paul makes his case, he touches on several themes that he will later develop: idol meat in 1 Corinthians 8–10 and the imagery of our bodies as "members of Christ" (1 Cor 6:15) in chapter 12, while 1 Corinthians 15 will describe more how "God raised the Lord and will also raise us by his power" (1 Cor 6:14).

Celibacy, Marriage, and Divorce
(1 Cor 7)

A failure to integrate body and spirit also produced an inappropriate asceticism in the church. Married couples repressed their sexual relationship, believing it to be incompatible with their spiritual lives. Others discouraged marriage and even sought divorce for the sake of heightened spirituality.

Paul probably encouraged marriage in his previous letter as part of his warnings against immorality. Perceiving this as contradicting his earlier support of celibacy, the church challenges Paul. Or, possibly, church members had independently developed a doctrine of sexual abstinence. Regardless, the Corinthians have written Paul with questions about sex and marriage.

The topics change abruptly in 1 Corinthians 7 as Paul runs down their list of questions: "Should not married couples abstain from sex?" (v. 1); "Should not the unmarried and widows remain single like you, Paul?" (v. 8); "Should not Christian couples divorce in order to be more spiritual?" (v. 10); "If we are married to unbelievers, should we not dissolve the unholy union?" (v. 12). Finally, they ask about "virgins" (v. 25), although Paul's response is so obscure that we cannot be certain of the situation in question.

Paul's answers show a pattern. He first lays down a general life principle. Then he allows exceptions. In each case he gives the rationale, noting whether he speaks a "command of the Lord" or his personal opinion.

Concerning Abstinent Couples (1 Cor 7:1-7)

Seven times Paul introduces a topic in 1 Corinthians with the expression "Now concerning..." (Greek—peri de; see Figure 4-1). Like other Greek letter writers, Paul uses this formula to return to a matter raised in previous correspondence.

Usually just a single catchword is needed to identify the topic. In the first case, however, Paul appears to quote an entire sentence from the Corinthian letter: "Now concerning the matters about which you wrote: 'It is well for a man not to touch a woman'" (1 Cor 7:1).

"Touching a woman" is a euphemism for having sexual contact (cf. also Gen 20:6; Prov 6:29), comparable to sexual intercourse being described as "having" someone (1 Cor 5:1; 7:2; cf. Mk 6:18; Jn 4:18). In other words, the Corinthians have said to Paul: "It is good for men not to have sex with women." According to some in the Corinthian church, this is good advice even for the married.

Paul accepts this statement, but with *major* qualifications. While on first reading it is difficult to decide what is Paul's principle and what is his exception, identifying a rhetorical device in this paragraph aids our interpretation.

Verses 1-6 form an A-B-A structure known as a "chiasm." A chiasm is a series of assertions that move into and then out of a central point. The sequence of thought reverses after the central point, creating a balance and focus to the argumentation. Note the parallelism of the chiasm in 1 Corinthians 7:1-6:

Seven times Paul introduces a topic in 1 Corinthians with the expression "Now concerning..." (Greek—*peri de*). The formula reintroduces a matter raised in previous correspondence.

* * * *

"Now concerning the matters about which you wrote: 'It is good for a man not to touch a woman.'"—*7:1*

"Now concerning virgins..."—*7:25*

"Now concerning food sacrificed to idols..."—*8:1*

"As to the eating of food offered to idols..."—*8:4*

"Now concerning spiritual gifts..."—*12:1*

"Now concerning the collection for the saints..."—*16:1*

"Now concerning our brother Apollos..."—*16:12*

FIGURE 4-1

v. 1   A¹   It is well for a man not to touch a woman.

v. 2   B¹   But because of cases of sexual immorality...

C¹   each man should have his own wife
and each woman her own husband...

v. 3   D¹   The husband should give his
wife her conjugal rights...
likewise the wife...

v. 4   D²   The wife does not have
authority over her own body
...likewise the husband...

v. 5   C²   Do not deprive one another except
perhaps by agreement for a set time...

B²   so that Satan will not tempt you...

v. 6   A²   I say this as a concession...

The central point of this chiasm is found in the "C" and "D" elements: husbands and wives should give themselves sexually to each other. The reasons for recommending marital intercourse are offered in the "B" elements: to avoid sexual immorality and Satan's temptations due to a lack of self-control. Paul's exception to the rule is found in the corresponding "A" elements: couples may abstain from sex for a temporary period to devote themselves to prayer. The A¹ element (v. 1) helps us understand the nature of the concession in A² (v. 6).

In other words, Paul sets out the principle of marital intercourse as a norm (1 Cor 7:2-5). The exception is occasional abstinence by mutual agreement for spiritual development (1 Cor 7:1, 6). Paul recommends celibacy and singleness, but he recognizes that the ability to remain celibate is a gift from God (1 Cor 7:7). Others are given the gift of sexual union in marriage. Problems arise when people switch the contexts for each gift: sexual fulfillment without marriage and abstinence within it.

Concerning the Unmarried and the Widows (1 Cor 7:8-9)

Attention now turns to "the unmarried and the widows" (1 Cor 7:8). Most readers assume this section describes both those who have never been married and those whose spouses have died. Yet it is likely that Paul has in mind only widowers and widows, addressing each gender in parallel as he does in the rest of this chapter. By New Testament times, the Greek word for widower had disappeared from use. The word *agamos* (unmarried) replaced it in reference to men while the feminine counterpart *chera* (widow) remained current.

Should the widowed remarry? Paul provides both a straightforward answer and an exception to this question. In principle, they should remain unmarried as Paul has (1 Cor 7:8). However, those who are not restraining their sexual drives should marry (1 Cor 7:9).

The rationale for remarriage is that "it is better to marry than to be aflame with passion" (1 Cor 7:9). Literally, the Greek says "it is better to marry than to burn." As most translations attest, very few interpreters see this as a reference to "burning in judgment" (cf. 1 Cor 3:12-15; Is 1:25; Jer 9:7; Dan 11:35). Instead, Paul probably means that marriage is preferable to being consumed by unexpressed, or wrongly expressed, sexual desire (cf. Sir 23:16).

Paul's marital status comes into question here. The apostle wrote as an "unmarried" man (1 Cor 7:8). Was he never married, a widower, or divorced? Most scholars conclude that because Paul was a rabbi he was once married—marriage was required of rabbis. If so, then Paul's wife had since died, or, possibly, she left him when he became a Christian, in which case his comments in 1 Corinthians 7:15 are autobiographical.

Concerning Divorce Among Christian Couples (1 Cor 7:10-11)

Both the church and Paul appreciate celibacy, but Paul maintains that singleness is the only appropriate context for the celibate lifestyle. Should couples who have become Christian therefore divorce in favor of a "more spiritual" life of celibacy?

Paul's governing principle is unequivocal: Christian couples should not divorce. As well, his "exception" is not an exception: it offers no grounds to end a marriage. Paul simply recognizes that divorce will sometimes still happen. In these cases, he rules out remarriage to another and encourages reconciliation.

Paul may refuse to compromise because the command is given by, as he puts it, "not I but the Lord" (1 Cor 7:10). He is likely referring to the narrative preserved in Mark 10:2-12 (cf. also Mt 19:1-9 and 5:31-32). This is one of the few times in Paul's letters where he appeals to a saying of Jesus. At this time, the gospels were not yet written. Paul's knowledge of the oral traditions of Jesus would have been based on limited interaction with the Jerusalem apostles.

Again Paul speaks separately to the man and the woman, yet here he *begins* with the wife and only she is given an "exception" clause. Furthermore, he tells the wife not to *"separate"* from her husband, while he tells the husband not to *"divorce"* his wife. Paul's language probably reflects his Jewish background. In the synagogue community, a woman could not actually divorce her husband without his consent. In Greek society, she could, but such action was rare. Regardless, modern distinctions between separation and divorce cannot be applied. Here the words are synonymous; Paul uses them interchangeably of both genders in his next paragraph.

Concerning Divorce From Unbelievers (1 Cor 7:12-16)

Particularly in the first generation of any Christian community, it would be common that only one spouse in a marriage was a believer. In such instances, the biblical idea of becoming "one flesh" through sexual union and Paul's directions to avoid immoral people could further support the case for singleness, celibacy, and, in this case, divorce.

Again, Paul upholds the principle of no divorce (1 Cor 7:12-13). He grants an exception when the unbeliever initiates the separation. Paul derives the authority for these directions not from a saying of Jesus (cf. 1 Cor 7:10) but from his personal apostolic status (1 Cor 7:12), which he defends as "trustworthy" (1 Cor 7:25) and in "the Spirit of God" (1 Cor 7:40).

The rationale in 1 Corinthians 7:14 suggests that some thought marriage to an unbeliever would defile the believer. Paul reverses the argument. The believer's union with God consecrates his or her unbelieving partner. The unbeliever is "made holy" not to the point of personal salvation, which v. 16 describes only as a future possibility, but as some sort of divine blessing or protection by association with God's people (cf. Rom 11:16). Starting with a premise the Corinthians apparently accept, Paul argues that just as the children of a "mixed" marriage are "holy," not "unclean," God's grace extends into the life of the unbelieving spouse.

Incidentally, 1 Corinthians 7:14 has been used to support the doctrine of infant baptism. Yet this passage nowhere refers to the rite. What is more, if Paul were referring only to baptized children, his argument would break down: children made holy *by baptism* would not make their *unbaptized* parent holy.

Paul concedes divorce when the unbeliever initiates it: "But if the unbelieving partner separates, let it be so; in such a case the believer is not bound" (1 Cor 7:15). The reference to being bound, or literally "enslaved," has been strongly debated. All agree that Paul is at least saying the believer is not "enslaved" to maintaining a marriage even the unbeliever doesn't want. Some argue further that the believer is free to remarry. Paul does not address that question. He is speaking to those who decry all marriage for religious reasons, not to those who want out of one marriage to enter another.

Even when making the concession for divorce, Paul ends on a note of reconciliation: "[But] it is to peace that God has called you. Wife, for all you know, you might save your husband. Husband, for all you know, you might save your wife" (1 Cor 7:15-16). God calls Christians to harmony and not disunity. Remaining married at least preserves the potential for the unbeliever's salvation.

Because the Greek frames v. 16 as open-ended questions, a few interpreters turn Paul's optimism into pessimism. They understand him to say, "If the unbeliever wants a divorce, don't contest it. After all, we should take the peaceful alternative and not fight to keep the marriage. In the end, how do you know you will save your partner anyway?" Yet such a reading not only pushes the grammatical limits of the Greek, but it critically weakens Paul's central argument for keeping the marriage intact.

Clearly, Paul never recommends divorce. Yet, he is dealing only with those who are proposing divorce for religious and ascetic reasons. Paul does not address, for example, the questions of divorce on the grounds of adultery or abuse. Nor does he address the issue of remarriage in these contexts.

Concerning "Virgins" (1 Cor 7:25-38)

The final question on marital life concerns "virgins." Unfortunately, Paul responds with such vague language that we cannot confidently reconstruct the situation or even the marital status of the people involved. The obscure Greek grammar and vocabulary leave us with at least three possibilities:

(1) Heads of households who are inappropriately withholding permission for their virgin daughters or slaves to marry;

(2) Engaged couples who had subsequently agreed to remain unmarried for spiritual reasons but are now finding celibacy difficult to maintain;

(3) Married couples who had pledged abstinence as each other's "virgin" but now wish to "marry" in the sexual sense.

Most scholars opt for the "engaged couple" theory, although the "spiritual marriage" view does have a precedent in 1 Corinthians 7:1-7. In vv. 1-7 and 25-38, Paul allows for both celibacy and sexual expression. However, the two passages differ on what is the principle and what is the exception. Earlier, celibacy was the exception; now it is the ruling principle. So, it is best to understand "virgins" as unmarried but engaged couples.

For the fifth time, Paul urges his readers to maintain their present marital status. "Virgins" should remain single and celibate. Yet, Paul again allows an exception for those who cannot contain their sexual desire (1 Cor 7:36). Marriage is no sin (1 Cor 7:28, 36). As Paul puts it, "He who marries does well; and he who refrains from marriage will do better" (1 Cor 7:38).

Other Advice (1 Cor 7:17-24, 29-35)

While answering the Corinthian questions, Paul twice makes general comments that restate his fundamental theme. In 1 Corinthians 7:17-24 he calls his readers not to worry about the position in life they find themselves, whether they be married or single, circumcised or uncircumcised, slave or free.

Scholars divide, however, on interpretations of Paul's ambiguously worded advice to slaves in v. 21. Is he telling them to use their position as slaves *even if* they have the chance for freedom, or is he saying that they should make use of the opportunity for freedom? The first option fits the general theme of remaining in one's present condition. Still, the second seems another reasonable exception for Paul to make.

In 1 Corinthians 7:29-35, the apostle gives an eschatological urgency to his exhortations. "The appointed time has grown short," he explains, "...the present form of this world is passing away" (1 Cor 7:26, 31). Because of the imminent end, Paul wants his readers "free from anxieties" (1 Cor 7:32) and in a state of "unhindered devotion to the Lord" (1 Cor 7:35). For some this means they should remain married; for others it means continued celibacy.

Conclusion

The Corinthians took immorality and asceticism to extremes. These apparently incompatible tendencies both stemmed from the inability to relate properly the physical life to the spiritual. To address resulting ethical problems, Paul carefully balanced his words. He had to avoid saying something to quench the blaze of one error that would fuel the fire of another. Next, the question of eating idol meat promises the same challenge.

STUDY QUESTIONS

1. According to 1 Corinthians 5:1-5, Paul hopes to see certain results from the excommunication of the incestuous man. What might these be for the man? — for the church?

2. Twice Paul speaks of the body as a temple (1 Cor 3:16-17 and 6:19-20). What are the differences and similarities in these two uses of the metaphor?

3. List at least four of Paul's statements in 1 Corinthians 6:12-20 that show the dignity of our physical bodies.

4. How does Paul's expectation of the return of Christ affect his view of litigation? How does it affect his view of marriage? Is his eschatology relevant to your perspective on these same issues?

5. In what way does the specific context limit present applications of Paul's teaching on divorce and remarriage in 1 Corinthians 7:10-16? Can you derive some timeless, universal principles from his teaching here?

6. According to his comments in 1 Corinthians 7, does Paul see a place for asceticism in the Christian life?

7. Sometimes Paul directs the church based on a saying of Jesus (cf. 1 Cor 7:10). Other times it is from his personal apostolic status (cf. 1 Cor 7:12, 25). Is there any indication that he considers his commands to the church any less authoritative than those of Jesus?

8. Offer some examples from 1 Corinthians 7 that differentiate between Paul's "commands" and his "opinions."

Chapter 5

THE CHURCH EATING IDOL MEAT
(1 Corinthians 8–10)

Introduction

The setting changes from the bedroom to the dining room for the next question from the Corinthians. They have asked Paul about "food sacrificed to idols" (1 Cor 8:1, 4). Some Christians in Corinth believed that it was wrong to eat meat that had been sacrificed in the pagan temples. Other church members felt free to eat such meat. Whom would the apostle support?

His answer is not straightforward. In chapters 8 and 9 Paul acknowledges freedom to eat unless "weak" Christians are scandalized. Yet in chapter 10 he warns that *no one* should provoke the Lord by eating the meat of idol worship.

Paul's apparent vacillation is due in part to his conviction that *where* one ate and *why* one ate were more important than *what* one ate. Since people ate "idol meat" in a variety of settings, at times its consumption by Christians was wrong and at other times it was allowable. In 1 Corinthians 8–10 Paul carefully balances freedom in Christ, sensitivity to others, and the spiritual realities underlying worship.

Knowledge, Freedom, and Consideration
(1 Cor 8-9)

In Corinth, most food available had some connection with pagan worship (see Figure 5-1). Whether eaten at the temple or bought in the marketplace, someone would have initially sacrificed a portion of the

In New Testament times, most meat available had some connection with pagan worship whether it was eaten at a temple or elsewhere:

The Pagan Temple

The temple hosted a variety of activities within its precincts. Participants could expect food at all of these gatherings:

1. **At a worship service —**
   These services, devoted explicitly to the worship of a god or goddess, divided the meat of the sacrifice into three portions: (i) to be burned on the altar; (ii) to be eaten by the worshipers; (iii) to be put on the "table of the god" for use by temple priests and servants.

2. **At a public festival —**
   Political transitions, athletic events, theatrical presentations, and building dedications often involved the temples in their celebrations. Again, sacrifices would be made and banquets held in honor of the occasion. The meat at the banquets would be dedicated to the gods.

3. **At a private celebration —**
   Many wealthier patrons would rent the temple banquet facilities to host private functions such as birthdays, weddings, funerals, and simple parties. Friends and neighbors would be issued written invitations. Before the meal, a sacrifice in honor of the host god or goddess was observed.

Even after all those who gathered at the temple had eaten, and those who served in the temple had taken what they needed, there was often meat left over. This surplus would be sold through the public marketplace.

The Club Meeting

All voluntary associations — trade, social, and burial clubs — met together regularly in their halls for social and business purposes. They chose a god or goddess to oversee their meetings and sacrificed accordingly at their banquets.

The Marketplace

Much of the meat bought at the public market was temple surplus and therefore "idol meat" in the strictest sense. In addition, however, almost all food brought to the market could be considered by scrupulous Jews and Christians as "idolatrous" because its pagan owners had likely dedicated the flock, herd, or crop with a representative sacrifice at a temple.

The Home

If Christians bought meat at the marketplace for private consumption, or if they were invited to dine at a pagan's home, then the meat on the table would probably have some connection with idolatrous worship. Jews and Christians wishing to avoid *all* association with idolatrous sacrifices would have to raise and slaughter their own meat.

FIGURE 5-1

flock, herd, animal, or crop in honor of a god or goddess. Using the surplus of food from sacrificial worship, pagan temples catered to the community as banquet halls for a variety of social functions including funerals, weddings, birthdays, and simple parties.

Jews and Christians wishing to avoid *all* association with idolatrous sacrifices would have to raise and slaughter their meat themselves. They would also have to withdraw from the hospitality of their pagan neighbors. Invitations to the pagan home, trade meeting, or temple — for any occasion involving a meal — would have to be declined.

Daunted by these restrictions, the Corinthians have asked Paul about food sacrificed to idols (cf. the *peri de* of 1 Cor 8:1, 4). With qualifications, Paul quotes from their letter: "All of us possess knowledge" (1 Cor 8:1); "No idol in the world really exists" (1 Cor 8:4); "There is no God but one" (1 Cor 8:4); "Food will not bring us close to God" (1 Cor 8:8; cf. 6:13); "We are no worse off if we do not eat, and no better off if we do" (1 Cor 8:9); "All things are lawful" (1 Cor 10:23; cf. 6:12).

These slogans show that many church members ate idol meat — yet now they feel compelled to defend their actions. Critics included Jewish Christians influenced by Judaism's dietary regulations and Greek Christians haunted by their former worship of pagan gods. Perhaps Paul even cautioned against the practice, in his previous letter, as a response to mounting tension on this issue in the churches.

Earlier, Christians in Jerusalem had questioned the propriety of eating meat sacrificed to idols. To facilitate Jewish-Gentile table fellowship in the church, the apostles agreed that Paul should direct his churches to "abstain from what has been sacrificed to idols and from blood and from what is strangled" (Acts 15:29).

Though the apostolic decree addressed the matter of idol meat, Paul does not appeal to it with the Corinthians. Some scholars suggest that, in spite of Luke's description (cf. Acts 15:1-35), Paul was unaware of the agreement. More likely, however, he judged that a dictum from distant Jerusalem, directed to Antioch, would have had little weight among the contentious Corinthians.

Standing on personal apostolic authority, Paul argues from basic theological and ethical principles. To begin, he accepts the premise touted in Corinth that "all of us possess knowledge" (1 Cor 8:1) and such knowledge brings "liberty" to eat (1 Cor 8:9). Yet if that is all we know, says Paul, then our knowledge is deficient.

Knowledge is perfected by love. Paul states: "Knowledge puffs up, but love builds up. Anyone who claims to know *something* does not yet have the necessary knowledge, but anyone who loves *God* is known *by him* [or "knows *him*"] (1 Cor 8:2-3). The words in italics are absent in a few of our earliest and most reliable manuscripts. The shorter reading is preferable: Paul is saying that anyone who loves also knows. The longer reading, though less appropriate to the context, nonetheless teaches that love rather than knowledge distinguishes God's people.

The Corinthians are inflated by their knowledge that there is "no God but one…and one Lord, Jesus Christ" (1 Cor 8:4-6). All things exist from and for the Father through the Lord Jesus Christ. Since there are no other gods, "no idol in the world really exists" (1 Cor 8:4). If there are no idols, some Corinthians reason, then idol meat is simply meat.

Paul agrees. Yet, other believers don't have this knowledge; this is where love comes in (1 Cor 8:7-13). Love dictates that those with knowledge abstain from idol meat in the presence of the "weaker" members of Christ's body. Idol meat still prompts some in the community of faith to consider pagan gods. They cannot partake of the meat in good conscience. Other Christians who eat indiscriminately can provoke them to eat anyway—with damaging consequences. The weak defile their consciences, stumble, fall, and are destroyed (1 Cor 8:7, 9, 11, 13).

Paul holds the knowledgeable accountable; their behavior is sinful. "When you thus sin against members of your family, and wound their conscience when it is weak, you sin against Christ" (1 Cor 8:12). The misguided application of a monotheistic faith has ironic results: far from honoring their one Lord, the knowledgeable are offending him. Paul will further warn of the danger of this error in chapter 10.

As Christ gave his life for all believers (1 Cor 8:11), so the strong should give up their freedom to eat idol meat for the sake of the weak. Paul does not ask for a sacrifice he has not himself made. 1 Corinthians 9 points out that, as an apostle, Paul has certain freedoms and rights—all he willingly sets aside for the sake of the gospel.

Though Paul has given up some of his apostolic rights, he reminds the Corinthians that he is still an apostle. He has the credentials: he has seen the Lord (cf. Gal 1:16; Acts 9:3-5; 22:6-9; 26:13-15) and has founded churches. The Corinthians cannot argue, for the existence of their church proves his position. As he points out: "you are the seal of my apostleship in the Lord" (1 Cor 9:2).

In defense of his personal freedom, Paul reserves the rights he does not use. Specifically, he lists the apostolic rights "to food and drink…to be accompanied by a believing wife…[and] to refrain from working for a living" (1 Cor 9:4-6).

Considering the issue in chapters 8 and 10, some interpreters understand "food and drink" to be a reference to "idolatrous" food. In other words, Paul is claiming the freedom to eat food associated with idolatry. Others, however, read "food and drink" as a reference to meals provided by host churches for their apostles. This second interpretation better fits the immediate topic of 1 Corinthians 9:5-14.

His comments about being "accompanied by a believing wife" (1 Cor 9:5) also can be understood two ways: either Paul is reserving the option to marry or, presuming that choice, he is further claiming the right to have a wife travel with him at the expense of the churches. Again, the second reading is more appropriate, given the context.

Paul notes that most other apostles, including Cephas and "the brothers of the Lord" (1 Cor 9:5), brought along their wives. If James is one of Jesus' brothers whom Paul has in mind (cf. Gal 1:19 and Mt 13:55), then this is one of several instances where Paul cites Cephas and James together as apostolic examples (cf. 1 Cor 15:5-7; Gal 1:18-19; 2:9-14).

Barnabas and Paul live differently than the Jerusalem apostles. Commissioned to go to the Gentiles (Gal 2:9), these two chose to work a trade while ministering free of charge. Still, Paul insists that they still have the right *not* to work two jobs. Churches are responsible for the room and board of apostles and their spouses.

A simple sense of fairness demands that those who give to the church should receive from it. To support this principle Paul summons the authorities of common practice, scripture, and Jesus' command (1 Cor 9:7-14). Precedents are found in many spheres of life: soldiers receive their necessities; farmers help themselves to their produce; priests eat from temple offerings (see Figure 5-2). According to Deuteronomy 25:4, quoted by Paul, even animals have this right: "You shall not muzzle an ox while it is treading out the grain."

Employing a rabbinic style of interpretation, Paul contends that God, unconcerned for oxen, decreed this "entirely for our sake" (1 Cor 9:10). Scholars debate whether Paul is reinterpreting scripture with a disregard for its original intent, exaggerating for effect, or, more likely, using rabbinic methods of case law to extend the command. Unlike midrashic allegories, here the initial principle is not changed — it is reapplied.

The apostle crowns his case with a command from Christ that "those who proclaim the gospel should get their living by the gospel" (1 Cor 9:14; cf. Lk 10:7; Mt 10:10). His rights established, Paul still does not try to claim the actual benefits. Instead, he proceeds to explain why he intentionally surrenders his entitlements (1 Cor 9:15-27).

In the course of defending his right to live at the expense of the church, Paul draws from common practice in many spheres of society:

> **The soldier** serves at the expense of the army (v. 7).

> **The vineyard planter** eats the fruit he produces (v. 7).

> **The shepherd** drinks the milk of his flock (v. 7).

> **The ox** eats the grain it is harnessed to tread (v. 9).

> **The plower and thresher** share in the crop (v. 10).

> **Temple servants** eat from the altar sacrifices (v. 13).

Having established his rights, Paul draws from athletic imagery, probably associated with the Isthmian games, to explain why he does not use them:

> **Runners** train themselves rigorously to win the race and claim the prize: a wreath of celery. They give up everything else and focus on that one goal. Likewise Paul exercises self-discipline and singular purpose, but his wreath will not wither (vv. 24-26).

> **Boxers** do not box the air while fighting in the ring, nor does Paul flail aimlessly. He subjects himself to strict discipline and makes sure his efforts count, lest he be disqualified (vv. 26-27).

FIGURE 5-2

Paul acts in the interests of both the Corinthians and himself. God compels him to preach. He is free to accept payment, but he takes pride in preaching free of charge. By doing so, he creates no financial burden for others. What is more, he remains indebted to no one to do the task God has assigned him.

Being "free with respect to all," Paul still makes himself "a slave to all" (1 Cor 9:19). He explains that he will give up his freedoms to enter the world of those he must reach with the gospel. For example, he will conduct himself differently among Jewish people than he will with Gentiles (1 Cor 9:20-21).

If following the religious laws of Judaism will open the doors to the synagogue community, Paul will follow them. If those same laws are a barrier to faith in Christ among Gentiles, he will discard them. Paul is quick to qualify his actions in either case: he regards himself as neither "under the law" nor "lawless"—always he lives by "Christ's law" (1 Cor 9:21).

Paul brings the principle of accommodation full circle to apply to the Corinthian situation: "To the weak, I became weak, so that I might win the weak" (1 Cor 9:22). In other words, if the eating of idol meat compromises weaker people, then the strong should not eat it.

Not only the weak benefit; the strong also will gain from their consideration. As Paul puts it, they will "share in the blessings" of the gospel (1 Cor 9:23). Capitalizing on Corinthian pride in the Isthmian games, Paul likens ministry in the gospel to athletic competition. The reward comes only to those with a singular purpose and self-control.

With the promise comes a caution. Paul confesses that he disciplines himself "so that after proclaiming to others I myself should not be disqualified" (1 Cor 9:27). With these words, the apostle warns that God will hold his people accountable for the faithfulness of their ministry (cf. 1 Cor 3:10-17). Paul now proceeds to relate the "disqualification" to idolatry.

Idolatry and the Table of the Lord
(1 Cor 10:1-22)

"I do not want you to be unaware..." (1 Cor 10:1). As elsewhere, this phrase introduces information new to the readers (cf. Rom 1:13; 11:25; 1 Cor 12:1; 2 Cor 1:8; 1 Thes 4:13). What follows is the familiar story of the exodus, newly interpreted for the Corinthian situation.

Using a typological method of interpretation similar to Jewish midrash, Paul shows how the history of Israel prefigures that of the church "on whom the ends of the ages have come" (1 Cor 10:11).

Specifically, Paul interprets the exodus to teach that baptism and the eucharist do not protect Christians from the dangers of idolatry. The Corinthians dare not presume on God's grace while participating in worship services honoring idols at pagan temples.

Paul makes several connections between the Israelites and the Corinthians (see Figure 5-3). Just as the Israelites entered the cloud and the sea, Corinthian believers entered the waters of baptism. In the same way that the wilderness wanderers received "spiritual food and drink" provided by God, so too the Corinthian church celebrates the Lord's supper of bread and wine. Paul even goes as far to say that the rock that provided the water to Israel "was Christ" (1 Cor 10:4).

The comparisons between Israel and the Corinthian church take an ominous turn at this point. Some Israelites sinned against God by turning to idolatry and immorality; some Corinthian Christians are making the same mistake. In the desert some of God's people complained; in Corinth his people are grumbling about losing their rights in Christ. For their rebellion, thousands of the Israelites fell and were destroyed. "So," says Paul to his readers, "if you think you are standing, watch that you do not fall" (1 Cor 10:12).

Significantly, instead of referring to the golden calf, Paul quotes from Exodus 32:6 to describe the Israelite idolatry: "The people sat down to eat and drink and they rose up to play" (1 Cor 10:7). Paul has focused on the festive meals associated with worship, for this is the issue in Corinth.

On the one hand, all Corinthian Christians are sharing in the blood and body of Christ through the elements of the eucharist (1 Cor 10:16-17). On the other hand, some are also sharing in the meals of pagan worship. Though the idols which are the center of the ritual sacrifice do not actually exist, demonic powers of evil receive honor from them (1 Cor 10:20; cf. Deut 32:17). The two worship meals are mutually exclusive: "You cannot drink of the cup of the Lord and the cup of demons. You cannot partake of the table of the Lord and the table of demons" (1 Cor 10:21).

It is not idols, or even demons, that the Corinthians must fear most: it is the Lord. He is a jealous God that will not allow worshipers to share his place of honor with anything else (1 Cor 10:22; cf. Ex 20:4-5; Deut 32:21; Is 42:8). He will save and protect his people. When they are tempted to turn away from him, he will faithfully provide them with strength and guidance to endure (1 Cor 10:13). Yet, when provoked by idolatry among his people, his judgment is sure and strong. "Therefore, my dear friends," Paul writes, "flee from the worship of idols" (1 Cor 10:14).

Referring to the wilderness rebellion of the people of Israel, Paul tells the Corinthians: "These things occurred as *examples* (Greek—*'typoi'*) for us..." (1 Cor 10:7, 11). New Testament writers often drew parallels between the saving work of God as recorded in the Old Testament and the work of Christ. They understood Israel's experience to prefigure that of the church.

1 Corinthians 10:1-12 illustrates Paul's use of typological interpretation in direct application to the Corinthian Christians:

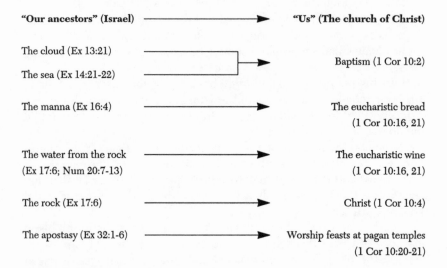

"Our ancestors" (Israel)	→	"Us" (The church of Christ)
The cloud (Ex 13:21)		
The sea (Ex 14:21-22)	→	Baptism (1 Cor 10:2)
The manna (Ex 16:4)	→	The eucharistic bread (1 Cor 10:16, 21)
The water from the rock (Ex 17:6; Num 20:7-13)	→	The eucharistic wine (1 Cor 10:16, 21)
The rock (Ex 17:6)	→	Christ (1 Cor 10:4)
The apostasy (Ex 32:1-6)	→	Worship feasts at pagan temples (1 Cor 10:20-21)

Paul says the rock that gave water to Israel "followed them" (1 Cor 10:7). Although this is not recorded in the Old Testament, Talmudic literature describes the rock climbing mountains and descending into the valleys with the Israelites as they traveled (*Tosephta Sukka* 3:11). By going on to say "... and the rock was Christ" (1 Cor 10:7), Paul strengthens the connection between God's saving action in the exodus and in Christ.

With this construct, Paul uses the exodus to teach that baptism and the eucharist do not protect Christians from the dangers of idolatry. Unless they want to suffer the same fate as idolatrous Israelites, the Corinthians dare not presume on God's grace while participating in religious feasts at pagan temples.

FIGURE 5-3

Conclusion
(1 Cor 10:23–11:1)

Chapters 8–10 give many reasons why a Christian is free to eat idol meat. They also present forceful arguments against the practice. In the final analysis, Paul affirms personal freedom based on the knowledge that idols do not exist and "all things are lawful" (1 Cor 10:23). However, he adds that our relationship to God and others conditions such freedom. For Paul, the context determines when Christians can eat idol meat. Several examples illustrate Paul's guiding principles:

Eat with a clear conscience all meat bought in the marketplace. Though the meat may have some association with a pagan sacrifice, Paul quotes Psalm 24:1 to note that ultimately the Lord provided it (1 Cor 10:25-26). All food can be eaten with thanksgiving to the creator (cf. 1 Cor 10:30).

Accept invitations to dine at a pagan's home and do not ask about the meal served. Should others point out that the food "has been offered in sacrifice," then abstain from eating for *their* sake (1 Cor 10:27-29). They may think that eating the sacrifice condones idolatry.

Use similar discernment and consideration when attending social functions at a pagan temple (1 Cor 8:10). However, never participate in temple meals that are part of the explicit worship of a pagan god. These idolatrous feasts jeopardize the Christian's relationship to God.

Paul's concluding paragraph on the issue of idol meat offers three guidelines that can be applied to any question of Christian behavior: "do everything for the glory of God ... give no offense to Jews or to Greeks or to the church of God ... be imitators of me, as I am of Christ" (1 Cor 10:31–11:1). In other words, Christians must worship only the Lord. They are to adopt a lifestyle that will bring as many as possible into a saving relationship with God. When needing guidance, they can follow the example of Christ and his servants.

STUDY QUESTIONS

1. List at least four contexts in which meat that had been sacrificed to idols might be inadvertently eaten by a Christian.

2. Why might a "weaker" *Gentile* Christian be offended by eating idol meat? Why might a "weaker" *Jewish* Christian?

3. What knowledge are some Corinthians claiming that justifies the eating of idol meat? What is more important than knowledge? Why?

4. Read 1 Corinthians 9:1. What are two criteria of apostleship implied in Paul's words here?

5. Describe in your words the specific rights of Christian leaders that Paul defends. Why must he defend them?

6. Read 1 Corinthians 9:15-18. What grounds does Paul have for "boasting"?

7. Read 1 Corinthians 10:1-12. In what way did Israel put the Lord to the test (1 Cor 10:9)? In what way are the Corinthians doing the same thing?

8. Explain the promise of 1 Corinthians 10:13. How does this fit in with the context of chapter 10?

9. List all the warnings in chapters 8–10 of judgment, falling, or being destroyed. Compare them to the promises of reward, blessing, and being saved. What message is Paul conveying in these references?

Chapter 6

THE CHURCH AT WORSHIP:
WOMEN AND MEN, RICH AND POOR
(1 Corinthians 11)

Introduction

To this point in the letter, Paul has been dealing with problems in the day-to-day lives of Corinthian Christians. Now he begins a four-chapter section dealing with the church at worship. The apostle focuses on three aspects of corporate worship: wearing head-coverings in prayer (1 Cor 11:2-16); cultivating unity at the Lord's supper (1 Cor 11:17-34); and exercising spiritual gifts (1 Cor 12–14).

All three features suffer from a lack of discernment in Corinth. The church does not make some distinctions that it should, and yet makes others that it should not; it nullifies differences that God created between genders while discriminating against the poor at the Lord's supper. As for spiritual gifts, we shall see in the next chapter that the enthusiastic worshipers do not recognize the need for balance, order, and variety (1 Cor 12–14).

Women and Men Praying and Prophesying
(1 Cor 11:2-16)

The gospel of Jesus Christ promised more freedom to women than either Greek or Jewish society gave. Paul proclaimed, "There is no longer Jew or Greek, there is no longer slave or free, there is no longer male and female; for all of you are one in Christ Jesus" (Gal 3:28).

Judging by 1 Corinthians 11:2-16, the women of Corinth misunderstood this good news.

Shedding the trappings of femininity, Christian women entered worship looking like men—without the customary veils on their head. Paul finds this behavior inappropriate. Yet, instead of expressing surprise and dismay, he begins with praise for the congregation: *"I commend you* because you remember me in everything and maintain the traditions just as I handed them on to you" (1 Cor 11:2).

This verse has a negative counterpart in v. 17: "Now in the following instructions *I do not commend you.* ..." A few scholars believe that these phrases belong side by side and speculate that the material in between (1 Cor 11:3-16) is a later insertion to the letter. In other words, they conclude that Paul never addressed the issue of women's veils. According to this view, Paul contrasts the Corinthian perspective on idol meat with which he agrees (1 Cor 11:2) to disturbing rumors about their abuse of the Lord's supper (1 Cor 11:17).

Yet more likely 1 Corinthians 11:2 reflects a statement in the church's letter to Paul. In context it confirms the women's right to participate actively in worship alongside men, just as Paul originally taught. Still, Paul's reaffirmation only prefaces further instruction. The apostle realizes that he must introduce a fuller perspective on gender distinctiveness and equality.

"I want you to understand," begins the apostle, "that Christ is the head of every man, and the husband [or *man*] is the head of his wife [or *the woman*], and God is the head of Christ" (1 Cor 11:3). The repetition of "head" in this sentence marks the focus for the rest of the passage. Figuratively, the Greek word for "head" (*kephale*) can mean "source," "origin," "first in sequence," "furthest extremity," or "authoritative leader." In this paragraph, Paul appears to have the sense of "source" in mind (cf. esp. 1 Cor 11:8, 12).

Using the term both literally and figuratively, Paul enjoins the Corinthians to show on their *physical head* that they recognize their *figurative head*. For the woman, this means wearing a veil when praying or prophesying. For the man, this means leaving his shorter hair uncovered. In other words, Paul is directing the church to maintain cultural conventions of appearance that distinguish between the sexes.

In first century Greek, Roman, and Jewish societies, women customarily wore long hair and head-coverings. By contrast, men kept their hair short and uncovered. Short or shaved hair on a woman was universally scandalous, often associated with lesbianism. Contrary to the speculations of some commentators, there is no evidence from the time to suggest that shaved heads identified prostitutes.

Christian women in Corinth would recoil at the thought of shaving their heads, as Paul's comments show. Knowing this, he argues that a woman removing her veil in worship is like having her hair cropped or even shaved; these practices are all "disgraceful" (1 Cor 11:5-6, 14-15).

Paul appeals to the two creation accounts of Genesis to support his argument that women should not try to look like men. Male and female were *both* created "in the image of God" (Gen 1:27), but the woman was taken "out of man" (Gen 2:23). Combining these two traditions, Paul says that a man "is the image and reflection [or *glory*] of God; but woman is the reflection [or *glory*] of man" (1 Cor 11:7).

Respect for the differences between man and woman acknowledges the sequence of creation. This in turn honors God, the ultimate source of all creation. Conversely, blurring the distinction between man and woman obscures the design of creation and thus detracts from the creator.

"For this reason," deduces Paul, "a woman ought to have a symbol of authority on her head, because of the angels" (1 Cor 11:10). This sentence is far from clear for modern readers since two of its phrases are very ambiguous. Our understanding of "authority" or "angels" affects our interpretation of the other.

The Greek word translated "authority" may also mean "right" or "power" and in context must refer to the veil. The veil, then, symbolizes one of three things: the woman's inherent right to pray and prophesy, the woman's submission to the authority over her, or the woman's protective power against malevolent angelic forces. The first of these options is most appropriate.

Explanations of wearing a veil "because of the angels" range from the mundane to the supernatural. One suggestion is that, since the Greek word for "angel" literally means "messenger," Paul wants women to wear veils so as not to offend delegates from other churches, particularly from Jerusalem. The context and the cryptic nature of Paul's language all but rule out this solution.

Other interpreters see here an allusion to the story of the evil "sons of God" who had sex with human women (Gen 6:1-7). According to this view, unless the Corinthian women want to suffer the same fate and consequent judgment, they should cover themselves with veils. Yet, the lustful spiritual beings in Genesis are not called angels, nor do they fit other biblical traditions about angels.

Paul surely has in mind "good" angels. Perhaps Paul, like the Jewish sectarians at Qumran, envisions these servants of God to oversee church worship and wants the women to show respect in their presence (cf. 1 QSa 2:8ff). Or maybe angels maintain the order of creation and

Paul does not want the women to resist them. Yet another interpretation best corresponds to what we know of the Corinthian church and its relation to angels.

Many Corinthians believed that they had already entered the new era Christ came to establish. They spiritualized their existence to the point that they lived as they thought angels would live. Among other things this meant they spoke in "tongues of angels" (1 Cor 13:1) and abstained from marriage and sex "like angels in heaven" (Mt 22:30; cf. 1 Cor 7:1-7, 29, 36-38). Therefore, Paul probably mentions angels here in chapter 11 mindful of their genderlessness.

In other words, the removal of gender distinctions in Corinth was another misguided move to be like the angels. The apostle must remind them that they are human beings, and not angels. When women remove their veils, they not only blur the distinctions between male and female, but they further obscure the God-ordained differences between humanity and the angelic order (see Figure 6-1). This refusal to maintain gender distinctions honors neither creator nor creation.

Altogether, v. 10 tells the women that they don't have to be like men or angels; as *women* they have the authority to pray and prophesy. They do not need to remove their veil to claim this right.

Lest readers misunderstand "head" (1 Cor 11:3) and "authority" (1 Cor 11:10) to mean unilateral male domination over women, Paul clarifies himself. In the church, gender does not dictate the direction of subordination or dependence. Christian men and women are interdependent (1 Cor 11:11). Even with "head" signifying "source," after creation women became men's immediate source of life (1 Cor 11:12).

Paul has affirmed gender distinctiveness, equality, and mutuality. Christian women in Corinth can affirm these same values by wearing a veil. As a final appeal, Paul leaves theological considerations and marshals the support of "nature itself" and the practice of other churches (1 Cor 11:13-16). Here "nature" cannot refer to biological factors: variations in hair length between genders are a matter of style and not physiology. Observing cultural propriety helps the Corinthians honor the differences God created between man and woman.

Rich and Poor at the Lord's Table
(1 Cor 11:17-34)

Even while the Corinthians have refused the conventions of their culture that distinguish between the sexes, they make social-economic distinctions that divide their church and ruin their observance of the

Paul tells the Corinthians, "Christ is the head of every man, and the man is the head of the woman, and God is the head of Christ" (1 Cor 11:3). He goes on to say that a woman ought to wear a veil on her head "because of the angels" (1 Cor 11:10).

These cryptic statements fit together as part of a call to maintain the divinely ordained human attributes of gender distinctiveness, equality, and mutuality (1 Cor 11:3-16).

God	God	God
Christ	Christ	Christ
Angels	Angels	Angels
Man	Man	Man
Woman	Woman	Woman

Through Christ, God created the angels, men, and women. Each created being is distinctive and fits within an order that glorifies the creator as ultimate source.	When women or men refuse to acknowledge their gender in ways their culture deems appropriate, they obscure the created differences between male and female. Rather than reflecting the glory of God, they detract from it.	In turn, genderless men and women blur the distinctions between humanity and angels, since angels are not sexual beings. By trying to be like the angels, the Corinthians honor neither the creator nor creation.

FIGURE 6-1

Lord's supper. In both cases, Paul must realign their perspective. Again, the Corinthians need discernment regarding the nature of the eucharist and its relation to the community of faith.

This one passage offers more teaching on the Lord's supper than any other in the New Testament. Yet, Paul aims his statements at a very specific problem. Any universal, timeless doctrines based on 1 Corinthians 11:17-24 must show a full appreciation of the original context.

Similar to reports from "Chloe's people" (1 Cor 1:11-12), other rumors of factions in the Corinthian church have reached Paul. As surprising as the nature of the division is, "to some extent" Paul believes the news (1 Cor 11:18). To him it is further evidence that some Corinthian believers lack an adequate appreciation of the body of Christ to which they belong (1 Cor 11:19). Some scholars take Paul to mean, in v. 19, that the apostle even considered the divisions a precursor of divine eschatological judgment.

In the early church, congregations gathered in the homes of wealthy hosts regularly for communal meals (cf. Acts 2:46). Each person brought food and drink to share in common with the others. During this "love feast," as it came to be called (Jude 12), Christians observed the Lord's supper with symbolic words and actions. The entire affair was a celebration of unity with Christ and, through him, with one another.

Wealthier members of the Corinthian church brought plenty to the feast while the poor could provide very little. Arrival times and the floor plan of the typical Corinthian house compounded this disparity. With more leisure time at their disposal, the rich could gather at their host's home earlier than the slaves and freedmen who worked longer hours. So, the meal would start for a privileged few in the *triclinium*, or inner dining room, without the rest of the church present (see Figure 6-2).

Late-comers arrived with their meager contributions only to discover the early arrivals gorged and drunk. The poor had to settle in the *atrium*, or outer court, with little or nothing to eat. The church's observance of the eucharist, even if it were possible, would not be a cause for celebration and remembrance.

Paul concludes it would be better if the Corinthians never bothered to gather for the Lord's supper than to continue with this behavior (1 Cor 11:17). He tells them, "When you come together, it is not really to eat the Lord's supper. For when the time comes to eat, each of you goes ahead with *your own supper* ..." (1 Cor 11:20-21).

The Greek grammar emphasizes that the Corinthians are eating their "*own* supper." By his choice of words, Paul stresses that each individual regards the food he or she brought as his or her *own* rather than

A typical villa floor plan from Corinth's Roman period

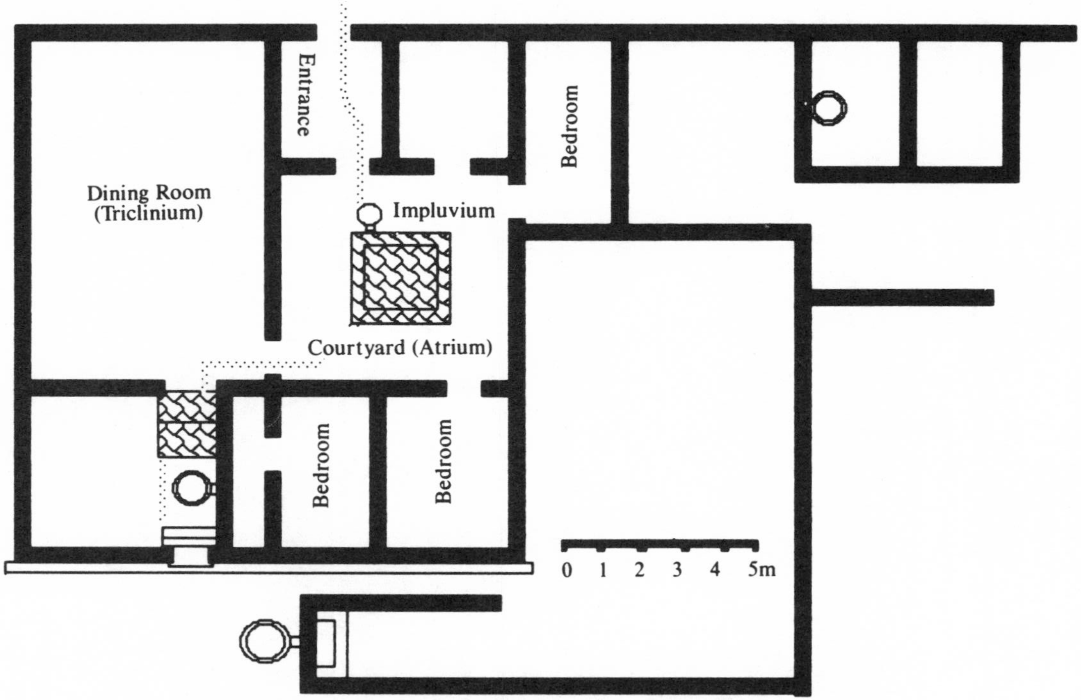

Entrance

Dining Room
(Triclinium)

Impluvium

Bedroom

Courtyard (Atrium)

Bedroom

Bedroom

0 1 2 3 4 5m

FIGURE 6-2

as part of the common meal. There may even be more to the point: Paul wanted them to recognize that their meal was no longer the *Lord's* supper. If all members did not share in the "one bread," then it was not the "table of the Lord" (cf. 1 Cor 10:17-21).

Instead of building up the community of faith, some in Corinth have torn it down. They "show contempt for the church of God and humiliate those who have nothing" (1 Cor 11:22). Paul's criticism is categorical; he can find nothing to commend in their observance of the eucharist. He must go back to basics to correct this disorder.

Taking nothing for granted, Paul recounts for them the fundamental account of the eucharist begun by the Lord just before his crucifixion (1 Cor 11:23-26). This is a rare instance where Paul appeals to an incident directly from the earthly life of Jesus. He uses technical expressions about "receiving" and "handing on," suggesting he had relayed an oral tradition that did not originate with him (cf. 1 Cor 15:1-3).

Evidence from the gospels confirms that Paul reflects an early account transmitted verbatim throughout the church (see Figure 6-3). Although Paul follows the same basic sequence as Matthew and Mark, only Luke and Paul have Jesus say, "Do this in remembrance of me" (1 Cor 11:24-25; Lk 22:19). Paul repeats the phrase, signaling his concern that the eucharist serve as a memorial in Jesus' honor.

Paul alone describes the observance of the Lord's supper as an ongoing proclamation of the death of Christ. In other words, the eucharist has ramifications for the church's view of the past, present, and future. Paul wants the Corinthians to *remember* Jesus' death for them whenever they gather to eat and drink. By doing so, they are covenanting together through Christ and declaring the gospel as they await his return.

The observance of the eucharist in Corinth has degenerated to the point that there is neither remembrance, nor covenant, nor proclamation. They are taking the Lord's supper "in an unworthy manner" (1 Cor 11:27). The consequences of such unworthy participation are severe.

Because of the unity that exists between all Christians and Jesus, taking the Lord's supper with no consideration for fellow believers displays disrespect for "the body and blood of the Lord" (1 Cor 11:27). God will judge this behavior and discipline his people accordingly. "For this reason," observes Paul, "many of you are weak and ill, and some have died" (1 Cor 11:30).

As difficult as this statement may be for modern readers to accept, it is not difficult to understand: the physical suffering of some Corinthian Christians is due to their abuse of the eucharist. Indeed, the biblical view of the person is holistic. Spiritual, social, emotional, and physical

Parallel Accounts of the Institution of the Lord's Supper

1 Cor 11:23-26	Mt 26:26-29	Mk 14:22-25	Lk 22:14-20
. . . the Lord Jesus on the night when he was betrayed took a loaf of bread, and when he had given thanks, he broke it and said,	While they were eating, *Jesus* took a loaf of bread and after blessing it he broke it, gave it to *the disciples*, and said,	While they were eating, he took a loaf of bread, and after blessing it he broke it, gave it to them, and said,	When the hour came, he took his place at the table, and the apostles with him. He said to them,
			"I have eagerly desired to eat this Passover with you before I suffer; for I tell you, I will not eat it until it is fulfilled in the kingdom of God." Then he took a cup, and after giving thanks he said, *"Take this and divide it among yourselves;* for I tell you that from now on I will not drink of the fruit of the vine until the kingdom of God comes."
"This is my body *that is for you. Do this in remembrance of me."*	"Take, *eat*; this is my body."	"Take; this is my body."	
In the same way he took the cup also, after supper, saying,	Then he took a cup, and after giving thanks he gave it to them, saying,	Then he took a cup, and after giving thanks he gave it to them, and all of them drank from it.	
"This cup is the new covenant in my blood. *Do this in remembrance of me." For as often as you eat this bread and drink this cup, you proclaim the Lord's death until he comes.*	*"Drink from it, all of you;* for this is my blood of the covenant, which is poured out for many *for the forgiveness of sins.* I tell you, I will never again drink of this fruit of the vine until that day when I drink it new *with you* in my Father's kingdom."	He said to them, "This is my blood of the covenant, which is poured out for many. I tell you, I will never again drink of the fruit of the vine until that day when I drink it new in the kingdom of God."	Then he took a loaf of bread, and when he had given thanks, he broke it and gave it to them, saying, "This is my body, *which is given for you. Do this in remembrance of me."* And he did the same with the cup after supper saying, "This cup that is poured out for you is the new covenant in my blood. . . ."

The words in italics mark significant differences between the wordings of the parallel accounts.

1. Luke's account is longest, referring to *two* cups and providing more comment from Jesus to the disciples.
2. Paul's account is shortest, yet he repeats the words "Do this in remembrance of me." This phrase is found elsewhere only once, in Luke.
3. Both Paul and Luke have Jesus saying, "This is my body . . . *for you.*"
4. Paul alone describes the Lord's supper as an ongoing practice that proclaims the Lord's death.
5. All four versions incorporate a reference to a future hope; the gospels frame it in "kingdom" language while Paul speaks of Christ's second coming. Instead of speaking of the "fruit of the vine" in this section, he refers simply to the "cup."

Paul stresses the ramifications of the Lord's supper for the church's view of the past, present, and future. In particular, he is concerned that the Corinthians *remember* Jesus' death for them whenever they gather for the eucharist. Every time they observe the Lord's supper, they covenant together and proclaim the gospel as they await the Lord's return.

FIGURE 6-3

factors are integrated so that dysfunction in one of these areas affects the others.

God's judgment on believers who abuse the Lord's supper should correct, not condemn. They can avoid *his* judgment if they exercise their own. They must ask themselves when they take the Lord's supper if they are "discerning the body" (1 Cor 11:29).

Paul's reference here to "the body" can refer either to the eucharistic loaf, the body of Jesus hanging on the cross, or the fellowship of believers. In other words, "to eat and drink without discerning the body" may mean receiving the eucharistic bread unaware while reveling in the feast. Or it can mean accepting the Lord's supper without reflecting on the physical suffering of Christ. The context best supports the third interpretation: to take the Lord's supper without discerning the body is to observe it with no consideration for the church, the body of Christ (cf. 1 Cor 10:17; 12:12-27).

Before receiving the eucharist, believers must determine whether they are living in unity with their brothers and sisters in the body of Christ. Paul ends with some practical advice for those who are eager to party in their exclusive cliques: wait for everyone else or feast at home (1 Cor 11:33-34). To exclude others from the celebration of the eucharist is to despise the church, disregard Christ's sacrifice for all, and incur God's judgment.

Conclusion

Believers at Corinth had not properly integrated their new life in Christ with their gender identity or their social status. As a result, when they gathered for worship they violated God's design in creation and denigrated his church. Paul gives them some guidelines for making better distinctions in the corporate life of the church. They are to respect the created order but transcend social status.

Created differences between man and woman are still in force and should be respected in our worship. Yet this does not subordinate women to men. In the church of Christ, the two genders are distinct, mutually dependent, and equal.

Social differences should never be a basis for acceptance in the church. A unified, covenanting community is the only context for the eucharist. When some from the body are neglected at the table, then it ceases to be the Lord's supper.

Celebrating unity in diversity is crucial for worship in the body of Christ. As we will see in the following chapter, this is no more evident than in the exercise of spiritual gifts.

STUDY QUESTIONS

1. Why were Christian women in Corinth removing their veils in worship? What did the veil symbolize? What did their removal of the veil indicate?

2. Paul uses the word "head" both literally and figuratively in 1 Corinthians 11:2-16. List the places where he uses it literally. List the figurative uses. Where he uses it figuratively, what possible meanings might he be implying?

3. Read 1 Corinthians 11:10 and answer the following two questions:
   a. Whose authority is symbolized by the veil—the man's or the woman's? Explain your answer.
   b. There are at least five ways to explain Paul's reference to "angels." List them and choose the one you think is best. Give the reasons for your choice.

4. What principles does Paul affirm regarding gender identity and worship in the church? How would you apply those principles to life in the church today?

5. What three things can the word "body" refer to in 1 Corinthians 11:17-34?

6. Who is abusing the Lord's supper in Corinth? How are they doing it? How would the floor plan of the typical Corinthian home contribute to this problem?

7. Compare Paul's account of the institution of the Lord's supper with those found in the gospels. In particular, what does Paul stress? How is this related to the situation in Corinth?

8. According to Paul, what corrective steps must the Corinthians take to redeem their observance of the eucharist?

9. Do you see similar potential for problems in the observance of the eucharist in your church today?

Chapter 7

THE CHURCH AT WORSHIP: SPIRITUAL GIFTS
(1 Corinthians 12–14)

Introduction

Whatever else it was, the assembled church in Corinth was exuberant. Christian women prayed and prophesied freely — without veils on their heads. The eucharist became a gala gathering — for those who could afford it. Still, there was a more spectacular sign of Corinthian enthusiasm — unrestrained ecstatic spiritual manifestations emerged.

Feeling moved by the Spirit, individuals in worship would spontaneously break into praise, prayer, or prophecy. Many would speak in a language intelligible neither to themselves nor to others. Often, more than one person would speak at a time. No one offered interpretations of the strange tongues. Unity, discernment, order, and meaning gave way to individualism, delirium, chaos, and nonsense. Christian worshipers in Corinth behaved as though they were out of their minds (1 Cor 14:23).

Interest in spiritual manifestations ran high enough to prompt the church to ask Paul about them, as the *peri de* of 1 Corinthians 12:1 attests. Yet Paul's response suggests as well that Paul is correcting a serious problem that the Corinthians do not acknowledge. Their preoccupation with the spiritual gift of tongues shows that they are overlooking more important aspects of worship in the body of Christ.

Paul moves them beyond their fixation on tongues to an appreciation of the diversity of spiritual gifts (1 Cor 12). He commends love as the ultimate spiritual quality (1 Cor 13) and returns to the form that tongues and prophecy will take when conditioned by consideration for others (1 Cor 14).

Unity and Diversity
(1 Cor 12)

Twice in his first paragraph Paul uses a phrase that shows he is revealing something new to his readers: "I do not want you to be uninformed... I want you to understand" (1 Cor 12:1, 3). For the first time Corinthians hear that no one under the power of the Spirit of God can speak a word against Christ and all who praise the Lord do so by the Spirit (1 Cor 12:3). In other words, the one Spirit of God works to bear witness in a variety of forms to the lordship of Christ.

This revelation must be understood in reference to ecstatic speech. "Speaking in tongues," or *glossolalia*, has always been a phenomenon of many religions and Paul alludes to its practice among pagans in Corinth (1 Cor 12:2). Possessed by one spirit or another, entranced devotees would act uncontrollably and speak as the spirits directed.

Corinthian Christians have imported their background of pagan spirituality to worship in the church. While not rejecting the validity of speaking in tongues, Paul sharply distinguishes between frenzied fervor and true worship directed by the Spirit of God. Behind the variety of expressions in Christian worship, there should be only one Spirit with one purpose (1 Cor 12:4-7).

Neither variety of expression nor unity of purpose characterized worship in the church at Corinth. For all the confusion, most in the church were doing the same thing: speaking in gibberish. Yet individuals followed their separate agendas, oblivious to the general order and direction of corporate worship. So, Paul must simultaneously unify their focus and diversify their practice.

God is the *one* source for all the gifts and ministries exercised in his church. Note the threefold way in which Paul refers to God in vv. 4-6: all the activities in the church are empowered by "the same *Spirit*," "the same *Lord*," and "the same *God*." Even within God, there is diversity within unity. Although Paul does not explicitly describe "the Trinity" as the church knows it, his language lays the foundation for the doctrine. Through the three expressions of his being, God distributes gifts, assigns service, and energizes his people.

As well as a single source behind all the worship activities of the church, there also is a collective purpose. As Paul says, "To each is given the manifestation of the Spirit for the *common good*" (1 Cor 12:7). In other words, spiritual gifts should build up the worshiping community as a whole. They are not given to individuals for self-centered goals.

God's Spirit, the only legitimate source, dispenses a diversity of gifts to accomplish his singular mission. Paul lists some gifts necessary for the church: wisdom, knowledge, faith, healing, miracles, prophecy, discernment of spirits, tongues, and interpretation of tongues (1 Cor 12:8-10). A comparison of this list with others shows that Paul was neither thinking exhaustively, nor establishing a particular priority of order (see Figure 7-1). Rather, the apostle gives examples to show that many types of activities are needed to build up the church and glorify the Lord.

Apart from naming them, Paul does not detail the exact nature of the various gifts. Tantalized by mere hints, interpreters from diverse theological backgrounds have offered extensive comments on each gift as it applies to church practice today. *All* such speculations necessarily go beyond the limits of the biblical text itself.

Most of the spiritual gifts Paul cites in 1 Corinthians focus on speech. As 1 Corinthians 14 will show, his main concern is that these "spiritual utterances" are meaningful to the whole congregation. Thinking more generally for the moment, Paul also lists gifts such as healing and miraculous powers.

The mention of the gift of healing may have prompted him to develop the imagery of the physical body and its many members in vv. 12-27. Saying we are all parts of one body, Paul likens the individual to a foot, hand, ear, eye, nose, head, or genital organ. Corinthian readers would be reminded of the hundreds of clay models of the various body parts offered for healing in the local temple of Asclepius, the god of healing (see chapter 2, Figure 2-1).

"If one member suffers, all suffer together with it; if one member is honored, all rejoice together with it" (1 Cor 12:26). Unlike dismembered, suffering limbs represented at the Asclepion, the church is a united, living body—a single living organism of diverse members joined in a mutually dependent life. Health issues from wholeness and, most importantly, union with *Christ*.

Other Greek writers used the metaphor of the body to describe social or political organizations. Yet Paul pushes the imagery beyond all other comparisons when he equates the body of the church with Christ's body. "Just as the body is one and has many members, so it is with *Christ* . . . you are the body of *Christ*" (1 Cor 12:12, 27).

Incorporating individual believers together into the continuing life of the risen Lord, Paul lays the foundation for what will become his dominant understanding of the church: it *is* the body of Christ. By the time he writes his later letters, his "body language" is no longer illustrative, it is descriptive. In reality, the church is Christ's body. What is

All believers in Christ are given the Holy Spirit and are to bear the same "fruit of the Spirit" in their lives (Gal 5:22-23). More specifically, however, Paul teaches that God, in his grace, has empowered each believer by his Spirit to perform distinctive and varying tasks in the life of the church. In several places he lists some of these gifts.

1 Cor 12:7-11	*1 Cor 12:28-31*	*Rom 12:6-8*	*Eph 4:11*
wisdom	apostles	prophecy	apostles
knowledge	prophets	ministry	prophets
faith	teachers	teaching	evangelists
healing	deeds of power	exhorting	pastors–teachers
working of miracles	healing	giving	
prophecy	assistance	leading	
discernment of spirits	leadership	compassion	
tongues	tongues		
interpretation of tongues	interpretation of tongues		

Unique to this list are the gifts of wisdom, knowledge, faith, and discernment. The Corinthian church's deficiencies in these areas probably motivate their mention.	Paul begins by enumerating an order: "first . . . second . . . third," but then speaks more generally.	As in the previous list, sometimes Paul designates the gift, sometimes he designates the person who practices the gift.	Describing gifts in terms of the people who practice them, this passage teaches that the ascended *Christ* has given these gifts.
Note that the gift of prophecy is placed farther down this list than it is in the others.	This particular order is not repeated elsewhere.	"Exhorting," "giving," and "compassion" appear as gifts.	"Evangelists" are introduced.
Each gift is either a gift of utterance or miraculous power.	Besides the gifts of utterance and miraculous power, Paul notes more "practical" gifts like "assistance" and "leadership."	In all cases, he further ascribes a desired attribute in the exercise of each gift.	Grammatically it is unclear whether pastors are to be distinguished from teachers.
His main point is that *each* person is allotted a gift by the Spirit.	His main point is that not all have the same gift.	His main point is that we must all display the grace of God as we practice our different gifts.	The main point is that Christ's gifts were given for the building up of his body.

A comparison of these lists shows that Paul was not thinking exhaustively in any particular instance, nor was he establishing a static priority of order in importance. All the gifts are to be practiced in relation to others and are meant to build up the body of Christ, the church.

FIGURE 7-1

more, the head is not just one among many congregational members. *Christ* himself is the head. Ephesians 4:15-16 puts it graphically:

> We must grow up in every way into him who is the head, into Christ, from whom the whole body, joined and knit together by every ligament with which it is equipped, as each part is working properly, promotes the body's growth in building itself up in love.

As Paul writes 1 Corinthians, he wants his readers to appreciate their diversity of function in a unified whole. Fixating on one or two particular spiritual gifts, and practicing them indiscriminately, divides the body. Paul has "a still more excellent way" to show them (1 Cor 12:31).

Love: A More Excellent Way
(1 Cor 13)

Perhaps the best known passage of Paul's letters, 1 Corinthians 13 has found an honored place among the literary classics. As polished prose, it transcends its epistolary context and continues to inspire audiences wherever the situation calls for noble praise of selfless, optimistic love. Its thirteen verses poignantly convey a concise, powerful, and poetic message that needs no explanation.

Yet, when the chapter stands alone, its intended significance is usually lost on those who hear it. Removed from its context, it offers no explicit *Christian* teaching. Yet, even if it was originally composed independently of 1 Corinthians, as some literary critics argue, Paul has offered it as the central focus of his teaching on *spiritual gifts* in the body of Christ.

All spiritual gifts are useless unless they stem from love (1 Cor 13:1-3). Speaking in tongues without love is mere noise like that sounded by Corinth's famous bronze gongs and cymbals. Prophesying without love is not inspired. Demonstrating understanding and knowledge is vain apart from love. The exercise of loveless faith is hollow. Giving to others, even to the point of bodily sacrifice, profits no one if it is not motivated by love.

What is this crucial quality called "love"? The term used in this chapter, *agape*, is one of several words for "love" in Greek. Its closest synonym, *philia*, denotes affection based on friendship. In comparison, *agape* is a more general term that does not necessarily specify a mutual relationship. While the New Testament uses both words to describe bonds between people as well as between God and people, *agape* was favored for describing Christian love. It conveyed a sense of respect for the object of love regardless of shared affections or personal attraction.

Using this most general and inclusive word for love, Paul personifies *agape* and describes "her" by what she does and does not do. Fifteen verbs follow in vv. 4-7. Love waits patiently and acts kindly. She neither envies, brags, puffs herself up, nor disgraces herself. Love never seeks her own advantage. She cannot be quickly irritated and harbors no grudges. Love does not enjoy wickedness but celebrates the truth. She always supports, trusts, hopes, and perseveres.

In other words, love is a way of life. What is more, it is the only way of life that will last. 1 Corinthians 13:8-13 develops a contrast between the present age and the age to come. Some scholars argue that Paul's reference to the coming of "the complete" in v. 8 refers to either the completion of the New Testament canon or the maturation of church office and structure. Yet neither interpretation fits into Paul's argument or perspective. Instead, he is speaking eschatologically.

In the present age, spiritual gifts such as prophecy, tongues, and knowledge afford us incomplete and indirect access to God. When we are in direct communion with him, these gifts will no longer be needed. Yet love, the greatest way of life, will continue to operate in all our relationships.

Paul uses two images to describe our transition from this age to the next. First he speaks of the growth from childhood to adulthood: "When I was a child, I spoke like a child, I thought like a child, I reasoned like a child; when I became an adult, I put away childish ways" (1 Cor 13:11). For the church in Corinth, obsessed with being "mature" yet acting like children, these words would be especially pertinent (cf. 1 Cor 3:1-2). Someday they would outgrow their need to express themselves with spiritual gifts — but they would always live in love.

Second, the apostle compares the present perspective to that of looking in a mirror: "For now we see in a mirror dimly, but then we will see face to face" (1 Cor 13:12; cf. 2 Cor 3:18). His analogy is apt, for highly polished Corinthian bronze was prized throughout the Mediterranean for use in mirrors. Still, images in the best of these metal mirrors would only approximate the realities they reflect. Likewise, the revelations of prophecy, knowledge, and tongues are partial and temporary. They will be unnecessary when believers enter God's presence. "Faith" will become sight, "hope" will be fulfilled, and "love" will continue (1 Cor 13:13).

Edification, Sense, and Order
(1 Cor 14)

With love in place as the foundation for life in the church, Paul returns to the form "spiritual utterances" should take. He is particularly concerned about prophecy and tongues. Under the force of love, clear guiding principles for their practice emerge. These gifts should edify, not divide; they should make sense, not nonsense; and they should be expressed with order, not disarray.

According to these criteria, the gift of prophecy is pre-eminent. By its very nature it builds community, since through it the prophet directs *other* worshipers. Prophecies are immediately meaningful since they come in the language of the audience. Because prophets can exercise self-control (1 Cor 11:32), they can speak one at a time, "so that *all* may learn and *all* be encouraged" (1 Cor 14:31).

Paul assumes his Corinthian readers know from his previous teaching exactly what he means when he refers to prophecy. Unfortunately, modern readers are not privy to that background. As a result, current conjectures about prophecy vary. For example, many assume that prophesying means predicting the future. Others limit it to expository preaching. Neither view is adequate in light of the biblical text.

A prophecy is a spontaneous message from God given to a person inspired by the Holy Spirit for the benefit of a group of worshipers. According to 1 Corinthians 14, prophecy builds up, encourages, consoles, reproves, teaches, discloses people's secrets, and calls to account.

In contrast to prophecy, tongues by themselves do not build community, make sense, or maintain order. Instead, they can splinter a congregation as individuals become isolated in their own spiritual realms. Those who speak in tongues utter unintelligible sounds that, at best, strengthen their personal devotion to God. The meaning of the tongue is lost even to the speaker (cf. 1 Cor 14:2, 14). When "the whole church comes together, and all speak in tongues," onlookers, seeing the discord, could only conclude that Christians were lunatics (1 Cor 14:23).

Sounds with no perceived arrangement are unintelligible. For example, says Paul, haphazard notes from a flute or harp do not make music. Unless a bugle issues a clear battle call, its sound will not rally the troops. Likewise, speaking in tongues that no one understands is like "speaking into the air" (1 Cor 14:9).

Unless the speaker and hearer both know the language, they remain alienated, foreigners to each other (1 Cor 14:11). Because Paul compares foreign languages and tongues, some interpreters conclude that tongues are actual human languages yet unknown to the speaker.

As evidence, they cite Acts 2:1-11 where Spirit-filled believers miraculously spoke in foreign languages, testifying to visitors from other countries about God's saving power.

To equate the "other languages" of Acts 2:4 with the tongues exercised in Corinth is to miss Paul's point. He is drawing only a loose analogy: *like* a foreign language, tongues are incomprehensible to the audience. The correlation ends there. Unlike the other languages of Acts, tongues in Corinth are not an instrument of public outreach. They are "mysteries in the Spirit" addressed to God alone (1 Cor 14:2; cf. Rom 8:26-27). They edify *the speakers*, but not necessarily those who hear them (1 Cor 14:4).

Far from benefiting outsiders, tongues can serve to drive them away from the church. Expressing it in a way that is easily misunderstood, Paul says tongues "are a sign for...unbelievers, while prophecy is...for believers" (1 Cor 14:22). For unbelievers, tongues do not point to the presence of God in the midst of his people. Instead, as Isaiah prophesied, "strange tongues" will confirm their skepticism (1 Cor 14:21; cf. Is 28:11-12).

Instead of repelling unbelievers with tongues, Paul insists that the Corinthians convert their ecstatic speech into a meaningful sign that elicits faith. They may do this by following each tongue with an interpretation (cf. 1 Cor 14:5, 13, 27-28). When interpreted for the group, tongues function as prophecy. Then outsiders become believers and more optimistic Old Testament prophecies are fulfilled: "After the secrets of the unbeliever's heart are disclosed, that person will bow down before God and worship him, declaring, 'God is really among you'" (1 Cor 14:25; cf. Is 45:14; Zech 8:23).

Having provided a theological rationale for modifying Corinthian worship, Paul concludes with some practical advice (1 Cor 14:26-40). Order must reign. Whether someone sings, teaches, speaks in tongues, interprets, prophesies, or evaluates the prophecy, they should speak one at a time while the rest are silent.

Three times in this section Paul calls for silence. First, tongues-speakers are to "be silent" if there is no one to interpret (1 Cor 14:28). Second, prophets who have been speaking should "be silent" when another receives a new revelation (1 Cor 14:30). Third, women are told to "be silent" while in church (1 Cor 14:34). Paul's words about women are unexpected and abrupt in this context:

> As in all the churches of the saints, women should be silent in
> the churches. For they are not permitted to speak, but should
> be subordinate, as the law also says. If there is anything they

desire to know, let them ask their husbands at home. For it is shameful for a woman to speak in church (1 Cor 14:34-35).

Since in this letter Paul has already stipulated guidelines for the public prayers and prophecies of women (cf. 1 Cor 11:2-16), the prohibition of chapter 14 poses a problem. On first reading, the two passages blatantly contradict each other.

Interpreters face three conclusions. Either Paul was absurdly inconsistent; or he did not write one of the passages; or the two texts address different situations. The first option is extremely unlikely and cannot be taken seriously.

The second option has some textual support, albeit weak: a few western Mediterranean manuscripts dating from the sixth century place vv. 34-35 after v. 40. The transposition may suggest that this was originally a non-Pauline marginal gloss that eventually found two separate places in the actual text of the letter.

The third option has the most support. Assuming women were allowed to pray and prophesy in church, chapter 14 must be forbidding another kind of speaking by women in the church. In these two verses, Paul uses the general term in Greek for talking: *lalein*. In contrast to *legein*, which always refers to the meaningful speech, *lalein* can refer simply to the sounds produced by people, animals, and even inanimate objects.

Paul is probably referring to women "chattering" in church or speaking at the same time as others. Consistent with his direction to others in this chapter, the apostle commands talkative women to be quiet and submit themselves to orderly behavior while in worship. Because they are behaving wrongly, Paul invokes "the law" (1 Cor 14:34). Most interpreters agree that this is an allusion to the curse of Genesis 3:16. As long as certain women act self-centered, they will remain in submission.

Conclusion

Paul had to correct the chaos of Corinthian worship. Many church members needed direction, including unveiled prophetesses behaving like men, selfish drunkards celebrating the eucharist, ecstatic speakers uttering nonsense simultaneously, and women chatting in the congregation.

An appreciation of others in worship would restore order in the congregation. So, Paul has called the Corinthians to recognize both the unity and diversity that comes from being part of the body of Christ. He has shown them the ultimate way to live — in love. The way of love conditions worship so that it always builds up the church and honors Jesus as Lord.

STUDY QUESTIONS

1. Both diversity and unity are to be aspects of corporate worship in the Christian church. In what way is there to be unity? In what way is there to be diversity?

2. What might be the possible background to Paul's imagery of the body in 1 Corinthians 12:12-26? How is this imagery further developed in later New Testament letters?

3. List the fifteen verbs that Paul uses to describe love in 1 Corinthians 13:4-7.

4. Offer your own definition and description of *agape* love according to 1 Corinthians 13.

5. "When the complete comes, the partial will come to an end" (1 Cor 13:8). What does Paul mean by "the complete"? Do you believe that "the complete" has come yet?

6. Do you believe that all the spiritual gifts Paul lists should be operative in the church today? Substantiate your answer.

7. Define and describe "prophecy" based solely on information gleaned from Paul's letters.

8. The value of "spiritual utterances" in corporate worship is measured against three criteria in 1 Corinthians 14. List these criteria.

9. Compare and contrast the tongues of Acts 2 with those of 1 Corinthians 12–14.

10. How would you interpret Paul's directions to women in 1 Corinthians 14:34-35 in light of those found in 11:2-16?

Chapter 8

THE CHURCH FACING DEATH AND BEYOND:
THE RESURRECTION
(1 Corinthians 15)

Introduction

Paul's agenda for writing is coming to an end. Throughout the letter he has touched on a wide spectrum of Christian living in the home, in public, and in the church. It is fitting that his last major section deals with the end of this life.

What happens when Christians die? Initially, the first generation of Christians, including Paul, did not have a definite answer to this question. The doctrine of the resurrection developed because of the unexpected delay in Christ's second coming. In 1 Thessalonians 4:13-18, for example, it is months after his initial founding visit before Paul teaches for the first time about resurrection. He is responding to their concern about the unexpected death of Christians.

Similarly in Corinth, Paul had introduced the principle of Christian resurrection, perhaps in his previous letter to the church. In reaction, some have challenged him. Either they have written Paul to ask how a decomposing corpse can be raised again, or he has heard rumors about their objections (1 Cor 15:12, 35).

Three convictions may have spurred the Corinthian reaction. As in Thessalonica (cf. 1 Thes 4:13-18), Corinthian Christians may have thought that those who survived until Christ's return would enter God's kingdom but those who died would be lost. Or, with most other Greeks, perhaps Corinthian Christians rejected the prospect of bodily resurrection in favor of an immortal soul finally free from the body.

More precisely, as shown in earlier passages, some Corinthian Christians believed that they had already transcended the physical world and were living a fully spiritual life. From their perspective, both death and resurrection were inconsequential aspects of Christian existence. They could comprehend neither the need nor the nature of a resurrected body.

Paul responds by arguing that the resurrection of Christians is an inevitable and necessary result of Christ's resurrection. The body will be transformed through resurrection to enable Christians to experience a spiritual life beyond anything they can even imagine.

The Fact of Resurrection
(1 Cor 15:1-34)

In 1 Corinthians 15:1-34, Paul presents the case for the bodily resurrection. As with other theological or pastoral questions, Paul finds an answer in what he knows of Christ: Jesus Christ, the resurrected one, would be the resurrecter for those who died in him.

The first two verses lay the foundation for the approach Paul will make. He reminds the Corinthians about the "good news" that united them with Christ. Without proclaiming and accepting this good news, the Christian faith is "in vain" (cf. 1 Cor 15:2, 10, 14, 17, 58).

What is this good news? It divides into three parts: Jesus died for our sins (1 Cor 15:3), he was buried (1 Cor 15:4), and he was raised from the dead on the third day (1 Cor 15:4). Christ died for *our* sins, not his. He was buried, proof that he was indeed dead. The power of these first two facts depends on the reality of the third. All else stands or falls on Christ's actual resurrection.

The tradition about the sacrificial death and resurrection of Christ did not originate with Paul. It comes from an early oral creed that he received and, in turn, passed on to the Corinthians (1 Cor 15:1, 30; cf. 11:23-26). In other words, he is participating in a widespread teaching. Because 1 Corinthians is one of the earliest documents in the New Testament, this passage is the most ancient account of the death and resurrection of Christ available to us. It arises within the first two decades of the actual events.

Paul maintains that the tradition of Christ's bodily resurrection rests on two types of testimony: written prophecy and eyewitness accounts. He appeals first to the testimony of the Old Testament. Christ's death and resurrection was "in accordance with the scriptures" (1 Cor 15:3-4).

Several passages include prophecies concerning the messiah. For example, Psalm 16:8-11 offers the hope of resurrection for the Lord's "faithful one." Hosea 6:2 describes the messiah reviving his people, stating "on the third day he will raise us up, that we may live before him."

Probably the most significant Old Testament scripture passage that points to Christ is Isaiah 52:13–53:12. This prophecy speaks of the death of God's servant, the messiah, for sinners. After his death, "he shall see his offspring, and shall prolong his days.... Out of his anguish he shall see light" (Is 53:10-11).

The sacrificial death and resurrection of Christ was divinely planned, and the world received hints about it hundreds of years ahead of time. Yet, God's revelation in the Old Testament was not the only evidence for the resurrection.

Paul draws from the testimony of hundreds of eyewitnesses in different places and different times. He lists six resurrection appearances. First, Paul says that Jesus appeared to Peter, then to the rest of the twelve (1 Cor 15:5). After that, at one time and place, he appeared to more than five hundred people. If the Corinthians wanted to corroborate Paul's report, he invites them to ask some of these witnesses; most of them were still alive (1 Cor 15:6).

Jesus also appeared to his brother James and again to the apostles (1 Cor 15:7). Further, Paul reminds the Corinthians that he too met the resurrected glorified Lord many years later (1 Cor 15:8). He likely recalls this so that no one could attribute the early reports of the resurrection to the troubled emotion of early believers. Despair did not "resurrect" Christ's presence in the hearts of bereaved believers.

The apostle strikes several jarring notes of self-disparagement in describing Christ's resurrection appearance to him. He calls himself "one untimely born... the least of the apostles, unfit to be called an apostle, because I persecuted the church of God" (1 Cor 15:8-9).

The reference to an untimely birth does not simply mean that, compared to the other apostles, Paul assumed his apostleship outside the expected time-frame. The Greek word Paul uses, *ektroma*, evokes revulsion: it refers to miscarriages, stillbirths, and abortions. Since Paul calls himself "*the* abortion," with the definite article, he may be using an epithet cast on him by scornful critics.

Rather than deny his faults, Paul highlights them to show God's grace (1 Cor 15:10-11). With subtle irony, he reminds the Corinthians that they have come to believe through him, "the least of the apostles" (cf. also 1 Cor 1:26-31; 2:1-5; 4:8-13). He will take the same tack, more vigorously, in 2 Corinthians 10–13. God's saving strength shines brightest from the weak.

According to 1 Corinthians 15:12-29, the resurrection of Christ is the ultimate sign of God's redemptive power. Christ's resurrection gives those in Christ hope of a resurrection. If there is no hope of resurrection, then the Christian message is stripped of its essentials.

If Christ was not raised, Paul says:	*If Christ was raised, Paul says:*
"Our preaching is in vain" (v. 14).	"Resurrection of the dead has come" (v. 21).
"Your faith is in vain" (vv. 14, 17).	"All will be made alive in Christ" (v. 22).
"We are misrepresenting God" (v. 15).	"Then comes the end, when Christ hands over the kingdom to God the Father, after he has destroyed every ruler and every authority and power" (v. 24).
"You are still in your sins" (v. 17).	"The last enemy to be destroyed is death" (v. 26).
"Those who have died in Christ have perished" (v. 18).	"When all things are subjected to him, then the Son himself will also be subjected to the one who put all things in subjection under him, so that God will be all in all" (v. 28).
"We are of all people most to be pitied" (v. 19).	

FIGURE 8-1

The resurrection of Christ is the ultimate sign of God's redemptive power. Christ's resurrection gives those in Christ hope of a resurrection. If there is no hope of resurrection, then the Christian message loses its essentials. Paul could not be more direct when, in 1 Corinthians 15:12-19, he spells out the ramifications of denying this fundamental tenet of the Christian faith (see Figure 8-1).

When skeptics dispute the reality of resurrection, says Paul, they do not make the gospel any easier to accept. They do not make Christianity more meaningful and relevant. Rather, they hold Christians up as spectacles for everybody to ridicule. They make Christian faith empty and useless.

Deniers of resurrection leave us with our sins unforgiven, reasons Paul. They imply that we still will be condemned because no one paid the debt and claimed the complete victory over the deadly powers of evil. They claim that the only life we have to live is the one we live right now, and Christians are wasting it away in a grand delusion. Ultimately, and worst of all, they implicate God in their lies.

If, however, we proclaim that Christ has been raised from the dead, argues Paul, then we proclaim much more (1 Cor 15:20-28). The resurrection of Christ offers promise to those who have died: he is the "first fruits" of a larger resurrection harvest. His resurrection gives meaning and substance to our faith, offering forgiveness for sin and victory over death.

Just as death has come to the human race through one man, Adam, victory over death comes through one man, Christ. The parallel between Adam and Christ teaches that resurrection is as inevitable for those "in Christ" as is death for all humanity. Secondarily, Paul's analogy affirms the *humanity* of Christ. The resurrection of Christ was the resurrection of a human being; therefore Christians can hope for a similar experience.

If Christ has been raised from the dead, reasons Paul, then all in Christ will also be raised into the presence of God. Those who have died will come to life; those who are still alive will be transformed (cf. 1 Cor 15:51-53), to live in an entirely new order.

The risen Christ has the power to break sin's deadly stranglehold over creation. He will abolish all evil, suffering, pain, deceit, ignorance, and oppression that mark earthly life. Quoting a messianic Psalm, Paul says Christ will "put all things in subjection under his feet" (1 Cor 15:27; cf. Ps 8:6). Through the resurrection, death, the last enemy of God, will evaporate. Brought before God by the reigning Son, all creation will bow down and worship him. God will be "all in all" (1 Cor 15:28).

Paul's argument now moves into a new arena, with one of the most puzzling sentences in the New Testament. He asks if there will be no resurrection of the dead, then why do certain people in Corinth "receive baptism on behalf of the dead?" (1 Cor 15:29). What was baptism for the dead? How does it relate to the New Testament teaching on baptism and salvation? Does Paul agree with the practice?

Scripture nowhere else alludes to the practice and Paul mentions it only in passing here. We may never know with certainty why and how Corinthians baptized for the dead. For good reason, then, the Christian church has not perpetuated the practice that some Corinthians had apparently observed.

With so little information to draw on, scholarly reconstructions of the practice are speculative and varied. The most natural reading of the Greek suggests that some people are baptizing by proxy for the sake of those who have already died. The beneficiaries of the rite may have come to faith in Christ but had yet to be baptized before dying. Or they may have been deceased unbelievers of Christian friends or family members.

A few commentators propose that unbelievers are being baptized so that they can be reunited after death with their deceased Christian friends. Still other interpreters maintain that "the dead" in v. 29 means nothing more than "the (dead) body." In other words, Paul asks why those who deny the resurrection would still baptize their bodies if corpses have no end but the grave. While this last interpretation removes the theological difficulties of v. 29, it hardly does justice to Paul's choice of words. Nowhere else does he use the adjective "dead" as a synonym for the physical body.

In any case, Paul neither condemns nor condones "baptism on behalf of the dead." He simply points out that even the practice of some in Corinth betrays a hope for the body after death. Without a physical resurrection, a bodily baptism is meaningless.

Likewise, without a physical resurrection, Paul considers his evangelistic activities as meaningless. If he has no hope of life after death, why does he continually endure mortal danger for the sake of his ministry? Getting specific, Paul asks, "If with merely human hopes I fought with wild animals at Ephesus, what would have I gained by it?" (1 Cor 15:32).

Although contests against hungry lions were staged in the Ephesian arena, Paul is probably speaking metaphorically of *human* opponents in the Asian capital (cf. 1 Cor 16:9). As a Roman citizen, he could not receive the sentence of death in the arena except before the Caesar in Rome. Still, mob rule in Ephesus could be just as deadly (cf. Acts 19:23-41; 2 Cor 1:8-9).

"If the dead are not raised," says Paul, "'let us eat and drink, for tomorrow we die'" (1 Cor 15:32). The apostle is quoting from Isaiah 22:13, but it also reflects well-known Epicurean philosophy prevailing in Corinthian society (see chapter 3, Figure 3-3).

Paul co-opts another familiar saying to conclude his call to belief in the resurrection. As the Greek poet Menander wrote, "Bad company ruins good morals" (*Thais* fr. 218; cf. 1 Cor 15:33). From this epigram we can conclude that some Corinthian Christians are challenging the idea of Christian resurrection because of conversations with non-Christians. This unbelief has implications for the present life, for it leads to bad ethics (1 Cor 15:34).

The bodily resurrection of Christians is not only a reasonable outcome of the resurrection of Christ, it is a necessary part of the saving plan of God. Christians need a resurrected body of a different nature to experience the spiritual life in all its fullness, as Paul now explains.

The Nature of Resurrection
(1 Cor 15:35-50)

This section begins with two questions: "How are the dead raised? With what kind of body do they come?" (1 Cor 15:35). Paul derides the one who asks, calling him "Fool!" (1 Cor 15:36). The intense rhetoric shows that he is not posing hypothetical questions for the sake of argument. Rather, he is responding to actual Corinthian objections framed as questions.

Paul answers that the body undergoes a radical transformation at its resurrection. To explain, he draws three analogies from the seeds, animals, and stars to illustrate different aspects of the nature of the resurrection body.

As did Jesus, Paul invokes a familiar religious symbol of life springing from death: the germinating seed (1 Cor 15:36-38; Jn 12:24, see also Figure 8-2). Jesus uses the imagery to teach that the Son of God, like a kernel of wheat, *must* die and be buried to produce a rich harvest. Paul stresses the change that occurs between the seed and the plant it sprouts.

The apostle compares the body before death to a "bare seed" (1 Cor 15:37). After it enters the earth, God clothes it with a body "as he has chosen, and to each kind of seed its own body" (1 Cor 15:38). The body that has risen is of a recognizably different order than the seed from which it grows.

The germinating seed is a familiar religious symbol of life springing from death. The Judeo-Christian tradition used the imagery to teach various aspects of resurrection.

Paul cites the example of the seed and plant to illustrate the change that occurs between that which is buried and the new life it sprouts —

> *"What you sow does not come to life unless it dies. And as for what you sow, you do not sow the body that is to be, but a bare seed, perhaps of wheat or some other grain. But God gives it a body as he has chosen, and to each kind of seed its own body"* (1 Cor 15:36-38).

* * * *

Jesus uses the imagery to teach that he, like a kernel of wheat, *must* die and be buried to produce a rich harvest. If he does not die, there will be no life for others; he alone will live. —

> *"Very truly I tell you, unless a grain of wheat falls into the earth and dies, it remains just a single grain; but if it dies, it bears much fruit"* (Jn 12:24).

* * * *

The Babylonian Talmud reports Rabbi Meir's response to the question, "Will the dead be raised naked?" —

> *"If a grain of wheat was buried naked and comes out of the ground abundantly clothed, how much more will the righteous be dressed in their clothes?"* (Sanhedrin 90b).

In 2 Corinthians, Paul talks about putting on clothes in the resurrection, although he does not use the imagery of a seed. —

> *". . . while we are still in this tent, we groan under our burden, because we wish not to be unclothed but to be further clothed, so that what is mortal might be swallowed up by life"* (2 Cor 5:4).

FIGURE 8-2

The resurrection body differs as much from the physical body as does the flesh of humans, animals, birds, and fish differ from one another (1 Cor 15:39). Each body has a nature and a "glory" suited to its environment. Even heavenly bodies that exist in the same environment radiate different glories, observes Paul. "There is one glory of the sun, and another glory of the moon, and another glory of the stars; indeed, star differs from star in glory" (1 Cor 15:40).

Picking up on the theme of glory, Paul goes on to contrast the glorious nature of the resurrected body with the mortal body (see Figure 8-3). The body that is buried is perishable, dishonored, weak, and physical; it is raised imperishable, glorious, powerful, and spiritual (1 Cor 15:42-44). In particular, Paul stresses the *imperishable* nature of the resurrected body (1 Cor 15:42, 50, 52, 53, 54). With these descriptions, Paul is not denouncing the physical body. Rather, he is highlighting the body's magnificent transformation at the resurrection.

What is physical will become spiritual, yet it will still be a bodily existence. Most interpreters agree that when Paul describes the resurrection body as "spiritual" he is not saying that the new body *consists* of spirit. Instead, he is saying that the resurrected body has transcended the natural order of existence. It is a "supernatural" body fit for life in the eternal, spiritual realm.

To show the relationship between "physical" and "spiritual" life, Paul again draws a parallel between Adam and Christ (1 Cor 15:45-49; cf. 15:21-22). In midrashic fashion, he quotes a text from the Torah and builds on it: "'The first man, Adam, became a living being'; the last Adam became a life-giving spirit..." (1 Cor 15:45; cf. Gen 2:7).

Just as the first Adam was "a man of dust," we too begin life with an earthly existence. Yet those in Christ also will experience a heavenly existence. Paul implies that his readers are already "of heaven" but their spiritual lives have yet to be fully realized.

A textual variant in v. 49 poses the question of whether life "in the image of the man of heaven" can be a present reality. Most manuscripts, including the earliest and most reliable, read Paul's statement as an exhortation: "...*let us* also bear the image of the man of heaven." A few other manuscripts simply predict that "...*we will* also bear the image of the man of heaven."

Most scholars opt for the second reading. They reason that from v. 35 Paul has been *describing* the resurrection body, not issuing ethical injunctions. Yet if we adopt the reading with the overwhelming manuscript support, then we see a familiar pattern. As in 1 Corinthians 15:1-34, Paul concludes a doctrinal section with its moral implications, urging the Corinthians to begin living eternal life in the image of Christ.

"Someone will ask 'How are the dead raised? With what kind of body do they come?'" (1 Cor 15:35). Paul answers this question by using the metaphor of a seed: "What you sow does not come to life unless it dies...you do not sow the body that is to be, but a bare seed" (1 Cor 15:36-37). The imagery effectively communicates both the continuity and the transformation that exist between what is sown and what is raised (1 Cor 15:42-49).

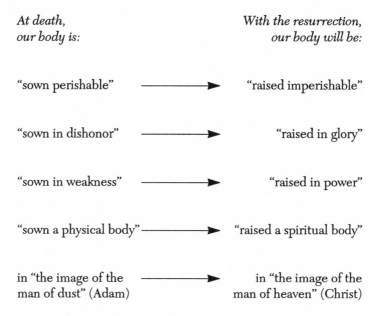

*At death,
our body is:*

*With the resurrection,
our body will be:*

"sown perishable" ———————▶ "raised imperishable"

"sown in dishonor" ———————▶ "raised in glory"

"sown in weakness" ———————▶ "raised in power"

"sown a physical body"———————▶ "raised a spiritual body"

in "the image of the ———————▶ in "the image of the
man of dust" (Adam)   man of heaven" (Christ)

Paul's description of the body before resurrection as "dishonorable" and "weak" is relative to the resurrected body. The earthly body is suited for the present life but unable to experience immortal life in the kingdom of God.

FIGURE 8-3

Conclusion
(1 Cor 15:51-58)

To this point, Paul has been teaching about what happens when a Christian dies and is buried. Now he proceeds to say to his readers, for the first time, that the resurrection hope holds promise even for those who will not die. "Listen, I will tell you a mystery! We will not all die, but we will all be changed..." (1 Cor 15:51).

The mystery that he reveals echoes his earlier words to the Thessalonian church, although he writes for different reasons. In 1 Thessalonians 4:13-18, he comforts a bereaved church without hope in resurrection. In Corinth, he corrects a smug church disdainful of a resurrection. He teaches the Thessalonians that all, whether dead or alive, will be caught up to meet the returning Lord. In 1 Corinthians he proceeds to say that at this time, *all* will undergo a necessary spiritual transformation.

Paul's apocalyptic timetable in 1 Corinthians 15:52 corrects the Corinthian realized eschatology. While those in Christ have already entered the spiritual life, they must wait until Christ's coming to apprehend it fully. When the end of this age comes, death will be vanquished.

Loose quotations from two Old Testament prophets celebrate the victory over death. "Death has been swallowed up in victory" (1 Cor 15:54; cf. Is 25:8). Paul follows this announcement with a taunt: "Where, O death, is your victory? Where, O death, is your sting?" (1 Cor 15:55; cf. Hos 13:14). With the coming of Christ, death loses all its power. It is not to be feared; it is not the end of life; it is not even necessary.

An easily misunderstood statement follows in v. 56: "The sting of death is sin, and the power of sin is the law." Paul is *not* damning the Mosaic law as sinful. Elsewhere he calls the law "holy, just, and good" (Rom 7:12). The law is the power of sin because its high standards expose the extent of humanity's sinfulness. It leads people to turn to Christ for grace and forgiveness. With faith in Christ, sin and the law can no longer join forces to pass the sentence of death.

As his concluding comment shows, Paul wants to motivate believers in their Christian walk with his teaching on the resurrection. People can choose to work "in vain" or "in the Lord" (1 Cor 15:58). A Christian faith without a resurrection hope is an empty faith. A Christian faith with a resurrection hope is a faith that gives a purpose to our present life and a promise of bodily existence beyond the grave.

STUDY QUESTIONS

1. Read 1 Corinthians 15:3-4. What three elements of the good news did Paul receive and pass on to the Corinthians? What is significant about each of these statements?

2. Paul appeals to two types of testimony to substantiate the resurrection of Christ. What are they?

3. In what way does Paul distinguish himself from the other apostles who witnessed the resurrected Christ?

4. According to Paul, can you deny the resurrection of Christ and still be a Christian? Explain your answer.

5. Describe at least four suggested interpretations of the practice of "baptism on behalf of the dead."

6. Read Figure 8-2. How do Jesus', Rabbi Meir's, and Paul's use of the seed analogy differ? What is Paul's main point in this analogy?

7. Compare 1 Thessalonians 4:13-18 with 1 Corinthians 15:50-58. What does 1 Corinthians add to the teaching of 1 Thessalonians?

8. Compare Paul's quotations from the Old Testament in 1 Corinthians 15:45, 54, and 55 with their actual wording in the Old Testament. What emphases are made by Paul's changes?

9. Does knowing that your body will be resurrected and changed affect the way you will live your present life? If so, in what way?

Chapter 9

TRANSITIONS
(1 Corinthians 16 —
Introduction to 2 Corinthians)

Introduction

Paul has addressed the main issues that prompted him to write. Two minor items of business remain. Apparently, the Corinthians have asked Paul about arrangements for the collection for Christians in Jerusalem. They have also requested that Apollos make a return visit to Corinth.

After responding to these requests in 1 Corinthians 16, Paul typically concludes his letter with travel plans, closing exhortations, and personal greetings. Understandably concerned about their attitudes and behavior, he announces plans to visit the Corinthians within the year. Meanwhile, he hopes that this letter will prepare the way for a warm welcome and an extended stay.

Unfortunately, as 2 Corinthians reveals, Paul's hopes were not fulfilled. Between the writing of 1 and 2 Corinthians, his relationship with the church degenerates. He, Timothy, and Titus make separate visits to Corinth to settle matters.

Eventually, Paul and the church are reconciled, but only after some painful exchanges. In the face of a renewed challenge to his apostolic authority, Paul must write again on the nature of Christian ministry.

Plans for Ministry
(1 Cor 16)

Two issues in 1 Corinthians 16 anticipate further visits to Corinth by Paul or members of his team. Both have been raised before, and

Paul uses the phrase *"peri de"* to reintroduce the matters (1 Cor 16:1, 12, see also chapter 4, Figure 4-1).

The first question put to Paul concerns "the collection for the saints" (1 Cor 16:1). This project arose from Paul's visit to Jerusalem when he introduced his Gentile mission to the other apostles. While in Judea, he agreed to collect money from the Asian and Greek churches to help the famine-stricken Christians in Jerusalem.

In his previous letter, Paul must have announced the collection to Corinth. Yet, before they open their purses the Corinthians ask about *how* they should go about collecting the money. It is difficult to tell whether they are wondering about the mechanics of the collection or they have concerns about the legitimacy of the enterprise. Later, when Paul writes 2 Corinthians 8–9, the Corinthians have yet to participate fully in the project.

Now, in 1 Corinthians, Paul responds diplomatically. He offers clear directions while giving the church complete discretion in handling the funds. By subtly mentioning the Galatian churches, Paul assures the Corinthians that they are not the only church he is soliciting.

Every Sunday the Corinthians were to set aside money they could spare so that when Paul arrived a fund would already exist. Like other churches, Corinth has the option of sending a contingent with the money to Jerusalem (1 Cor 16:3). Paul offers to lead the delegation, or, at the least, write letters of introduction for the travelers. Such letters were a normal part of business dealings in the Roman era (cf. Acts 21:25; Rom 16:1-2; esp. 2 Cor 8:16-24).

Earlier in 1 Corinthians, Paul *threatened* the Corinthians with a visit (1 Cor 4:18-21). Now he is more conciliatory as he explains why he is delaying the trip. As he writes in Ephesus, it is early spring. Mounting opportunities and opposition in the Asian capital demand the apostle's attention. He hopes to be free to travel in the fall, after the feast of Pentecost.

Going overland through Macedonia, Paul wants to arrive in Corinth for an extended winter stay. Twice in vv. 6 and 7 he says he wants to spend a considerable amount of time with the Corinthians. Paul sees this as an important visit for the sake of his relationship with the church.

Paul adds that when the time comes for him to leave Corinth, he expects them to cover his travel expenses. This is what the common phrase "send me on my way" meant (1 Cor 16:6; cf. Acts 15:3; Rom 15:24; 1 Cor 16:11; 2 Cor 1:16; Tit 3:13; 3 Jn 6). Judging by his earlier comments in 1 Corinthians 9:4-18, this is the first time Paul will ask for personal financial support from the church.

According to 1 Corinthians 4:17, Paul is sending Timothy to Corinth. As he concludes the letter, he again urges the church to accept the young man's authority as Paul's envoy (1 Cor 16:10-11). Clearly, Paul is worried about the reception Timothy might receive and he reminds them that Timothy will be returning to Paul with a report.

If the Corinthians could choose an apostolic delegate to host, they would nominate Apollos. They have already requested his return, as the *peri de* of 1 Corinthians 16:12 attests. Considering the personality cults in the Corinthian church, that Paul "strongly urged" him to go is an unequivocal vote of confidence in Apollos. Also, that Apollos declined at this time is a sign of the Alexandrian's wisdom. He would not fuel the fire of rivalries in Corinth.

With the business now addressed, Paul concludes his letter in a typical pattern: hortatory remarks (vv. 13-18); greetings (vv. 19-20); autograph (v. 21); and benediction (v. 23). To his standard form, he adds a warning (v. 22) and a personal wish of love (v. 24).

1 Corinthians 16:15-18 implies that Stephanas and his associates have been loyal to Paul in the midst of the tensions in Corinth. Paul clearly regards Stephanas as a leader and asks the Corinthians to treat him accordingly. We know nothing about the two other men except that Fortunatus was Roman and Achaicus was from southern Greece. Their names were common, especially among slaves and freedmen.

Paul tells the Corinthians that "the churches of Asia send greetings" (1 Cor 16:19). This is the only place in Paul's letters where he sends greetings from *all* the churches of a province. The letter thus ends as it opens: with a stress on unity with those in every place who profess faith. Divided loyalties have no place either in the local church or in the church universal of which the Corinthians are a part.

Aquila and Prisca, who were former residents in Corinth (Acts 18:1-3), send greetings. As v. 19 shows, they are now hosting a church in their home in Ephesus. As well, the couple had lived in Rome until the emperor Claudius expelled all Jews in A.D. 49. They must have been wealthy since they traveled so widely and owned homes large enough to accommodate fellow Christians in each city.

Finally, Paul takes the reed pen from his secretary, perhaps Sosthenes (1 Cor 1:1). The apostle supplies his autograph (cf. Gal 6:11; Col 4:18; 2 Thes 3:17) and personally curses non-Christian antagonists (1 Cor 16:22). Then, ending on a positive note, he invokes an eschatological prayer: "*Maranatha.*"

Depending on the division of the Aramaic transliteration, Paul is either stating "Our Lord has come" (*Maran atha*) or, more likely, praying "Our Lord, come!" (*Marana tha*; cf. Rev 22:20; *Didache* 10:6). In either case he gives Jesus the title *Mar*, which the Hebrew (Aramaic) language reserved for God. It is with hope in the Lord's return that Paul signs off with a benediction of grace and love for his readers (1 Cor 16:23-24).

The Contexts, Composition, and Themes of 2 Corinthians

Nothing turned out the way Paul planned after he sent 1 Corinthians. The letter was not well received. Timothy quickly returned from Corinth with bad news. Circumstances in Ephesus thwarted Paul's announced visit to Corinth. Attitudes in the congregation degenerated. Paul's leadership faced a major challenge from outsiders and the apostle reacted angrily. 2 Corinthians reflects a long and painful process of conflict and eventual reconciliation.

2 Corinthians shows that Paul's fears about Timothy's reception were founded and Timothy was disappointed. Although the letter does not recall Timothy's visit, it alludes to a challenge to the young man's integrity (2 Cor 1:19). As well, Paul's abrupt and "painful visit" (2 Cor 2:1) presupposes Timothy's early return to Ephesus with a discouraging report.

Writing retrospectively in 2 Corinthians, Paul explains the reasons for his change in plans (2 Cor 1:8–2:2). Rather than wait until after Pentecost (1 Cor 16:8), he felt it necessary to make a disciplinary visit immediately. After a short and stormy encounter, Paul backtracked to Ephesus.

Two factors played a part in Paul's decision not to winter in Corinth as he had initially planned. First, he and his team became embroiled in a life-threatening "affliction" in Asia and he was not free to leave (2 Cor 1:8-11). Second, as he says, "it was to spare you that I did not come again to Corinth...so I made up my mind not to make you another painful visit" (2 Cor 1:23–2:1). In other words, the painful visit did not settle the issues and Paul left Corinth still upset.

Instead of another personal confrontation, Paul sends Titus to Corinth with a painful letter (2 Cor 2:3-11; 7:8-13). Paul hoped that this would prompt Corinthian repentance and allow a more congenial visit in the future. However, overcome by anxiety, Paul could not wait for an arranged rendezvous in Troas; he enters Macedonia to find Titus (2 Cor 2:12-13). When the two meet, Titus shares consoling news of Corinthian repentance (2 Cor 7:5-16). The grieving church has even disciplined one of its offenders (2 Cor 2:5-9; 7:11-12).

With the burden of worry lifted, Paul offers the reconciling message of 2 Corinthians 1–9. Titus carries it back with directions to complete the collection for Jerusalem (2 Cor 8:6, 16-24). At this point, Paul remains in Macedonia. He does, however, announce intentions to visit Corinth a third time (2 Cor 12:14; 13:1) and Acts 20:2-3 reports that Paul stopped over in Greece, likely Corinth, for three months.

Nothing more is heard of the Corinthians until Clement of Rome writes to the church more than forty years later. He writes because the church had split under the influence of "a few rash and self-willed individuals" (1 Clement 1:1). With 1 Corinthians in mind, the bishop of Rome appeals to "the letter of blessed Paul the apostle" (1 Clem 47:1-3).

Interestingly, there is no evidence that Clement knew of 2 Corinthians. Yet, by the middle of the second century, 2 Corinthians circulated as part of the Pauline collection. This observation, and others more compelling, lead to the conclusion that 2 Corinthians is a later compilation of at least two letters.

The Composite Nature of 2 Corinthians

Even a superficial reading of 2 Corinthians reveals a dramatic change in tone between chapters 1–9 and 10–13. Paul changes from a conciliatory pastor to a confrontational protagonist. Relief gives way to anger; threats replace reassurances. What is more, Paul's travel plans vary. In chapters 1–9 he speaks of refraining from a visit (2 Cor 1:23; 2:1) while 2 Corinthians 10:2 announces an imminent trip (cf. also 2 Cor 10:11; 12:14; 13:2, 10).

Paul is not the only one who changes at chapter 10; the church does as well. In chapters 1–9, the Corinthians are repentant and obedient (cf. 2 Cor 7). Chapters 10–13 reflect an arrogant, rebellious congregation led astray by some "super-apostles" who are challenging Paul's leadership (cf. 2 Cor 11:1-5).

These contrasts convince all but a few scholars that Paul wrote the two sections at different times. Most consider chapters 10–13 to be the severe letter written *before* 2 Corinthians 1–9 (see Figure 9-1). Others maintain that Paul wrote 2 Corinthians 10–13 *after* 2 Corinthians 1–9 in response to yet another crisis in Corinth.

Part of a *third* letter also may be embedded in 2 Corinthians. Sometime after Paul evangelized Corinth, but before he wrote 1 Corinthians, he wrote the so-called "previous letter" (1 Cor 5:9). In it he warned the church to avoid immorality and idolatry. This early letter is either totally lost or partially preserved in 2 Corinthians 6:14–7:1.

Two clues suggest that a fragment of the previous letter lies here. First, 2 Corinthians 6:14–7:1 completely derails an otherwise unbroken train of thought running through chapters 6 and 7. Without the jarring

Was 2 Corinthians 10–13 Written Before 1–9?

In 2 Corinthians 2:3-11 and 7:8-13, Paul refers to a previous letter sent with "much distress and anguish of heart and with many tears" (2 Cor 2:4). He wrote it immediately after a "painful visit" (2 Cor 2:1) in the hopes it would prompt Corinthian repentance and allow a more congenial visit in the future. His severe letter works and the Corinthians respond with grief, repentance, discipline, and obedience (2 Cor 7:7-13). Relieved, Paul responds with the reconciling message of 2 Corinthians 1–9.

Chapters 10–13, however, do not follow smoothly. A comparison of the comments in the two sections have convinced most scholars that 2 Corinthians 10–13 comprises the severe letter written *before* 2 Corinthians 1–9. Notice how well statements in chapters 1–9 read as fitting resolutions to tensions reflected in chapters 10–13.

2 Corinthians **10–13**	2 Corinthians **1–9**
"Examine yourselves to see *whether you are living in the faith* . . ." (2 Cor 13:5).	". . . we are workers with you for your joy, *because you stand firm in the faith*" (2 Cor 1:24).
"We are ready to punish every disobedience *when your obedience is complete*" (2 Cor 10:6).	"I wrote for this reason: to test you and to know *whether you are obedient in everything*" (2 Cor 2:9)
"I fear that when I come, I may find you not as I wish . . . there may perhaps be quarreling, jealousy, anger, selfishness, slander, gossip, conceit, and disorder. . . . *I may have to mourn* over many who have previously sinned and have *not repented* of their impurity, sexual immorality, and licentiousness . . . (2 Cor 12:20-21).	"*Now I rejoice*, not because you were grieved, but because your grief led to *repentance*; for you felt a godly grief. . . . For see what earnestness this godly grief has produced in you, what eagerness to clear yourselves, what indignation, what alarm, what longing, what zeal, what punishment! At every point you have proved yourselves guiltless in the matter" (2 Cor 7:9-11).
"Since many boast according to human standards, *I will also boast*. . . . Indeed *you should have been* the ones *commending me*, for I am not at all inferior to these super-apostles . . ." (2 Cor 12:11).	"Are we beginning to *commend* ourselves *again*? . . . *We are not commending ourselves to you again*, but giving *you* an opportunity to *boast about us* . . ." (2 Cor 3:1; 5:12).
"I warned those who sinned previously and all the others, and I warn them now, while absent, as I did on my second visit, that *if I come again, I will not be lenient*" (2 Cor 13:2).	". . . *it was to spare you that I did not come again* to Corinth . . . so I made up my mind not to make you *another painful visit*" (2 Cor 1:23–2:1).
"So *I write* these things while I am away from you, so that *when I come, I may not have to be severe* . . ." (2 Cor 13:10).	"*I wrote* as I did, so that *when I came I might not suffer pain* . . ." (2 Cor 2:3).

FIGURE 9-1

interruption, the two sentences of 6:13 and 7:2 would fit together seamlessly: "In return—I speak to you as children—open wide your hearts also.... Make room in your hearts for us; we have wronged no one, we have corrupted no one, we have taken advantage of no one."

Second, the concerns of the interjection parallel those of the previous letter. Paul wrote 1 Corinthians to answer questions about his previous letter: what did he mean when he said the church was to avoid people who were immoral (1 Cor 5:9-11), unbelieving (1 Cor 7:12-16), or idolatrous (1 Cor 8, 10)? A reading of 2 Corinthians 6:14–7:1 raises the same questions.

As compelling as the evidence is, theories about the composite nature of 2 Corinthians remain theories. Such reconstructions may help in understanding the contexts and origins of the document. They may illumine obscure comments in the text. Still, responsible interpreters must deal ultimately with the final form of 2 Corinthians. From at least the second century, the "single letter" as it now stands has shaped faith and practice in the Christian church everywhere.

The Themes of 2 Corinthians

The question of literary unity aside, 2 Corinthians displays all aspects of Pauline letter structure. It has a salutation, thanksgiving, body, and conclusion (see Figure 9-2). The topics of the letter have a wide range, but they all relate to Paul's sense of Christian ministry.

Whether he describes past adversities, present reconciliations, or future hopes, Paul consistently models the nature of true ministry. Whatever he has done, it was for the sake of the church. Whatever he asks of the Corinthians, it is for the sake of Christ's body, the church universal. Whatever glory there is in ministry belongs to Christ.

He tells the Corinthians that his suffering is "for your consolation and salvation" (2 Cor 1:6). When ministry involves suffering, it leads to consolation and reconciliation. God has "reconciled us to himself through Christ, and has given us the ministry of reconciliation" (2 Cor 5:18).

Paul implores the Corinthians to participate in the collection for Jerusalem as a ministry of the gospel. "The rendering of this ministry," writes Paul, "not only supplies the needs of the saints but also overflows with many thanksgivings to God. Through the testing of this ministry you glorify God by your obedience to the confession of the gospel of Christ..." (2 Cor 9:12-13).

According to 2 Corinthians, even "boasting" has a place in true Christian ministry. Yet such boasting does not follow human standards. As in 1 Corinthians, Paul says, "Let the one who boasts boast in the

Salutation
(1:1-2)

- names the senders and recipients
  - relays greetings

Thanksgiving
(1:3-7)

- recalls past afflictions and God's consolation
- expresses hope for consolation of the readers
  - foreshadows concerns in the letter

Body
(1:8–13:10)

Whether a single or composite letter, 2 Corinthians revolves around the theme of "ministry."

- Recalling the Past: Affliction, Consolation, and Forgiveness (1:8–2:13)
- A Ministry of the New Covenant: Glory and Reconciliation (2:14–5:21)
- A Ministry of Righteousness, Suffering and Reassurance (6:1–7:16)
- A Ministry of Giving: The Collection (8:1–9:15)

- -

- A Ministry of Glory: The Grounds for Boasting (10:1–13:10)

Conclusion
(13:11-13)

Final Exhortations (13:11)
General Greetings (13:12)
Benediction (13:13)

FIGURE 9-2

Lord" (2 Cor 10:17; cf. 1 Cor 3:21). The Christian ministry glorifies the saving work of Christ that transforms human weakness into a sign of God's grace.

Conclusion

For Paul's sake, it would have been good if 1 Corinthians settled matters in Corinth. Yet, for the sake of the church in succeeding generations, it was better that he had to write more. The Corinthian correspondence provides a rare opportunity to be party to an extensive conversation dealing with many issues over several years. In particular, 2 Corinthians provides unparalleled insight into how Christ can mend broken relationships and restore his people to effective ministry.

STUDY QUESTIONS

1. List at least three remaining items of business that Paul addresses in 1 Corinthians 16.

2. Compare travel plans in 1 Corinthians 16 to those of 2 Corinthians 1–2 and 7. What are the differences between Paul's plans and what happened?

3. What evidence do we have that Timothy's visit to Corinth was troublesome?

4. What two factors played a part in Paul's decision not to spend the winter in Corinth as he had initially intended?

5. What are the two ways of understanding the phrase "Maranatha" in 1 Corinthians 16:22? Does this phrase imply anything about the divinity of Christ?

6. List at least four observations that suggest 2 Corinthians is a composite letter.

7. List three reasons why many interpreters think that 2 Corinthians 6:14–7:1 is part of the previous letter mentioned in 1 Corinthians 5:9.

8. Judging from comments in the letter itself, what was Paul's main reason for writing 2 Corinthians 1-9?... for writing 2 Corinthians 10-13?

Chapter 10

RECALLING THE PAST: AFFLICTION, CONSOLATION, AND FORGIVENESS
(2 Corinthians 1:1–2:13)

Introduction

Ambivalence sways Paul as he opens this letter. On the one hand, he expresses tremendous relief that he has come through a terrible ordeal in Asia. On the other hand, he anxiously broaches some sensitive unresolved issues that stand between him and Corinth. Paul must explain that, through none of his fault, the past distress has created the present tension.

His explanations offer theological insight into suffering, consolation, and forgiveness. Paul recognizes human limitations and affirms faith in God's sovereignty. And, on a personal level, his explanations show the depth of Paul's love for God and his church.

The Letter's Opening
(2 Cor 1:1-7)

As in 1 Corinthians, the formal opening of 2 Corinthians relays both routine information *and* significant themes. In particular, the greeting and thanksgiving sections confirm the basis for unity between Paul and the church. This will lead to an invitation to enter again a spirit of sharing.

In contrast to his other letters, Paul here does not elaborate his self-identification. He calls himself "an apostle of Christ Jesus by the will of

God" and cites Timothy as co-sender (2 Cor 1:1). At most, this subtly re-establishes apostolic authority for Paul and his young delegate.

Paul uncharacteristically expands the identification of recipients to include not just the Corinthians but "all the saints throughout Achaia" (2 Cor 1:1). By this, he guides his readers to regard themselves as part of the larger body of Christ. This greeting also implies that the Corinthians regularly related to Christians in outlying regions.

Instead of his customary "I thank God," Paul follows the greeting with "Blessed be the God..." (2 Cor 1:3). As with other thanksgivings, this paragraph praises God for his work in the church and in Paul's ministry. Here Paul is particularly thankful for God's consolation.

While he refers to suffering and affliction in every sentence of the thanksgiving (2 Cor 1:3-7), Paul does *not* feel sorry for himself. To the contrary, he celebrates the fact that suffering becomes a channel of God's grace. "For just as the sufferings of Christ are abundant for us, so also our consolation is abundant through Christ" (2 Cor 1:5).

As always, Christ stands at the center of the apostle's world. Paul understands his suffering from the perspective of "the sufferings of Christ." This may refer either to Christ's suffering for our sake or our suffering for Christ's sake. Both ideas fit well into Paul's theology, but the context here suggests that Paul considers himself to be enduring the sufferings of Christ.

Paul perceives a close mystical link between Christ and his follow-ers. We share in Christ's suffering so that we also may share in his glorification (Rom 8:17). Part of knowing Christ is "the sharing in his sufferings by becoming like him in his death" (Phil 3:10).

United with Christ, Paul can say, "In my flesh, I am completing what is lacking in Christ's afflictions for the sake of his body, that is, the church" (Col 1:24). As difficult as this statement is to interpret, it clear-ly affirms that participation in the suffering of Christ was an integral part of Paul's ministry.

Several factors may have contributed to the apostle's perspective on this shared suffering. There was a widespread apocalyptic belief that God's people would suffer "birth pangs" heralding the imminent return of the messiah (cf. Mk 13; Mt 24; Lk 17:22-37; 21:7-36; 1 Thes 5:1-11). As he awaited Christ's second coming, Paul expected tribulations to escalate.

Also, for Paul, the idea of the church as the body of Christ united the Lord and his people in suffering. On the road to Damascus, the exalted Christ confronted Paul with the words "I am Jesus, whom you are persecuting" (Acts 9:5; cf. also 22:8; 26:15). From that point, Paul could never separate Christ's suffering from the church's. As the body suffers, so does the head; as the head, so the body.

Suffering enables us to minister to others. "If we are being afflicted, it is for your consolation and salvation; if we are being consoled, it is for your consolation, which you experience when you patiently endure the same suffering that we are also suffering" (2 Cor 1:6). True ministry requires true empathy. Paul assumes that the Corinthians also would share in the sufferings of Christ, the mark of authentic service in the Christian life.

If Christian suffering is inevitable, so is the consolation that comes from Christ. Although some scholars think that the formal thanksgiving continues to v. 11, it is more compelling to see it end here on a note of hope, as in Paul's other letters: *"Our hope for you is unshaken*; for we know that as you share in our sufferings, so also you share in our consolation" (2 Cor 1:7).

An Affliction in Asia
(2 Cor 1:8-11)

The main body of the letter begins with important news that explains Paul's delay in coming to Corinth, signaled by the initial disclosure formula: "We don't want you to be unaware, brothers and sisters..." (2 Cor 1:8; cf. 1 Cor 10:1; 12:1; Rom 1:13; 11:25; 1 Thes 4:13).

Using the strongest possible language, Paul tells the church of a sustained life-threatening affliction he and his associates endured in Asia: "We were so utterly, unbearably crushed...we despaired of life itself...we had received the sentence of death...so deadly a peril..." (2 Cor 1:8-10).

Though striking, Paul's words do not reveal the exact nature of the danger. Some interpreters maintain that Paul is alluding to a serious illness, perhaps his "thorn in the flesh" (cf. 2 Cor 12:7-9). Yet the legal terminology and mention of others involved point to another type of trouble. Elsewhere we read of Paul and his team struggling against opponents in Ephesus (1 Cor 16:9).

Acts 19:23-40 reports a riot and arrest spurred on by silversmiths angered by Paul's interference in their business at the Ephesian temple of Artemis. Paul may have this crisis in mind when he says, "I fought with wild animals at Ephesus" (1 Cor 15:32). He also says that Prisca and Aquila, who worked with him in Ephesus, "risked their necks for my life" (Rom 16:4). Based on these and other indications, many scholars conclude that after sustained conflict Paul was imprisoned for at least several months in Ephesus. During this incarceration, facing the prospect of death, he may have written Philippians (cf. Phil 1:12-30).

In retrospect, Paul is glad for the Asian experience. It drove him to "rely not on ourselves but on God who raises the dead" (2 Cor 1:9). The apostle expects further peril, but he has confidence that God "will continue to rescue us" (2 Cor 1:10). Paul draws the Corinthians into the process. They can share in God's work of deliverance by praying for Paul, as many others do (2 Cor 1:11).

Paul's attitude through this ordeal is a model for the church. His trials cause him to lean on his Lord even more. He knows that he does not suffer alone; Christ and his body unite with him so that he may endure. Still, the effects of his detention have not been completely overcome. Sadly, some within the Corinthian church now question his word. He must recover their confidence in him.

Censure from Corinth
(2 Cor 1:12–2:11)

Was Paul lying when he said that he was coming for a winter stay in Corinth? Since the visit never happened, some Corinthians wondered. Was Paul unstable? A coward? Or not concerned for them? These questions prompted Paul to respond with a frank defense of his integrity, commitment, and care for the Corinthians.

Paul does not boast in his foresight or his personal agenda. Instead, he stands on his sincere openness before God and the church. He has always acted with a clear conscience, realizing the limits of his knowledge and acknowledging the gracious sovereignty of God (2 Cor 1:12). He tactfully suggests that the Corinthians need to do the same. They must recognize their limited understanding and have confidence in Paul (2 Cor 1:13-14).

The apostle intended to stop in Corinth not once but twice. The first stopover would be on the way to Macedonia. Then, returning from the north, Paul would stay in Corinth for the winter before heading to Jerusalem with the collection. He has already announced the second visit in 1 Corinthians 16:5-6. Yet the first visit seems a contradiction of 1 Corinthians 16:7. No doubt the unforeseen crisis in Corinth led to this short visit "in passing" to Macedonia.

Putting the best light on the situation, the two visits would mean the Corinthians "might have a double favor" (2 Cor 1:15). Literally the phrase speaks of "a second *grace*" and it can be understood in one of two ways. Either Paul intimates that the Corinthians will benefit twice from Paul's presence or, more likely, they will have a second chance to contribute to the collection.

As it turned out, Paul never made it to Corinth for the winter. Critics said Paul was making promises he never intended to keep. Was he "ready to say 'Yes, yes' and 'No, no' at the same time?" (2 Cor 1:17). Those words echoed the well-known lines of the Roman dramatist Terence, who describes the credo of a flattering scoundrel: "Whatever they say, I praise; if again they say the opposite, I praise that too. If one says no, I say no; if one says yes, I say yes. In fact I have given orders to myself to agree with them in everything" (*The Eunuch* 251-253; cf. also Cicero, *On Friendship* 25.93 and Plutarch, *How To Tell a Flatterer from a Friend*, 52b-53d).

Yet, an adamant Paul insists that he and his associates have consistently acted with integrity. "As God is faithful," he vows, "our word has not been 'Yes' and 'No'" (2 Cor 1:18). In other words, Paul has *always* said "Yes" — to God. The basis for his change in plans has been the will of God, the "promises of God," and the "glory of God" (2 Cor 1:20). Vv. 21-22 have a Trinitarian stress: "*God* establishes us with you in *Christ*...giving us his *Spirit*." The gift of the Spirit is "a first installment," says Paul (2 Cor 1:22). God guarantees, through his Spirit, that he will finish the work he has begun with Paul among the Corinthians.

Besides the trouble in Asia and divine prerogative, Paul's genuine love for the Corinthians also prevented a visit (see Figure 10-1). Ironically, it was better for all if they did not meet. "It was to spare you that I did not come again to Corinth....I made up my mind not to make you another painful visit" (2 Cor 1:23; 2:1). If Paul had shown up a third time, it would have been to exercise some regrettable discipline. As it was, the severe letter that replaced the visit was painful enough for both Paul and the congregation (2 Cor 2:3-5).

Now that the church has repented and Paul has forgiven them, he can speak more gently. He must ensure that reconciliation is complete. Unfortunately censure persists in Corinth, only now the congregation has turned its condemnation inward, on itself.

Forgiveness Within the Church (2 Cor 2:5-11)

Paul gets specific in 2 Corinthians 2:5-11 regarding a previous conflict. This passage reveals that a certain man in the Corinthian congregation had "caused pain" to Paul. The church also suffered because of his actions. Now, in the face of discipline that may go so far as to destroy the man, Paul comes to his rescue.

Who was this offender? Many scholars identify him with the incestuous man Paul excommunicated *in absentia* (1 Cor 5:1-5). This is possible, but it appears that the present culprit personally opposed Paul

In 1 Corinthians 16:5-11 Paul announces his intention to leave Asia and spend the winter in Corinth. After writing this, situations in the church and in Paul's life changed and he never made this visit. Critics charged Paul with a lack of integrity and concern for the Corinthian church. In 2 Corinthians 1–2, Paul responds by offering several good reasons for the change in plans.

An Affliction in Asia

While in Ephesus, Paul and his associates endured a sustained life-threatening affliction in Asia. He could not have used stronger language to describe his plight: "We were so utterly, unbearably crushed...we despaired of life itself...we had received the sentence of death... so deadly a peril..." (2 Cor 1:8-10).

Some interpreters maintain that Paul is alluding to a serious illness, perhaps his "thorn in the flesh" (cf. 2 Cor 12:7-9). Yet the legal terminology and mention of others involved point to another type of trouble. Elsewhere we read of Paul and his team in conflict with opponents in Ephesus (1 Cor 16:9).

Acts 19:23-40 reports a riot and arrest spurred on by silversmiths angered by Paul's interference in their business at the Ephesian temple of Artemis. Paul may have this crisis in mind when he says, "I fought with wild animals at Ephesus" (1 Cor 15:32). He also says that Prisca and Aquila, who worked with him in Ephesus, "risked their necks for my life" (Rom 16:4). On the basis of these and other indications, many scholars conclude that after sustained conflict Paul was imprisoned for at least several months in Ephesus.

The Sovereignty of God

Paul does not boast in his foresight or his personal agenda. Instead, he stands on his sincere openness before God and the church. He has always acted with a clear conscience, realizing the limits of his own knowledge and acknowledging the gracious sovereignty of God (2 Cor 1:12). He tactfully suggests that the Corinthians need to do the same. They must recognize their limited understanding and have confidence in him (2 Cor 1:13-14).

The apostle insists that he and his associates have consistently acted with integrity. "As God is faithful," he vows, "our word has not been 'Yes' and 'No'" (2 Cor 1:18). In other words, Paul has *always* said "Yes"—to God. The basis for his change in plans has been the will of God, the "promises of God," and the "glory of God" (2 Cor 1:20). Vv. 21-22 have a Trinitarian stress: "*God* establishes us with you in *Christ*...giving us his *Spirit*." The gift of the Spirit is "a first installment," says Paul (2 Cor 1:22). God guarantees, through his Spirit, that he will finish the work he has begun with Paul among the Corinthians.

The Welfare of the Church

Paul's genuine love for the Corinthians also prevented the visit. Ironically, it was better for all concerned if they did not meet. "It was to spare you that I did not come again to Corinth....I made up my mind not to make you another painful visit" (2 Cor 1:23; 2:1). If Paul had shown up a third time, it would have been to exercise some regrettable discipline.

FIGURE 10-1
---

during the period *between* the writing of 1 and 2 Corinthians. Perhaps the incestuous man mounted an attack on Paul in response to 1 Corinthians 5:1-5. He may have used Paul's absence to cast aspersions on his character and challenge his authority. In any event, Paul's severe letter decisively thwarted the agitator's defiance and won the obedience of the church (2 Cor 2:9; cf. also 7:12).

If 2 Corinthians 10–13 is the severe letter, it may illuminate the situation. While chapters 10–13 do not identify a particular individual, they call for church discipline because of pride, disobedience, and sexual immorality (2 Cor 12:20–13:9). If the Corinthians did not discipline themselves, Paul threatened to step in with a heavy hand: "I write these things while I am away from you, so that when I come, I may not have to be severe in using the authority that the Lord has given me for building up and not for tearing down" (2 Cor 13:10).

The discipline Paul effected in the church surpassed even the apostle's expectations. The individual who has "caused pain" to both Paul and the church is subsequently being subjected to "punishment by the majority" (2 Cor 2:5-6). The mention of a majority implies that the Corinthians have deliberated over the matter and most, but not all, have agreed to take action against the man.

They have disciplined enough, cautions Paul. Now they should extend grace to the offender. He runs the risk of being "overwhelmed by excessive sorrow" if the congregation does not reaffirm him (2 Cor 2:7-8).

Failure to forgive also may hurt the church. "What I have forgiven," says Paul, "has been for your sake" (2 Cor 2:10). He explains that an unforgiving spirit is a tool Satan uses to deceive and divide the church.

Certain principles surface in Paul's handling of this situation. Church discipline is not to be an instrument for *personal* restitution; Paul did not care for *his own* sake. Rather, discipline works for *corporate* restoration. It must be practiced in love, with the best interests of both the offender and the church in mind. Without a willingness to forgive, discipline will destroy the church.

Conclusion
(2 Cor 2:12-13)

Paul's failure to make a promised visit was a persistent sore point in Corinth. Some questioned his integrity and care for them. In response, Paul offered several reasons for the change in plans. He now ends his explanations with a final example of his concern for the Corinthians.

In spite of ministry opportunities in Asia, Paul pushed toward Corinth when he could (2 Cor 2:12). His "mind could not rest" until he heard from them (2 Cor 2:13). Titus was on his way back from Corinth to meet Paul in Troas, but Paul could not wait. His care for the Corinthians drove him to Macedonia in search of Titus.

The first two chapters of 2 Corinthians reveal an apostle who committed himself totally to the welfare of his churches. Paul wants the Corinthians to realize that they share with him in his ministry. Together, they are united in Christ. They suffer together the sufferings of Christ. They share the consolation offered through Christ. They are to forgive one another in the presence of Christ.

STUDY QUESTIONS

1. Describe the two ways the phrase "sufferings of Christ" can be understood in 2 Corinthians 1:5. Which interpretation would you choose?

2. Is suffering an inevitable part of ministry in the body of Christ? Substantiate your answer with Paul's comments in 2 Corinthians 1–2.

3. List at least three passages from the New Testament that suggest Paul's "affliction in Asia" involved an arrest, trial, and imprisonment.

4. The "double favor" of which Paul speaks in 2 Corinthians 1:15 can be understood in two ways. Summarize them.

5. What are three reasons Paul gives for not making his third visit to Corinth?

6. What evidence is there in the Corinthian correspondence that connects the incestuous man of 1 Corinthians 5:1-5 with the punished offender of 2 Corinthians 2:5-11? What evidence differentiates between the two situations?

7. Judging by his comments in 2 Corinthians 2:5-11, did Paul previously want the church to punish the man who caused him pain? Why does he now want the Corinthians to forgive him?

Chapter 11

A MINISTRY OF THE NEW COVENANT: GLORY AND RECONCILIATION
(2 Corinthians 2:14–5:21)

Introduction

The rendezvous with Titus in Macedonia brought good news of a restored relationship with the church. Paul's relief is evident as he writes this next section. In his fresh start with the church he describes the Christian ministry as one of new beginnings: a ministry of the new covenant, of the new creation, and of reconciliation.

Comparing the Mosaic law and life in Christ, Paul makes several distinctions between the new and the old (see Figure 11-1). God wrote the old covenant on tablets of stone; he writes the new on human hearts. The old ministry was a ministry of condemnation; the new is a ministry of justification. The old revelation of God's glory was veiled; the new fully reflects his glory.

Still, Paul's description of the new ministry in Christ is neither triumphalistic nor escapist. Paradoxically, God shows his strength most in our weakness. We contain our immortal treasure in clay jars. The new life comes *through* death; it does not avoid the grave. God, through Christ, confronts our weakness, sin, and death to transform them into strength, righteousness, and life. "For our sake he made him to be sin who knew no sin, so that in him we might become the righteousness of God" (2 Cor 5:21).

In 2 Corinthians 3–5 Paul develops the idea that God has established a new covenant with his people through Christ. Several allusions to the Old Testament show how the new life in Christ grows out of and transcends God's revelation in the Old Testament.

When God finished speaking with Moses on Mount Sinai, he gave him the two tablets of the covenant, tablets of stone, written with the finger of God (*Ex 31:18*).

...you show that you are a letter of Christ, prepared by us, written not with ink but with the Spirit of the living God, not on tablets of stone but on tablets of human hearts (*2 Cor 3:3*).

The days are surely coming, says the Lord, when I will make a new covenant with the house of Israel.... I will put my law within them, and I will write it on their hearts... (*Jer 31:31, 33*).

...our competence is from God, who has made us competent to be ministers of a new covenant, not of letter but of spirit... (*2 Cor 3:6*).

Moses came down from Mount Sinai. As he came down from the mountain with the two tablets of the covenant in his hand, Moses did not know that the skin of his face shone because he had been talking with God.... When Moses had finished speaking with them, he put a veil on his face, but whenever Moses went in before the Lord to speak with him, he would take the veil off... (*Ex 34:29, 33-34*).

Now if the ministry of death, chiseled in letters on stone tablets, came in glory so that the people of Israel could not gaze at Moses' face because of the glory of his face, a glory now set aside, how much more will the ministry of the Spirit come in glory? ...Since, then, we have such a hope, we act with great boldness, not like Moses who put a veil over his face to keep the people of Israel from gazing at the end of the glory that was being set aside...when one turns to the Lord, the veil is removed (*2 Cor 3:7, 12-13, 16*).

Then God said, "Let there be light"; and there was light. And God saw that the light was good; and God separated the light from the darkness (*Gen 1:3-4*).

For it is the God who said, "Let light shine out of darkness," who has shone in our hearts to give the light of the knowledge of the glory of God in the face of Jesus Christ (*2 Cor 4:6*).

Then the Lord God formed man from the dust of the ground, and breathed into his nostrils the breath of life; and the man became a living being (*Gen 2:7*).

But we have this treasure in clay jars, so that it may be made clear that this extraordinary power belongs to God and does not come from us (*2 Cor 4:7*).

FIGURE 11-1

I kept my faith, even when I said: "I am greatly afflicted" (*Ps 116:10*).

We are afflicted in every way.... But just as we have the same spirit of faith that is in accordance with scripture— "I believed, and so I spoke"—we also believe and so we speak (*2 Cor 4:8, 13*).

"When you make his life [an offering for] sin, he shall see his offspring.... The righteous one, my servant, shall make many righteous" (*Is 53:10-11*).

For our sake he made him to be sin who knew no sin, so that in him we might become the righteousness from God (*2 Cor 5:21*).

—————————— **FIGURE 11-1** ——————————

The New Covenant of Glory
(2 Cor 2:14–4:6)

Spurred on by the favor he has regained in Corinth, Paul offers thanks to God. The familiar Roman triumph, or victory procession, provides imagery for Paul's burst of praise. These triumphs were frequently held in honor of Roman generals when they returned after victory in the battlefield.

Entering Rome through the triumphal arch, the general and his entourage would lead their captives through the city to the Capitoline hill. There, they would offer a sacrifice to Jupiter, the god who gave victory. After this, the prisoners of war would be executed. For the celebrants, the odor of the burning sacrifice was the aroma of triumph; for the doomed captives, it was the smell of death.

Paul pictures himself as a conquered slave of Christ whom "God always leads...in a triumphal procession" (2 Cor 2:14). In other words, as a suffering apostle continually sentenced to death (cf. 1 Cor 4:9; 2 Cor 1:9; 4:11), he glorifies the victorious God. Adding another metaphor from the same context, Paul also describes himself as the odor of a burning sacrifice. The "aroma of Christ" he spreads is a fragrance of death to the perishing and a fragrance of life to those who are being saved (2 Cor 2:15-16).

The apostle counts it a privilege to be held captive by Christ. He gladly offers his life as a sacrifice in honor of God. This distinguishes

Paul from his opponents in Corinth. They are insincere "peddlers of God's word" (2 Cor 2:17). They solicit "letters of recommendation" from churches and cast aspersions on Paul's competence because he does not do the same (2 Cor 3:1-6).

Such letters of recommendation were a normal part of business dealings in the Roman era (cf. Acts 9:2; 18:27; 21:25; 22:5; Rom 16:1; 2 Cor 8:16-24). Still, Paul does not feel compelled to commend himself in this way. After all, he tells the Corinthians,

> You yourselves are our letter, written on our hearts, to be known and read by all; and you show that you are a letter of Christ, prepared by us, written not with ink but with the Spirit of the living God, not on tablets of stone but on tablets of human hearts (2 Cor 3:2-3).

These words allude to Exodus 31:18, which describes how God gave the Mosaic covenant as "two tablets of stone, written with the finger of God." In contrast, the new covenant in Christ is written "with the Spirit of the living God" on "tablets of human hearts." Paul's transition from speaking of letters to calling them tablets suggests that he was opposing his critics who sought to impose the law of Moses even on Gentile Christian life. Elsewhere in Paul's letters we read of "Judaizers" who have infiltrated Gentile churches, insisting on circumcision and observance of the Jewish law (cf. esp. Gal 3–5; Phil 3:1-11; 2 Cor 11).

Wherever Paul dealt with the issue, he argued that a turn to the Mosaic law would be regressive for Gentile Christians. Here in 2 Corinthians 3:7–4:6 he compares the fading glory of Moses to the surpassing glory of Christ. In the past, argues Paul, God had revealed his glory through Moses, but this revelation was "set aside" (2 Cor 3:7, 11, 13). A "greater" "permanent" glory that radiates from Christ now outshines the glory from Moses (2 Cor 3:10-11).

Exodus 34:29-35 recounts how, when Moses descended from Mount Sinai with the tablets, "the skin of his face shone because he had been talking with God" (Ex 34:29). After passing on the covenant to the Israelites, Moses veiled his face and removed the veil only when he would come again before God. Every time he returned from the presence of the Lord, his unveiled face would shine. After he delivered God's word to the people, he would again put on the veil.

Paul sees the veiling as an attempt to "keep the people of Israel from gazing at the end of the glory" (2 Cor 3:13). Was Moses hiding the fading of his glory or was he trying to stop the Israelites from fixating on a glory that was not ultimate? Paul does not say, but his analogy suggests that the Mosaic covenant was incomplete and looked forward to a greater glory in Christ.

The apostle goes on to note that even now the people of Israel have not seen beyond the glory of Moses. "To this very day," he says, "whenever Moses is read, a veil lies over their minds" (2 Cor 3:15). In other words, Jewish readers of the Old Testament do not see the transcendent glory of Christ embodied in the law of Moses. There is only one way to discover this greater glory: "When one turns to the Lord, the veil is removed" (2 Cor 3:16; cf. Ex 34:34).

In its original setting, Exodus 34:34 described Moses removing his veil when he came to speak with God. Paul recasts this sentence to teach that when people look beyond the Mosaic law and turn to "the Lord," they will see the full glory of God (2 Cor 3:16). When Paul speaks of "the Lord," he usually means Jesus Christ. Here he implies Christ (cf. 2 Cor 3:14; 4:4-6), but he extends his scope to include the Holy Spirit (2 Cor 3:17-18).

With Christ, the Holy Spirit has a central role in establishing the new covenant. "The Spirit of the living God" has written the "letter of Christ" on our hearts (2 Cor 3:3). "The letter kills, but the Spirit gives life" (2 Cor 3:6). The "ministry of the Spirit" comes in glory (2 Cor 3:8). "Where the Spirit of the Lord is, there is freedom" (2 Cor 3:17).

God has moved beyond the era of Moses to reveal his glory in Christ through the Holy Spirit. He has established a "new covenant" with his people (2 Cor 3:6; cf. Jer 31:31-34). We seal this covenant by turning to the Lord Jesus Christ as the Spirit leads. Those who turn to Christ then reflect God's glory like Moses. "All of us, with unveiled faces, seeing the glory of the Lord as though reflected in a mirror, are being transformed from one degree of glory to another..." (2 Cor 3:18).

Because Paul shares in this ministry of the new covenant he does not "lose heart" when criticized by others (2 Cor 4:1). To counter, he levels a few of his own oblique criticisms (cf. 2 Cor 2:17–3:6). Unlike his opponents, Paul and his team "have renounced the shameful things that one hides" (2 Cor 4:2). While many interpret this phrase to refer to subterfuge, it may be a euphemistic reference to circumcision with "the shameful things that one hides" referring to genitals (cf. also Phil 3:2, 19).

In contrast to the message of those who "practice cunning" or "falsify God's word," Paul's gospel stands open to all and true to scripture. Still, some disparage his preaching as misleading or unclear. In response, Paul reaffirms that his gospel remains veiled only to those who are perishing. "The god of this world has blinded the minds of the unbelievers, to keep them from seeing the light of the gospel of the glory of Christ" (2 Cor 4:4). *Satan*, not Paul, has obscured the gospel.

Paul likens the light of the gospel to the light of creation. He notes that the same God who said "Let there be light" (Gen 1:3) has also shone "in our hearts" the light of Jesus Christ (2 Cor 4:6). In other words, the God of creation is also the God of new creation.

Mortal and Immortal Bodies
(2 Cor 4:7–5:10)

At present, the new creation exists within the constraints of the old. Physical bodies, created from the "dust of the ground" (Gen 2:7), are the "clay jars" that contain the eternal treasure of new life in Christ (2 Cor 4:7). The earthenware to which Paul refers functioned for a variety of purposes. Cheap and fragile, the value of a clay pot was limited to what it contained.

So, too, the human body, notes Paul, is subject to afflictions, death, and decay. Yet, the very weakness of the physical body shows that the life of Jesus within the Christian is from God and *not* inherent to mortal human beings. "While we live," says Paul, "we are always being given up to death for Jesus' sake, so that the life of Jesus may be made visible in our mortal flesh" (2 Cor 4:11). In other words, the paradox of the Christian life surfaces again: new life in Christ germinates in the soil of suffering (cf. 2 Cor 1:3-11; 4:11).

Christian life straddles the present physical existence and the future spiritual one. We live between the "now" and the "not yet." The "outer nature is wasting away" while the "inner nature is being renewed day by day" (2 Cor 4:16). Christians have begun the spiritual life, but they must wait to apprehend it fully. Physical death completes the transition.

In 2 Corinthians 5:1-10, Paul develops the connection between our present bodies and our resurrection bodies. He compares the tent as a temporary dwelling to the permanent house "not made with hands, but eternal in the heavens" (2 Cor 5:1). Along with this imagery Paul speaks of clothing, mixing metaphors. In our present tent, Paul says, we wish "to be clothed with our heavenly dwelling" (2 Cor 5:2).

A difficult textual problem in 2 Corinthians 5:3 further compounds Paul's metaphor. Most manuscripts read "...when we have *put it on* [endusamenoi]* we will not be found naked." With the difference of a single letter, other manuscripts read "...when we have *taken it off* [ekdusamenoi]* we will not be found naked." Most scholars opt for the smoother second reading, given the context. A few, however, suggest that this verse alludes to "putting on" Christ in baptism (cf. Gal 3:27). Baptism, then, is the beginning of a clothing process that will be fully realized after physical death.

Readers may picture the building of a home over a tent *or* putting more clothes on over those already worn. If Paul had a choice, he would rather assume the new without having to discard the old. He does not wish to be found naked by losing the physical body in death. Instead, Paul yearns or "groans" to be further clothed by living until Christ's return, when the Lord will transform his people for immortal life (2 Cor 5:4; cf. 1 Cor 15:51-53; see also Figure 11-2).

Meanwhile, the gift of the Spirit serves as a guarantee that God will finish the work he has begun (2 Cor 5:5; cf. 2 Cor 1:22). Paul continues life "at home in the body" confident that some day he will be "at home with the Lord" (2 Cor 5:6-8). Philippians 1:20-26 conveys a similar perspective; Paul would prefer to go to be with the Lord, but as long as he lives "in the body" he will devote himself to the Lord's service. At the end, Christ will judge that service and reward it accordingly (2 Cor 5:10; cf. 1 Cor 3:1-15; 4:4-5).

A Ministry of Reconciliation
(2 Cor 5:11-21)

Faced with a future judgment, Paul strives to fulfill the ministry to which God has called him. The ministry is one of reconciliation — restoring broken relationships between God and his people and among his people. Reconciliation is possible only through Christ, who recreates life for all through his death and resurrection.

When Paul says a knowledge of "the fear of the Lord" (2 Cor 5:11) motivates his ministry, he is not referring to a dread of possible condemnation. A healthy fear of the Lord involves reverence, trust, and hope. Knowing that God, the trustworthy judge, will examine the motives and quality of everyone's ministry, Paul already opens his life completely to God in trust. He is confident that his heart is "well known to God" and he hopes the Corinthians will also recognize his true character (2 Cor 5:11).

Assured of the saving work of God and his part in it, Paul must "persuade others" (2 Cor 5:11). The context suggests that Paul must convince his audience not only to accept salvation through Christ but also to accept his integrity as an apostle. If they doubt the messenger, can they trust the message?

In the time between the writing of 1 and 2 Corinthians, Paul has developed in his thinking about the Christian's resurrection body. He paints the same general picture and he uses similar language about "putting on" immortality over mortality, but his perspective on the process of change has evolved. For example, in 2 Corinthians he says "our inner nature is being renewed day by day" (2 Cor 4:16) whereas in 1 Corinthians he speaks of the change that will occur "at the last trumpet" (1 Cor 15:52).

1 Corinthians 15:50-57	*2 Corinthians 4:16–5:5*

What I am saying, brothers and sisters, is this: flesh and blood cannot inherit the kingdom of God, nor does the perishable inherit the imperishable. Listen, I will tell you a mystery! We will not all die, but we will all be changed, in a moment, in the twinkling of an eye, at the last trumpet. For the trumpet will sound, and the dead will be raised imperishable, and we will be changed. For this perishable body must put on imperishability, and this mortal body must put on immortality. When this perishable body puts on imperishability, and this mortal body puts on immortality, then the saying that is written will be fulfilled:

> "Death has been swallowed up in victory."
> "Where, O death, is your victory?
> "Where, O death, is your sting?"

The sting of death is sin, and the power of sin is the law. But thanks be to God who gives us the victory through our Lord Jesus Christ.

Even though our outer nature is wasting away, our inner nature is being renewed day by day. For this slight momentary affliction is preparing us for an eternal weight of glory beyond all measure, because we do not look at what can be seen but at what cannot be seen; for what can be seen is temporary, but what cannot be seen is eternal.

For we know that if the earthly tent we live in is destroyed, we have a building from God, a house not made with hands, eternal in the heavens. For in this tent we groan, longing to be clothed with our heavenly dwelling—if indeed, when we have taken it off we will not be found naked. For while we are still in this tent, we groan under our burden, because we wish not to be unclothed but to be further clothed, so that what is mortal may be swallowed up by life. He who has prepared us for this very thing is God, who has given us the Spirit as a guarantee.

FIGURE 11-2

As we've already seen elsewhere (2 Cor 1:17-20; 2:17–3:3; 4:2-5), in 2 Corinthians 5:12-13 Paul responds to his detractors in Corinth. Paul hopes that he is well known enough to the Corinthians that he does not need to commend himself to them in the same manner the interlopers do. If anything, the Corinthian church should be doing the boasting about Paul to those who would denigrate the apostle to increase their stature.

That he says "we are not commending ourselves to you again" (2 Cor 5:12) suggests that he has previously boasted of his apostolic credentials. If Paul wrote 2 Corinthians 10–13 before 1–9, as seems likely, then Paul is probably referring to his self-recommendation in 2 Corinthians 11:16–12:13. Even as he wrote these words he apologized for his foolish pride. As 2 Corinthians 5:12 shows, the apostle does not want to succumb to such a spirit of boasting again.

In "outward appearance" (2 Cor 5:12), Paul is not as impressive as his opponents. Whatever else this may mean, it is linked to some sort of ecstatic spiritual manifestation. "If we are beside ourselves," writes Paul, "it is for God. If we are in our right mind, it is for you" (2 Cor 5:13).

Being "beside oneself" can refer either to being mentally deranged or to being caught up in a spiritual experience. Given what we know of both Paul and the Corinthians, here the phrase probably refers to speaking in tongues (cf. 1 Cor 12–14). If this be the case, then 2 Corinthians 5:13 can reflect one of two situations. People may have criticized Paul for his practice of ecstatic spiritual gifts, as if he were out of his mind (cf. 1 Cor 14:23).

Or, as most interpreters believe, critics may have impugned Paul because he did not make a public show of ecstatic behavior as much as others. Paul responds that for him spiritual ecstasy was a private matter between him and God. In public he chooses to speak intelligibly for the benefit of others (cf. 1 Cor 14:2, 18-19).

Motivation for Paul's ministry comes not from public honor but from "the love of Christ" (2 Cor 5:14). Does Paul mean *his love* for Christ compels him to preach or does *Christ's love* for him constrain him? Considering the rest of the sentence in v. 14, most interpreters agree that Paul is saying that an awareness of Christ's sacrifice of love encourages Paul to live for his Lord. Paul has therefore given two reasons for his apostolic service: his "fear" or reverence for God (2 Cor 5:11) and Christ's selfless love for all humanity.

Referring to Jesus Christ, Paul states, "We are convinced that one has died for all; therefore all have died" (2 Cor 5:14). The death of Christ marks the transition from the old way of life to the new. The old has passed away. There is no life apart from Christ. The death of Jesus was necessary and sufficient for all.

Christ's loving sacrifice for all calls for a reciprocal sacrifice from everyone. "He died for all, so that those who live might live no longer for themselves, but for him who died and was raised for them" (2 Cor 5:15). Two crucial aspects of salvation merge in this sentence. First, Christ died *for all*. He did not die just for a chosen few. To limit the inclusiveness of the word "all" is grammatically unjustifiable and theologically short-sighted.

Second, Christ's death for all is not effective for people unless they die to themselves and live for Christ. Christ's work requires a response. Just as Christ gave up his life and was raised, those who die to themselves will be raised to new life in Christ. These two aspects of the saving work of God cannot stand apart from one another. Christ's death for all means nothing for those who do not die to themselves and live for him.

Again the paradox of the Christian life surfaces. In sacrifice, there is gain; in weakness there is God's strength; in death to self there is Christ's life. Though by worldly standards the career of Jesus was short and ignominious, Christians know it brought salvation to the world. Likewise Christ's work in the lives of people changes the way we view ourselves and others (2 Cor 5:16). "So if anyone is in Christ, there is a new creation: everything old has passed away; everything has become new!" (2 Cor 5:17).

Since the fall of humanity, creation has suffered separation from God. Now, with creation made new through the initiative of God through Christ, reconciliation is possible. Paul stresses that "all this is from God" (2 Cor 5:18). God has made the first move to restore the relationship that humanity had broken.

In turn, those who become part of the new creation have a role in the ongoing ministry of reconciliation. They are to announce forgiveness and serve as "ambassadors for Christ" (2 Cor 5:20). As ambassadors are official envoys sent by a ruler to another country, so too Paul regards Christians as Christ's representatives sent into the world.

Although Paul began this paragraph speaking generally of the reconciling work of God in the world, he narrows his focus for a concluding statement directed specifically at his readers. As an apostle to the church he writes, "we entreat you on behalf of Christ, be reconciled to God!" (2 Cor 5:20).

These words are not simply a summary of Paul's gospel that he preaches everywhere. He is speaking directly to the Corinthians and his words reflect a long history of shaky relations between the apostle and the Corinthian church. To this point, 2 Corinthians has conveyed the apostle's relief at Corinthian repentance. Compared to their falling out after the writing of 1 Corinthians, Paul and the Corinthians are now much closer. Still, as the following chapters will show, Paul has yet to see evidence of full Christian reconciliation in Corinth.

The chapter ends with a concise yet grand summary of God's work of salvation through Christ: "For our sake he made him to be sin who knew no sin, so that in him we might become the righteousness of God" (2 Cor 5:21).

What does it mean that God "made him to be sin who knew no sin"? There are at least three possible interpretations. Perhaps God made Christ actually assume humanity's sinful nature. Or God may have treated his incarnated Son *as if* he were a sinner. Yet most scholars point out that "made him to be sin" is a shorter way of saying "made him to be an offering for sin." The same abbreviated construction is used in the Greek text of Isaiah 53:10 (cf. also Lev 7:1-10).

Paul is probably alluding to this well-known verse in Isaiah. The "Servant Songs" of Isaiah (Is 42:1-4; 49:1-6; 50:4-11; 52:13–53:12) provided writers of the New Testament with prophecies of the life and ministry of Christ. In particular, this fourth song describes the sacrifice of the servant for "the sin of many" (Is 53:12).

Through Christ, God has reversed the alienating effects of sin. He has sacrificed his Son so that humanity is not condemned. Instead, people can share in Christ's righteousness when they are incorporated in him. This identification with Christ forms the theological basis for Paul's pastoral ministry and his ethical exhortations.

Conclusion

Paul has written to the Corinthians in confidence and hope. Just as Christ had given him a new life years ago, he has now experienced another beginning with the church in Corinth. The sense of reconciliation with God and one another permeates this entire section of the letter.

Still, old problems persist. Interlopers continue to meddle in the church. They are criticizing Paul and calling for submission to the Mosaic law. They glory in the past and brag about their "apostolic" credentials.

Paul responds with a clear presentation of the nature of the saving work of Christ. He argues that the Christian life *is* a life of glory. Such glory, however, is a different kind of glory than his critics flaunt. It is a glory rooted in Christ and not the self. It shines through human weakness. It transforms sin and death into righteousness and life. Above all, it calls us to selfless living for Christ.

STUDY QUESTIONS

1. What two things does Paul describe himself as in the context of a Roman victory procession?

2. Based on his comments in 2 Corinthians 2–5, what are at least three criticisms that opponents in Corinth are making of Paul? What are at least three criticisms that Paul levels against his critics?

3. Contrast the glory of Moses to the glory of Christ in at least three ways. What similarities do they share?

4. Find at least three possible references to creation and new creation in 2 Corinthians 3–5.

5. In what ways are the Holy Spirit and Jesus Christ linked in 2 Corinthians 3-5?

6. Compare 1 Corinthians 15 with 2 Corinthians 4:7–5:10. How does Paul's description of the resurrection body differ in these two passages? What is the main point of each passage?

7. Define reconciliation in your own words. What function does God have in the process of reconciliation? What part does Christ have? What must Christians do in God's ministry of reconciliation?

Chapter 12

A MINISTRY OF RIGHTEOUSNESS, SUFFERING, AND REASSURANCE
(2 Corinthians 6–7)

Introduction

2 Corinthians began with expressions of consolation in the restored relationship between Paul and the church. After recounting Titus' good news from Corinth, Paul laid a theological foundation on which to rebuild a sense of joint ministry with the church. Now he draws his themes together by recounting the comforting report that originally prompted this letter.

Chapters 6–7 are not simply a rehearsal of Paul's opening words; they move his readers to deeper commitment to Paul and their shared ministry. If the Corinthians respond to some final appeals, the apostle is confident that their restoration will be complete. They must accept the legitimacy of his apostolic ministry, rededicate themselves to holy living, and open their hearts as wide to Paul as he has to them.

Righteous Endurance: The Mark of True Ministry
(2 Cor 6:1-13)

Paul continues the exhortation begun in his previous chapter: "As we work together...we urge you..." (2 Cor 6:1).

The Greek of this sentence does not identify specifically with whom Paul is working, and it is possible that he is referring to a partnership in ministry with the Corinthian church. 2 Corinthians 5:20, however, links Paul and God in a joint appeal to the Corinthians. So, most translations of 2 Corinthians 6:1 refer to God: "As we work together *with him*...." Partners with God in the work of reconciliation, Paul asks the Corinthians "also not to accept the grace of God in vain" (2 Cor 6:1).

As Paul has accepted the grace of God, the Corinthians "also" should. What is more, they are not to accept it "in vain." They are not to accept God's grace and yet live as if they had not; as recipients of divine grace, they are to exercise it in their attitude toward Paul and others just as Paul deals graciously with them.

This is a crucial moment in the relationship between the church and the apostle. To emphasize this, he quotes Isaiah 49:8:

> At an acceptable time I have listened to you,
> and on a day of salvation I have helped you.

Employing a rabbinic style of interpretation, Paul refocuses and escalates the impact of this statement to apply to the Corinthians: "See, now is the acceptable time; see, now is the day of salvation!" (2 Cor 6:2). In other words, as God's ambassador, Paul has brought the time of acceptance to the Corinthians. They now have the responsibility of accepting God's grace by receiving the Lord's apostle.

Paul's life presents no impediments to their acceptance of him, he argues (2 Cor 6:3). To this point in the letter, Paul has refused to commend himself. Rather, he has criticized those who resort to self-promotion (cf. 2 Cor 3:1-6). Yet now he sets down the proper criteria by which ministry is to be measured. By these standards, Paul says, "as servants of God we have commended ourselves in every way" (2 Cor 6:4).

As he has already shown, the Christian life is paradoxical (cf. 1 Cor 1:25–2:5; 4:8-13; 2 Cor 1:3-11; 4:7-12). New life comes through death. Suffering leads to salvation. God's power manifests itself whenever human weakness is most apparent. Therefore, the more severe the opposition Paul encounters in his mission, the more he displays God's blessing on his ministry.

Paul does not list his sufferings in 2 Corinthians 6:4-5 to elicit sympathy. As elsewhere, he cites his troubles only to validate his ministry and show how God remains faithful (cf. also 2 Cor 11:23-29). Slander, beatings, whippings, imprisonments, riots, stonings, shipwrecks, sleepless nights, hunger, thirst, and exposure—his scars are also his badges of honor.

Paul proudly bears these marks of a true minister. He endures everything for the sake of righteousness. As his adversities increased, so did the fruits of God's grace in his life. His struggles had yielded "purity, knowledge, patience, kindness, holiness of spirit, genuine love, truthful speech, and the power of God" (2 Cor 6:6-7). Yet, Paul wants the Corinthians to recognize his Christian love and service, particularly for them.

"Our heart is wide open to you. There is no restriction in our affections, but only in yours," writes Paul (2 Cor 6:11-12). The last phrase of v. 12 shows that the Corinthians have yet to reciprocate fully Paul's commitment. Their reservations about Paul have nagged at him since he began this letter. He has been leading up to a compassionate appeal: "I speak to you as to children — open wide your hearts also" (2 Cor 6:13).

An Exhortation To Separate from Unbelievers
(2 Cor 6:14–7:1)

A stern call to holiness abruptly interrupts Paul's plea for an open heart in 2 Corinthians 6:11-13. Striking like a lightning bolt from a clear sky, 2 Corinthians 6:14–7:1 jolts the reader with the danger of consorting with unbelievers. Then, just as abruptly, the warning is over and the theme of an open heart continues in 7:2.

Chapter 9 of this book presented the theory that 6:14–7:1 is a fragment of "the previous letter" to which Paul alludes in 1 Corinthians 5:9. Judging from the further explanations of 1 Corinthians, this previous letter warned the church to avoid immoral, unbelieving, and idolatrous people. Because the interjection of 2 Corinthians 6:14–7:1 raises these same concerns, it may have been originally part of the previous letter (see Figure 12-1).

Even if it were inserted later, 2 Corinthians 6:14–7:1 contributes to themes in its context. Paul has already stressed the importance of righteousness. Through Christ, we become "the righteousness of God" (2 Cor 5:21). Paul endures his afflictions by "purity. . . holiness of spirit . . . with the weapons of righteousness. . ." (2 Cor 6:6-7). As the apostle is righteous in his ministry, so the people of God must remain righteous in the world.

In context, we also might discern an apologetic for Paul. The unbelievers Paul wants the Corinthians to avoid may be those who denigrate servants of the Lord like him. To be reconciled with Paul means breaking away from these unrighteous critics.

Paul begins his exhortation with an image from the farmer's field. Just as the law of Moses forbade the yoking together of an ox and a donkey (Deut 22:10), Paul was prohibiting the teaming of a believer and an unbeliever. This does not mean, of course, that Christians were

Sometime after Paul evangelized Corinth, but before he wrote 1 Corinthians, he wrote the so-called "previous letter" (1 Cor 5:9). Judging from his responses in 1 Corinthians to questions from the church, the topics of the previous letter included immorality, unbelief, idolatry, spiritual gifts, resurrection, and the Jerusalem collection.

The previous letter is either totally lost or partially preserved in 2 Corinthians 6:14–7:1. This passage completely derails an otherwise unbroken train of thought running through 2 Corinthians 6–7. What is more, the concerns of the interjection parallel some of those from the previous letter as it is reflected in 1 Corinthians. Compare Paul's comments about unbelief, immorality, and idolatry in 2 Corinthians 6:14–7:1 to some counterparts in 1 Corinthians.

The Previous Letter (?) (2 Cor 6:14–7:1)	Explanations in 1 Corinthians
Do not be mismatched with unbelievers. For what partnership is there between righteousness and lawlessness? Or what fellowship is there between light and darkness? What agreement does Christ have with Beliar? Or what does a believer share with an unbeliever? What agreement has the temple of God with idols? For we are the temple of the living God; as God said, "I will live in them, and walk among them, and I will be their God, and they shall be my people. Therefore come out from them, and be separate from them, says the Lord, and touch nothing unclean; then I will welcome you, and I will be your father, and you shall be my sons and daughters, says the Lord Almighty." Since we have these promises, beloved, let us cleanse ourselves from every defilement of body and spirit, making holiness perfect in the fear of God.	I wrote to you in my letter not to associate with sexually immoral persons, not at all meaning the immoral of this world, or the greedy, and robbers, or idolaters, since you would then need to go out of the world. But now I am writing to you not to associate with anyone who bears the name of brother or sister who is sexually immoral or greedy, or is an idolater, reviler, drunkard, or robber. Do not even eat with such a one. For what have I to do with judging those outside? Is it not those who are inside that you are to judge? God will judge those outside. "Drive out the wicked person from among you" (1 Cor 5:9-11). ... if any believer has a wife who is an unbeliever, and she consents to live with him, he should not divorce her... but if the unbelieving partner separates, let it be so, in such a case the brother or sister is not bound (1 Cor 7:12-15). Are not those who eat the sacrifices partners in the altar?... I do not want you to be partners with demons. You cannot drink the cup of the Lord and the cup of demons. You cannot partake of the table of the Lord and the table of demons. Or are we provoking the Lord to jealousy? (1 Cor 10:18-22).

FIGURE 12-1

to have *no* contact with unbelievers (cf. 1 Cor 5:9-11). Rather, it is a warning against joining with unbelievers in a working relationship that required close partnership, harmonious agreement, and the sharing of resources (2 Cor 6:14-16). Judging from v. 16, Paul may be concerned particularly with Christian participation in idol worship.

Besides the contrast of belief with unbelief, Paul distinguishes Christians from the world with four other sets of opposites: righteousness versus lawlessness, light versus darkness, Christ versus Beliar, and the temple of God versus idols.

"Beliar," also known as "Belial," was a demonic being described in Jewish apocalyptic literature (see Figure 12-2). He is particularly prominent as a leader of the army of darkness in the "War Scroll" of the Qumran community. In several other documents, such as the *Testaments of the Twelve Patriarchs* and *The Ascension of Isaiah*, the name is used of Satan, or the devil.

People are either on the side of God or the side of Satan, argues Paul. They cannot concurrently align themselves with opposing forces. There is no common ground for a temple for God and for idols too.

Building on the idea that believers are "a temple of the living God" (cf. also 1 Cor 3:16-17; 6:19), Paul strings together several passages from the Old Testament (2 Cor 6:16-18; cf. Lev 26:12; Ez 37:27; Is 52:11; 2 Sam 7:14). He interprets these as promises that God will live and move among his people. He will adopt as his sons and daughters those who dissociate from the world and "touch nothing unclean" (2 Cor 6:17).

The promise of God's presence has an ethical corollary, concludes Paul. The privilege of being God's temple brings a responsibility to "cleanse ourselves from every defilement of body and spirit, making holiness perfect in the fear of God" (2 Cor 7:1). Some interpreters take "cleansing from defilement" to be synonymous with "making holiness perfect." If this is the case, then Paul is calling for moral perfection. Perfect holiness, however, more fundamentally refers to complete dedication to God. For such fidelity and reverence, moral cleansing is essential.

Consoling News from Titus
(2 Cor 7:2-16)

Though he has concerns about the loyalties of the Corinthians, Paul assures them that he regards them warmly. He has already told them that his heart is wide open to them (2 Cor 6:11). Now he com-

"Beliar" in Intertestamental Judaism

Satan is often called "Beliar" in Jewish intertestamental literature. Also known as "Belial," he is a central figure in the "War Scroll" of the Qumran community. In particular, compare Paul's exhortation in *2 Corinthians 6:14-15* with a few references in the *Testaments of the Twelve Patriarchs*:

> "What partnership is there between righteousness and lawlessness? Or what fellowship is there between light and darkness? What agreement does Christ have with Beliar?" (*2 Cor 6:14-15*).

* * *

> "And now, my children, you have heard everything. Choose for yourselves light or darkness, the law of the Lord or the works of Beliar" (*Testament of Levi 19:1*).

> "As a person's strength, so also is his work; as is his mind, so also is his skill. As is his plan, so also is his achievement; as is his heart, so is his speech; as is his eye, so also is his sleep; as is his soul, so also is his thought, whether on the law of the Lord or on the law of Beliar" (*Testament of Naphtali 1:6*).

> ". . . the Lord will be with you in the light, while Beliar will be with the Egyptians in the dark" (*Testament of Joseph 20:2*).

FIGURE 12-2

pletes his exhortation by again asking them to be open to him in return (2 Cor 7:3; cf. 2 Cor 6:13).

Paul insists that he has never done the Corinthians any harm, in contrast to his rivals who may have "wronged," "corrupted," and "taken advantage" of them (2 Cor 7:2-3). He is not criticizing the church for these problems. Rather, he has found the Corinthians a source of pride, consolation, and joy in the midst of his personal ordeals (2 Cor 7:4).

The news of repentance that Titus brought from Corinth allows Paul to praise the church. Paul has already alluded to this rendezvous with Titus in Macedonia (2 Cor 2:13), which marked a new beginning in the apostle's relationship with the congregation. Now he returns to that turning point and builds on it to gain the full allegiance of the Corinthians.

After the "deadly peril in Asia" (cf. 2 Cor 1:8-11), Paul moved on to Macedonia. Unfortunately, he found no relief there. "Our bodies had no rest, but we were afflicted in every way—disputes without and fears within" (2 Cor 7:5). Judging from further references in the next chapter, Paul and the Macedonian churches endured "a severe ordeal of affliction" that resulted in "extreme poverty" (2 Cor 8:1-2).

Part of Paul's "fears within" were worries about the severe letter he had sent to Corinth (2 Cor 7:5, 8). Was he too harsh? Would they repent or would they reject the letter? Would the church divide over it? Should he have taken the risk of complete alienation?

Paul confesses that he had second thoughts about sending the letter (2 Cor 7:8). Yet, now that Titus has returned with his good news, Paul can say he no longer regrets the missive. The pain the letter caused both him and the church was worth the reconciliation it effected.

In a bittersweet paragraph, the apostle describes his comfort in their grief (2 Cor 7:7-13). He assures them that he took no delight in their distress. Rather, he rejoiced to hear that they now shared Paul's sorrow for their sin. They saw their behavior as God saw it, and repented in "godly grief" (2 Cor 7:9).

Not all sorrow comes from seeing things from God's perspective, explains Paul. "Godly grief produces a repentance that leads to salvation and brings no regret, but worldly grief produces death" (2 Cor 7:10). In other words, people may be sorry for the consequences of their sin but, unless they then turn to God in repentance to find forgiveness, they will remain under the power of sin and death.

The Corinthian grief has borne the fruit of repentance. Paul commends their zealous efforts to undo the wrong they have done. Dismayed by their past behavior, they have reacted with zealous obedience and disciplined themselves (2 Cor 7:11).

Already in 2 Corinthians 2:5-11 Paul has acknowledged "the punishment by the majority" of a particular offender in the church. Now he raises the issue again (2 Cor 7:12), explaining that his severe letter was not meant to exact personal retribution. Paul is more concerned for corporate restoration. With such restoration evident, he calls for forgiveness and consolation.

Not only has the church's obedience comforted Paul, it has relieved Titus (2 Cor 7:13-15). To avoid another painful confrontation (2 Cor 2:1), he had sent Titus to Corinth in his place. Naturally, in such tense circumstances, Titus would have a certain amount of trepidation. Paul confesses to the Corinthians that, to encourage his associate, "I was somewhat boastful about you to him" (2 Cor 7:14).

Paul did not have to take back his words; the Corinthians felt rebuked by the severe letter, welcomed Titus, and obeyed Paul's correctives. Paul realized his highest hopes. "I rejoice," he concludes, "because I have complete confidence in you" (2 Cor 7:16).

Conclusion

Whether it be the minister or the congregation, holiness is required of God's people. Paul has made the case that he has always lived lovingly and righteously before God and the church. He calls for the same from the Corinthians.

Much ground had been lost and regained in the relationship between Paul and the church between the writing of 1 and 2 Corinthians. The apostle took stern measures to restore his ministry in Corinth. The risk paid off and now Paul felt secure enough to move ahead with a tangible test of Corinthian loyalty. Would they give sacrificially to his collection project?

STUDY QUESTIONS

1. How does Paul commend himself in 2 Corinthians 6:3-12? In what way is it different from how his critics commended themselves?

2. Compare 1 Corinthians 5:9-11 with 2 Corinthians 6:14–7:1 (Figure 12-1). What evidence supports the theory that 2 Corinthians 6:14–7:1 is part of the "previous letter" Paul explains in 1 Corinthians? What evidence detracts from this reconstruction?

3. What might Paul have in mind when he prohibits partnerships between believers and unbelievers (2 Cor 6:14–7:1)? How might this apply in the life of the Christian today?

4. Read 1 Corinthians 3:16-17, 6:19, and 2 Corinthians 6:16–7:1. How does Paul's use of the imagery of the temple vary in these three examples?

5. What role did Titus play in the reconciliation between Paul and the Corinthians before the writing of 2 Corinthians?

6. List all the references in 2 Corinthians 6–7 that describe Paul's feelings for the Corinthians. Summarize his attitude.

7. List all the references in 2 Corinthians 6–7 that reflect the Corinthians' feelings toward Paul. Summarize their attitude.

8. What evidence do you see in these two chapters that Paul is not content to leave the relationship between him and the church where it stands?

Chapter 13

A MINISTRY OF GIVING:
THE COLLECTION
(2 Corinthians 8–9)

Introduction

Having expressed his confidence in the Corinthians, Paul now asks them to prove that it is not misplaced. They can rise to the challenge by completing the collection for Jerusalem he requested more than a year ago. To this point, the Corinthians have questioned the enterprise and hesitated to contribute. The time has come, says Paul, to share their riches. "Therefore openly before the churches, show the proof of your love and our reasons for boasting about you" (2 Cor 8:24).

More than embarrassment was at issue for Paul and the Corinthians. The welfare of impoverished Christians was threatened. The Corinthian church would forfeit spiritual blessings if they did not donate. The unity and witness of the body of Christ depended on these gifts. Jerusalem's ratification of Paul's apostolic commission hinged, in part, on the relief project. Paul had to deliver the funds as he promised before he could move west to new fields of mission. These factors combined to make the contribution a fundamental expression of the nature of the church, its mission, and Paul's part in that mission.

Several letters of Paul refer to the collection (Gal 2:10; 1 Cor 16:1-4; Rom 15:27; see Figure 13-1), but 2 Corinthians has the most to say about it. In chapters 8–9, Paul issues an extended plea for cooperation. He sets up a friendly rivalry of generosity between Achaia and Macedonia. He assures the church of the project's integrity. Finally, he tells the Corinthians that their gifts will glorify God, and God will bless them accordingly.

The Contribution for the Saints in Jerusalem

Acts 11:27-30

After receiving news from Jerusalem of a famine, the Christian community in Antioch decided they would donate what they could for "relief to the believers in Judea" (Acts 11:29). Barnabas and Paul delivered the offering to the Jerusalem elders. This act of charity marks the beginning of "the collection for the saints" that Paul introduces to the churches of Galatia, Macedonia, and Achaia.

Galatians 2:1-10

Paul describes the visit to Jerusalem at which other church leaders recognized his apostolic commission (cf. also Acts 15:2-29). Jewish Christians agreed to welcome uncircumcised Gentile believers with a few conditions stipulated in the so-called "apostolic decree" (cf. Acts 15:20, 29; 21:25). In addition, Paul reports that the Jerusalem church asked "that we remember the poor, which was actually what I was eager to do" (Gal 2:10).

1 Corinthians 16:1-6

In his "previous letter," Paul introduced the Corinthians to the collection project. Before they open their purses the Corinthians have written Paul, asking *how* they should go about collecting the money. It is difficult to tell whether they are wondering about the mechanics of the collection or have concerns about the legitimacy of the enterprise.

Here, in 1 Corinthians, Paul responds diplomatically. He offers clear directions while giving the church complete discretion in handling the funds. By mentioning the Galatian churches, Paul assures the Corinthians that they are not the only church he is soliciting.

Every Sunday the Corinthians were to set aside money they could spare so that when Paul arrived, a fund would already exist. Like other churches, Corinth has the option of sending a contingent with the money to Jerusalem (1 Cor 16:3). Paul offers to lead the delegation, or, at the least, write letters of introduction for the travelers.

2 Corinthians 8–9

In a year since being told of the collection, the Corinthians have yet to contribute. The breakdown of relations between Paul and Corinth was doubtless a major factor in the delay. Now that they are reconciled, the apostle suggests that the church follow up on its promise to participate in the collection.

Paul is about to travel to Jerusalem with the offerings of other churches and the delegation will be stopping in Corinth en route. To avoid embarrassment, Paul urges the Corinthians to have an offering ready when he arrives. He is sending three men on ahead to help.

2 Corinthians 8–9 sets up a rivalry of generosity between Achaia and Macedonia. Paul assures the church of the integrity of the project and the men he is sending to coordinate it. Finally, he tells the Corinthians that their gifts will glorify God, and God will bless them accordingly.

Continued on next page

FIGURE 13-1

Romans 15:25-29

When Paul writes the church in Rome, he is in Corinth, about to leave for Jerusalem to deliver the collection. He explains why the Macedonians and Achaians were sending money to Jerusalem: "They were pleased to do this, and indeed owe it to them, for if the Gentiles have come to share in their spiritual blessings, they ought also to be of service to them in material things." In other words, Paul thought it was only fair that the Gentile churches help sustain the physical lives of the people who had a part in bringing them spiritual life.

After the collection is delivered, Paul intends to leave his ministry in the eastern Mediterranean and move west. He wants the Roman Christians to host him as he prepares for a mission to Spain (Rom 15:28-29).

Acts 24:17

Luke has not mentioned a Gentile collection for Jewish Christians since Acts 11:27-30, and scholars cannot agree on an explanation for Luke's silence about the collection.

Still, the book of Acts does describe a trip to Jerusalem by Paul and delegates from churches in Macedonia, Galatia, Asia, and Greece (Acts 20:4). As well, Luke reports Paul's reason for the visit: "I came to bring alms to my nation and offer sacrifices" (Acts 24:17). This may be an allusion to the offering for Jerusalem.

 FIGURE 13-1

The Appeal
(2 Cor 8:1-15)

Based on several factors, many scholars divide 2 Corinthians 8–9 into two separate letters. Some suggest that chapter 9 may have been a general appeal for circulation in the Achaian region, while chapter 8 was directed specifically to the church in Corinth. Still, most commentators conclude that it is best to see chapters 8 and 9 as a unified section following naturally from the previous discussion (see Figure 13-2).

Paul begins his appeal with a disclosure formula: "We want you to know..." (2 Cor 8:1); what follows is news to the Corinthians. Paul tells them of "a severe ordeal of affliction" among the churches of Macedonia. He has already mentioned how he endured "disputes without and fears within" while in Macedonia (2 Cor 7:5). His letters to the Macedonian churches show that persecution continued (Phil 1:28-30; 1 Thes 3:3-4; 2 Thes 1:4-6).

The crises left the churches poor but undaunted. In the midst of their struggles, they still gave sacrificially to the "ministry to the saints" (2 Cor 8:4). Paul had come to expect such generosity from Macedonians. In the past, the small congregation in Philippi had sent Paul to Thessalonica with financial support to carry on his mission. They followed this up with yet more gifts (Phil 4:10-19; 2 Cor 11:9). For their part, the Thessalonians had posted a bond to free Paul from prison during his initial visit (Acts 17:9).

As confident as Paul was of Macedonian generosity, he did not expect the diplomatic service they offered. "They gave themselves first to the Lord and, by the will of God, to us, so that we might urge Titus that, as he had already made a beginning, so he should also complete this generous undertaking among you" (2 Cor 8:5-6). In other words, as Paul will explain later, the Macedonians have offered to travel with Titus to complete the collection in Corinth (cf. 2 Cor 8:16-24; 9:2-5).

Not only does the church in Corinth have the example of the Macedonians to follow, but it will have them as witnesses to its offering. Paul reminds the Corinthians they have a reputation to maintain. "Now as you excel in everything—in faith, in speech, in knowledge, in utmost eagerness, and in our love for you—so we want you to excel also in this generous undertaking" (2 Cor 8:7). From the beginning, the Corinthians cultured a reputation for "faith," "speech," "knowledge" and spiritual enthusiasm (cf. esp. 1 Cor 1:5-7; 12:8-9).

We would expect that Paul would commend the Corinthians for their love for him, rather than telling them that they abound "in our love for you." In fact, most Greek manuscripts read "...your love for us." Scholars disagree on which reading is the original, although in keeping with basic hermeneutical principles most choose the more difficult one in context. It is easier to understand why scribes would change from the harder reading to the simpler one. Paul is probably saying that, since he loves them so much, they should be prepared to share that love.

Paul's point is straightforward: the Corinthians are renowned for their excellence in many areas. With such a wealth of spiritual gifts, it is only fitting that they abound in the grace to give to others. Even the Macedonians, with less to share, have *begged* for the chance to contribute. They are now coming to see what the Corinthians will do.

As compelling as Paul's case is, it stops short of commanding participation in the collection. He is "testing" the Corinthians against others (2 Cor 8:8) and offering his "advice" (2 Cor 8:10). The Christian faith models grace freely offered, not payments forcibly extracted.

Are 2 Corinthians 8 and 9 Separate Letters?

Based on the factors presented below, some scholars divide 2 Corinthians 8 and 9 into separate letters, though they do not agree on the order of composition or even destination.

Though the arguments for separate letters are weighty, the differences between the two chapters also can be explained in the context of a single letter. Considering the evidence, most commentators conclude that it is best to see chapters 8 and 9 as a unified section that follows naturally from the previous discussion.

Separate Letters	Single Composition
Because 2 Corinthians 9:2 speaks of the region of "Achaia" and does not name Corinth, chapter 9 may have been a general appeal written separately for circulation in the Achaian region, while chapter 8 was meant specifically for the church in Corinth.	2 Corinthians is addressed to Corinth, "including all the saints throughout Achaia" (2 Cor 1:1). Consistent with this salutation, 2 Corinthians 9:2 uses the regional designation to balance the reference to "the people of Macedonia."
2 Corinthians 9:1 reads as if it were a letter's first reference to the collection: "Now it is not necessary for me to write to you about the ministry of the saints."	Before the opening sentence of chapter 9, the last time Paul explicitly mentioned the "ministry of the saints" was 2 Corinthians 8:4. Paul has addressed many issues in between, and a repetition of the full phrase as a summary or for emphasis is not out of order. Some scholars even suggest that Paul may have paused in his composition of the letter between the two chapters. This would explain the fresh resumption in 2 Corinthians 9:1.
Chapter 9 repeats many of the same topics as chapter 8, yet it apparently presents them inconsistently. For example, in chapter 8, Paul vaunts the Macedonians before the Corinthians, whereas in chapter 9 he says that he has boasted about the Achaian zeal to the Macedonians.	It is not inconsistent for Paul to boast about the Macedonians to the Corinthians and also tell the Corinthians that he has boasted in Macedonia about a Corinthian willingness to give. He is simply giving the Corinthians several reasons to open their purses: the Macedonians have set the example and the Corinthians have a reputation to maintain.
In chapter 8, Paul says he is sending Titus and other brothers, presumably Macedonian delegates (2 Cor 8:18-19, 22), to administer the collection so Paul could not be suspected of fraud in any handling of the money. A different scenario is explained in chapter 9: "the brothers" are coming ahead of Paul to ready the collection so that when Paul arrives with other Macedonians, they would not witness any reluctance to give (2 Cor 9:2-5).	"The brothers" from Macedonia who are preceding Paul can serve more than one function. Along with Titus, in Paul's absence they can forthrightly assuage any doubts about the integrity of the campaign. At the same time, they can save both Paul and the Corinthians from embarrassment by soliciting funds before the apostle arrives with more Macedonian delegates. It is important to note that the reference to "the brothers" in chapter 9 assumes the readers already know who is coming, and Paul gives this information only in chapter 8.

FIGURE 13-2

To cite the ultimate example of this principle, Paul invokes the incarnation and saving work of Christ: "For you know the generous act of our Lord Jesus Christ, that though he was rich, yet for our sakes he became poor, so that by his poverty you might become rich" (2 Cor 8:9). The Lord voluntarily gave up his pre-existent glory and lived a human life with all its limitations. What is more, he offered even his human life on the cross so we might share in his eternal riches.

Apparently the Corinthians have come to agree with the grounds for the collection. A year ago they expressed their eagerness to respond graciously (2 Cor 8:10; 9:2). Yet the funds have not materialized. The breakdown of relations between Paul and Corinth was doubtless a major factor in the delay. Now that they are reconciled, the apostle suggests that it is time to follow up on their good intention with action (2 Cor 8:10-11).

If the Corinthians were hesitating because they did not think they had enough to offer, Paul assures them that willingness to give is more important than the amount given (2 Cor 8:12). Still, Paul knows that the church can afford a liberal donation from their "present abundance" (2 Cor 8:14). Compared to Christians in Jerusalem, and even Macedonia, the Corinthians are rich. So, Paul notes that they should give according to their means (2 Cor 8:11-12).

Paul is not asking that the Corinthians impoverish themselves to enrich others. Rather, he is calling for a balancing of resources. "It is a question of a fair balance between your present abundance and their need," writes Paul, "so that their abundance may be for your need" (2 Cor 8:14).

Presumably, Paul is speaking of a balance between Corinth and Jerusalem. Interpreters differ in their understanding of the "abundance" in Jerusalem that may meet a need in Corinth. Paul may be speaking hypothetically, suggesting that a time may come when the Corinthians would need the financial support of Jerusalem. Then Corinth would be glad for the principle of sharing the surplus among the saints.

Yet, the occasion for aid from Jerusalem to Corinth would be so remote that it detracts from Paul's argument. So, it is best to spiritualize the reference to Jerusalem's abundance and Corinth's need. This is what Paul does in Romans 15:27 when he explains why the Macedonians and Achaians were sending money to Jerusalem: "They were pleased to do this, and indeed owe it to them, for if the Gentiles have come to share in their spiritual blessings, they ought also to be of service to them in material things." In other words, it was only fair that Corinth help sustain the physical lives of the people who had a part in bringing them spiritual life.

Paul ends his initial plea for a fair sharing of resources with a quotation from the story of the manna from heaven (Ex 16). God told the people of Israel to gather an "omer" of manna for each person. Some gathered more, some less, but when they measured and ate it, each had exactly what he or she needed. "The one who had much did not have too much, and the one who had little did not have too little" (2 Cor 8:15; cf. Ex 16:18). Like Israel, Corinth was not to be concerned with gathering too much or having too little.

Endorsement of the Delegates
(2 Cor 8:16–9:5)

At the beginning of his appeal, Paul related the zeal of the Macedonians. They had even offered themselves to help Titus with the collection in Corinth (2 Cor 8:5-6). Now Paul tells them more.

Though having just left Corinth, Titus is returning to Corinth to report to Paul in Macedonia. Paul thought that the quick backtrack was necessary and that Titus was the best one on his team to make it. Titus welcomed Paul's request to return. "He not only accepted our appeal, but since he is more eager than ever, he is going to you of his own accord" (2 Cor 8:17).

Paul has carefully chosen his language to describe Titus' response. He wants the Corinthians to follow his example. As Titus accepted Paul's *appeal*, so should the Corinthians. As Titus is more *eager* than ever, so should be the church. As Titus is acting on *his own accord*, so must those in Corinth.

With Titus, the Macedonians are sending delegates. Among them is "the brother who is famous among all the churches for his proclaiming the good news" (2 Cor 8:18). The Greek does not specifically refer to "proclaiming," and it is best to understand this verse as a general reference to someone praised in all the churches for his "service" in the gospel. It is impossible to know his name, although scholars have made various suggestions, including Luke, Barnabas, Apollos, and the Macedonian Aristarchus (cf. Acts 19:29; 20:4; 27:2).

In v. 22, Paul describes a third member of the delegation. Again Paul does not name him but calls him "our brother," so he may have been someone from Paul's apostolic team. Like Titus, he is confident in the Corinthians and eager to go. In addition, he has proven himself "in many matters."

The team will go on ahead of Paul and ensure that the funds are properly solicited and managed (2 Cor 8:20). Paul must keep some distance from the actual collection process itself in Corinth. Here more intensely than anywhere, critics have questioned the apostle's personal financial arrangements (cf. 1 Cor 9:3-18). Paul has always acted with integrity before the Lord, but in Corinth that is not enough. He cannot allow even an opportunity for his honesty to be questioned (2 Cor 8:21).

Realizing the Corinthians may have reservations about these three men, Paul adds a few final commendations. Titus is his "partner" and "co-worker in your service" (2 Cor 8:23). Of course the Corinthians already know Titus, but Paul is stressing the close relationship between Titus and himself. He will speak for Paul among the Corinthians when the group arrives.

The two others are "messengers of the churches" (2 Cor 8:23). The word translated "messengers" is "*apostoloi*," but Paul is not using the term in the technical sense he does in other places (e.g. 1 Cor 9:1-2; 15:7-9; Gal 1:1). They are *delegates* sent by the churches to represent them in a particular assignment. What is more, they are "the glory of Christ" (2 Cor 8:23), perhaps a lofty way of saying that they also represent the Lord in this ministry within his body.

Because these three men are not acting independently, looking for their personal interests, Corinth must honor them as it would honor Paul, other churches, or even Christ himself. Paul directs the church to welcome the delegation openly (2 Cor 8:24). He asks for a demonstration of the Corinthian love and eagerness about which he has boasted.

The Corinthians have known about this project since Paul wrote his "previous letter" (2 Cor 9:1). When they first heard about it they agreed to participate, although they had some concerns about it. Paul answered their questions (1 Cor 16:1-4), and assumed their funds would be forthcoming. Now he tells the church that he has boasted about it to the Macedonians, "saying that Achaia has been ready since last year" (2 Cor 9:2).

Prompted by Corinthian eagerness, the Macedonians have responded most generously (2 Cor 8:1-6; 9:2). Paul is in an awkward situation: Corinth has yet to follow through on its commitment and the Macedonians are ready to come through on the way to Jerusalem. Both Paul and the Achaians stand to be humiliated should the Macedonians find that Corinth has done nothing for the collection in Corinth (2 Cor 9:3-4).

This is another reason the brothers are coming to Corinth ahead of Paul and the main travel party. "The brothers" must not only satisfy the Corinthian concern for the integrity of the collection, but they must make sure that the Corinthians keep their promise of a "bountiful gift"

(2 Cor 9:5). It must be ready before Paul arrives so that he does not have to coerce the Corinthians in the presence of the Macedonians.

The Blessings of Generosity
(2 Cor 9:6-15)

So far, Paul has provided the Corinthians with examples of sacrificial giving, assured them of the fairness of sharing, addressed their concerns about the integrity of the process, and appealed to their pride. Everything he has said has been to motivate contributions. He ends his case by stating a principle that should interest those more concerned with getting than giving.

"The point is this: the one who sows sparingly will also reap sparingly, and the one who sows bountifully will also reap bountifully" (2 Cor 9:6). The agricultural image of sowing what one reaps was common in the maxims of Paul's time. The apostle uses the principle to imply that the Corinthians will prosper if they give generously to the collection.

Paul goes on to explain that the attitude of the giver is important. As well, the returns on the gift multiply in their amount and vary in their nature. The givers, recipients, and God will all benefit from Corinthian obedience to this test of generosity.

God will honor donors who act thoughtfully and joyfully (2 Cor 9:7). Even if Paul is doing all he can to persuade, he is not forcing them. For encouragement, Paul cites a Proverb only found in the Septuagint, the Greek version of the Old Testament: "... God loves a cheerful giver" (2 Cor 9:7; cf. Prov 22:8, LXX).

Because God loves joyful benefactors, he will provide abundantly for them. He does this so that givers can give even more (2 Cor 9:8-11). Paul quotes Psalm 112:9 to show how God uses the generous person to help the poor and establish his righteousness everywhere (2 Cor 9:9). He continues the agricultural theme begun in v. 6: if the Corinthians scatter the seed that God supplies, it will multiply and God will "increase the harvest of your righteousness" (2 Cor 9:10).

Generosity benefits those who give and those who receive. Yet, more importantly, it brings praise to God (2 Cor 9:11-14). "The rendering of this ministry," says Paul, "overflows with many thanksgivings to God" (2 Cor 9:12). With their generosity, the Corinthians can "glorify God" and show their obedience to the gospel (2 Cor 9:13). Those who receive gifts from the church in Corinth will praise God for the grace that he has channeled through it (2 Cor 9:14).

Paul punctuates this last point with a burst of praise: "Thanks be to God for his indescribable gift!" (2 Cor 9:15). With that, he ends his appeal for the collection.

The "indescribable gift" for which Paul is so thankful is probably "the surpassing grace" he mentioned in the preceding sentence. This grace from God is manifest in many ways. As Paul has taught, grace is expressed in the generosity of those who contribute to the collection. So, in his concluding doxology, Paul thanks God for the collection from Corinth he expects *and* for the ultimate gift of his Son that makes all other offerings possible.

Conclusion

Although the contribution for Jerusalem was voluntary, it became an integral part of Paul's ministry among the churches of Galatia, Macedonia, and Achaia. As an act of charity, it expressed the unity of the church among Gentile believers in different regions as well as between the Gentile and Jewish churches.

The collection authenticated Paul's apostolic ministry in the eyes of the Judean Christians. He had agreed to the service as part of his negotiations in Jerusalem at the apostolic council. The completion of the project would mark the end of his ministry in the eastern Mediterranean. Paul would then be free to move west to Rome and on to Spain.

Specifically in Corinth, the offering was a test of obedience to the gospel and to Paul's apostolic authority. As Paul writes these chapters, he is confident that they will pass the test. Although we will never know the extent of their generosity, Romans 15:26 and Acts 20:4 both testify that Christians from the region eventually brought their gifts to Jerusalem with Paul.

STUDY QUESTIONS

1. Besides giving money for the collection, what else did the Macedonians offer to do for the project?

2. List at least two references in chapters 8 and 9 that suggest the Corinthians have ample resources from which to draw for the collection.

3. In a sentence each, summarize four reasons to give that these two chapters present.

4. What are two reasons Paul mentions for sending "the brothers" on ahead of him to Corinth?

5. List the three parties that gain from generosity. In what way does each benefit?

6. Why does God give more to those who share graciously with others?

7. List at least two ways of interpreting the "indescribable gift" for which Paul gives thanks in 2 Corinthians 9:15.

Chapter 14

A MINISTRY OF WEAKNESS:
THE GROUNDS FOR BOASTING
(2 Corinthians 10–13)

Introduction

The conciliator of 2 Corinthians 1–9 is the contender of 10–13. From his opening paragraph in chapter 10, a sarcastic Paul issues angry threats instead of gentle encouragement. This sudden change is best explained by separate occasions for the two sections. As discussed earlier (see chapter 9, Figure 9-1), 2 Corinthians 10–13 is probably the severe letter written between 1 Corinthians and 2 Corinthians 1–9 (cf. 2 Cor 2:4; 7:8).

"Boasting" dominates these four chapters. Paul deplores the way his arrogant opponents "measure themselves by one another" (2 Cor 10:12). Albeit apologetically, Paul also succumbs to self-commendation and shows how, by any criteria, he has more to brag about than these "super-apostles" (2 Cor 11:5). The apostle chastises his readers for submitting to a different gospel and questioning his authority. He charges them to repent or face his discipline on a third visit.

Critics in Corinth
(2 Cor 10:1–11:15)

Paul immediately confronts critics by the way he identifies himself in his opening sentence: "I myself, Paul, appeal to you by the meekness and gentleness of Christ—I who am humble when face to face with

you, but bold toward you when I am away..." (2 Cor 10:1). With this he
lets his readers know that he is aware of what people in Corinth are saying about him.

Throughout these chapters Paul cites his detractors. He notes that
there are those who say he is "acting according to human standards" (2
Cor 10:2). They also say, "His letters are weighty and strong, but his
bodily presence is weak, and his speech contemptible" (2 Cor 10:10).
They imply that Paul did not love the Corinthians (2 Cor 11:11), that he
"was crafty," and he took them in "by deceit" (2 Cor 12:16). They say he
took advantage of the church (2 Cor 12:17) while also denigrating him
for preaching free of charge (2 Cor 11:7-9).

To silence his critics, Paul defends himself and counters with a
scathing appraisal of his opponents.

First, he responds to the charge that he behaves "according to
human standards" (2 Cor 10:1-6). Paul uses the same phrase in 2
Corinthians 1:17 to refer to self-centered opportunism, or saying whatever was necessary for personal advantage. Although he is only human,
admits Paul, he still serves a higher cause than self-interest. He is in
spiritual warfare, using weapons of divine power to "destroy arguments
and every proud obstacle raised up against the knowledge of God" (2
Cor 10:4-5). With this military metaphor, Paul takes aim at the problem
in Corinth, warning "we are ready to punish every disobedience" (2 Cor
10:6). If Paul wrote 2 Corinthians 1–9 after this section, then he saw his
hope for obedience fulfilled (cf. 2 Cor 2:5-9; 7:9-15; see also chapter 9,
Figure 9-1).

At this point, however, the rebellious church is confident in itself
but has lost confidence in Paul. Face the facts, not the allegations,
stresses the apostle (2 Cor 10:7). If the Corinthians think that they are
Christ's, then certainly Paul, the one who introduced them to the Lord,
is Christ's as well. He has the God-given right to exercise his apostolic
authority over the church he has built up.

From the perspective of some in Corinth, Paul is quick to remind
them of his powerful leadership whenever he writes. Yet when he visits,
he's a different person; he is weak and inarticulate. This is the second
charge Paul disputes. He vows that "what we say by letter when absent,
we will also do when present" (2 Cor 10:11). In other words, he will
back his words with actions. Paul reminds them that the last time he
was in Corinth, he was stern. "I warned those who sinned previously
and all the others, and I warn them now while absent, *as I did when
present on my second visit*, that if I come again I will not be lenient" (2
Cor 13:2).

As for his skill as an orator, Paul concedes weakness (2 Cor 11:6; cf. 10:10). Still, his audience cannot confuse his unpolished rhetoric with a lack of genuine knowledge. He has consistently shown the Corinthians his understanding of the truth.

This is not the first time Paul makes this point. From the beginning of his ministry in Corinth, the church has compared his speech with the eloquence of others. Paul has responded by saying he has purposely avoided "lofty words," choosing instead to speak simply of the crucifixion of Jesus Christ (1 Cor 2:1-5). The power of the message lies not in the skill and style of the messenger but in the knowledge and power of God.

Not only did critics ridicule Paul for being a poor public speaker, but they maligned him because, unlike other itinerant philosophers, he did not collect fees for his preaching. "Did I sin by humbling myself . . . because I proclaimed God's good news to you free of charge?" Paul asks (2 Cor 11:7). The Corinthians may have thought that it demeaned their apostle, and therefore them, when he supported himself with the manual labor of tentmaking. Or perhaps they thought he was defrauding them with the collection for Jerusalem instead of openly soliciting personal support (2 Cor 11:16-18).

Paul assures the church that he has always acted in their best interests. Rather than burdening anyone with his financial needs, he worked at his trade wherever he traveled (Acts 18:1-4; 1 Cor 4:12; 1 Thes 2:9; 2 Thes 3:7-9). In addition, Paul tells the Corinthians, "I robbed other churches by accepting support from them in order to serve you" (2 Cor 11:8). In case they misinterpret his exaggeration, he explains that the generous Macedonians voluntarily met his needs while he ministered in Achaia (2 Cor 11:9; cf. Phil 4:10-20).

Unlike other apostles, Paul takes pride in foregoing his rights to support from Corinth (2 Cor 11:10; cf. 1 Cor 9). By so doing, he makes the gospel available to all, not just to those who can afford it. As well, he stands accountable to no one but God for his ministry. Above all, his free service to the Corinthians should prove his love for them (2 Cor 11:11).

Members within the congregation are not alone in casting aspersions on Paul. "Super-apostles," as he sarcastically calls them (2 Cor 11:5; 12:11), are spurring on the Corinthians. They have infiltrated the church, denigrated Paul, and impressed their audience with bold assertions. Focusing on these interlopers, Paul attacks their character, methods, and claims (2 Cor 10:12–11:15).

They show their folly by measuring their success in comparison to one another (2 Cor 10:12). Such mutual admiration is antithetical to the

Lord's standards and leads to empty boasts. As Paul has already taught, if anyone is to boast, he or she should boast in the Lord, from whom comes the only commendation that matters (2 Cor 10:17-18; cf. 1 Cor 1:31; 4:1-4).

Worse yet, these boasters are competing for followers in the territory that God has assigned to Paul (2 Cor 10:13). He was the first to arrive in Corinth, he founded the church, and now the late-comers take credit for "the labors of others" (2 Cor 10:15). As for Paul, he refuses to boast in the work of someone else. When he completes his ministry in Achaia, he will move on to preach in unevangelized lands (2 Cor 10:16; cf. Rom 15:20-21). He plans to move west to Spain, via Rome (Rom 15:23-29).

We can understand Paul's frustration considering the arrangement he forged with the other apostles in Jerusalem. As Galatians 2:7-9 reports, they had agreed that Paul would go to Gentile lands while the Judean leaders would preach to the circumcised. Paul had kept to the agreement, but unauthorized Judaizers claiming apostolic credentials had invaded Paul's churches. They touted their Jewish credentials (2 Cor 11:22), insisting on circumcision and the observance of the Jewish law (cf. also Gal 3–5; Phil 3:1-11).

The "super-apostles" were proclaiming a different gospel than Paul's. They came in another spirit and presented a distorted view of Christ (2 Cor 11:4). Paul sadly observes that the Corinthians are too ready to accept their claims. Deceived, the church that Paul betrothed to Christ is in danger of losing its first love (2 Cor 11:2-3). Paul will give the congregation directions on how to remedy this later. For now, he remains focused on these false apostles.

These apostolic charlatans do not love the church as Paul does. This is evident from their practice of soliciting money for their services. Paul reverses their criticism of his refusal to collect. How can they be Paul's equal when they do not give themselves freely to the church (2 Cor 11:12)?

Paul scorns these opponents with damning indictments. He calls them "false apostles" and "deceitful workers" (2 Cor 11:13). Even worse, he charges, they are Satan's ministers who disguise themselves as apostles of Christ just as "Satan disguises himself as an angel of light" (2 Cor 11:14). Here Paul draws from stories about Satan that circulated in extra-biblical documents (e.g. *The Life of Adam and Eve* 9:1; *Apocalypse of Moses* 11:3). He warns that the impostors will share the fate of their diabolical master (2 Cor 11:15).

Paul's Boasting
(2 Cor 11:16–12:13)

Using extreme irony, Paul prepares to "boast a little" (2 Cor 11:16). If the church in its wisdom listens to fools, then he will act like a fool. Paul acknowledges that he cannot boast "with the Lord's authority" (2 Cor 11:17), but it will be no worse than the folly of the Corinthians. After all, they have allowed pretentious false apostles to enslave them, prey upon them and "give them a slap in the face" (2 Cor 11:20). "To my shame, I must say," quips a sarcastic Paul, "we were too weak for that!" (2 Cor 11:21).

Having made it clear that he is stooping to a level beneath good sense and Christian standards, Paul accepts the challenge to measure himself against his opponents. He presents three areas of his life for comparison: his Jewish background, his service to Christ, and his experience of ecstatic spirituality.

"Are they Hebrews? So am I. Are they Israelites? So am I. Are they descendants of Abraham? So am I" (2 Cor 11:22). Besides what this says about Paul, it also reveals how the false apostles claimed that their Jewish credentials gave them authority in the church. Apart from whether Paul would agree with this reasoning, he claims the same credentials (cf. Rom 11:1; Phil 3:4-7; Acts 22:3; 26:4-6; see also Figure 14-1).

To be "Hebrew" is to speak Hebrew (Aramaic; cf. Acts 6:1), which was a sign of fidelity to Judaism. The designation also may refer to Jews born in Palestine as opposed to those of the diaspora, although Paul cannot be using it this way. Though Paul was born in Tarsus, he was raised in a Hebrew-speaking home (cf. Phil 3:5).

To be an "Israelite" is to be an ethnic Jew, born into the chosen people. The term was not limited to people from the land of Israel; it stressed participation in the social and religious life of Judaism. Whether from Palestine or not, Paul was a member of the nation of Israel.

To be a "descendant of Abraham" is to share in God's covenantal promises to Abraham (Gen 17). Both ethnic Israelites (Acts 13:26) and others who shared in Abraham's faith were his descendants (Rom 4:13-18; 9:6-8). Paul sees the promises to Abraham fulfilled in the gospel of Christ (Gal 3:16-18).

Paul was proud of his Jewish heritage, but he understood it in light of Christ. His opponents claimed the same, as Paul's fourth rhetorical question shows: "Are they ministers of Christ? I am talking like a madman — I am a better one..." (2 Cor 11:23). Clearly Paul feels awkward

Several times, Paul was forced to list his Jewish credentials, either to discredit critics who charged him with crimes against Judaism or to warn his readers of Judaizers.

- "Are they Hebrews? So am I. Are they Israelites? So am I. Are they descendants of Abraham? So am I" (2 Cor 11:22).

- "If anyone else has reason to be confident in the flesh, I have more: circumcised on the eighth day, a member of the people of Israel, of the tribe of Benjamin, a Hebrew born of Hebrews; as to the law, a Pharisee; as to zeal, a persecutor of the church; as to righteousness under the law, blameless" (Phil 3:4-6).

- "I myself am an Israelite, a descendant of Abraham, a member of the tribe of Benjamin" (Rom 11:1).

- "I advanced in Judaism beyond many among my own people of the same age, for I was far more zealous for the traditions of my ancestors" (Gal 1:14).

- "I am a Jew, born in Tarsus in Cilicia, but brought up in this city at the feet of Gamaliel, educated strictly according to our ancestral law, being zealous for God, just as all of you are today" (Acts 22:3).

- "All the Jews know my way of life from my youth, a life spent from the beginning among my own people and in Jerusalem. They have known for a long time, if they are willing to testify, that I have belonged to the strictest sect of our religion and lived as a Pharisee" (Acts 26:4-5).

FIGURE 14-1

with such boasting, but he is about to reverse the prevailing standards in Corinth of what it means to be a minister of Christ.

Hard work, persecution, suffering, danger, and weakness characterize true Christian service. Can the super-apostles match Paul's track record? He lists a daunting yet fascinating catalogue of adversities. In other places Paul offers similar descriptions, and Acts narrates some of them, but 2 Corinthians 11:23-29 is the longest and most detailed account of the sufferings of the apostle (cf. also 1 Cor 4:8-13; 2 Cor 1:8-11; 4:8-9; 6:4-5).

Paul speaks both in generalities and specifics. He describes toil, danger, and pain. He suffers physically, psychologically, and spiritually at the hands of enemies and at the mercy of the forces of nature. To understand some of Paul's comments, it helps to have an understanding of legal punishments in his time.

Flogging, or beating, often accompanied other punishments prescribed by the court. Yet, mobs also frequently flogged victims with no official sanction. Paul experienced "countless floggings, and was often near death" (2 Cor 11:23).

The five times that Paul was whipped with "forty lashes minus one," he was subject to synagogue discipline. Mosaic law allowed a maximum penalty of not more than forty lashes, "with the number of lashes proportionate to the offense" (Deut 25:2). The Mishnah prescribes thirty-nine lashes as a precaution against exceeding the law by a miscount (*Makkoth* 3:1-9).

Three times Paul was "beaten with rods" (2 Cor 11:25; cf. Acts 16:22). Under the direction of Roman magistrates, "lictors" would scourge criminals with wooden rods for municipal offenses. According to the law, Roman citizens were exempt from such punishments, although there are many examples of officials ignoring this restriction.

Stoning was a capital punishment prescribed in Jewish law for a variety of specific offenses (Deut 17:5; 22:22-24; *Sanhedrin* 7:56-60). As well, angry crowds would often resort to stoning without consideration of due procedure. In Paul's case, a mob stoned him and left him for dead in Lystra (Acts 14:19). Earlier, in Iconium, a mob of Jews and Gentiles had also tried to stone him after he incensed them with his preaching (Acts 14:1-6).

Besides the various persecutions and dangers of travel, the "daily pressure because of my anxiety for all the churches" (2 Cor 11:28) contributes to Paul's apostolic suffering. In part, this is a jab at the Corinthians, yet Paul also means it to show his weakness (2 Cor 11:29-30). That is why, almost as an afterthought, Paul includes the account of the narrow escape from the governor of Damascus (2 Cor 11:32-33; cf. Acts

9:23-25). Paul presents the picture of being let down in a basket through a window as evidence of his humiliation in ministry.

Even when Paul goes on to recount his "visions and revelations of the Lord," he concludes on a note of frailty (2 Cor 12:7-10). These ecstatic experiences could lead to a sense of spiritual pride but Paul is careful to distance himself from this danger. He may have visited "paradise" (2 Cor 12:3), but he has no inflated view of himself because of it.

Discreetly describing his experience in the third person, he speaks of "a person in Christ who fourteen years ago was caught up to the third heaven" (2 Cor 12:3). Twice he confesses that only God knows if he was in or out of his body. He heard "things that are not to be told, that no mortal is permitted to repeat" (2 Cor 12:4).

"The third heaven" is a term used in Jewish cosmologies to denote the highest heaven where God resides as compared to the atmospheric heaven and the stellar heaven (cf. 1 Kgs 8:27; 2 Chr 2:6; 6:18; Neh 9:6; Ps 148:4). The word "paradise" describes the same place in Jewish apocalyptic literature (cf. 2 *Enoch* 8 and *Apocalypse of Moses* 37:5). Because the spiritual realities Paul experienced were so sacred, he does not share them with his readers (2 Cor 12:4).

This was not the only spiritual vision Paul had (cf. Gal 1:16; 1 Cor 15:8; Acts 9:3-19; 16:9; 18:9-10; 22:17-21). Still, this was one of his most vivid and extraordinary. Since the vision occurred "fourteen years ago," before his council visit to Jerusalem, it was formative in Paul's ministry. Yet it cannot be considered apart from the "thorn in the flesh" that accompanied the ecstasy (2 Cor 12:7-8).

Paul describes this thorn as "a messenger of Satan" that keeps him "from being too elated" about his spiritual vision. Satan may have been the agent through whom the thorn came, but *the Lord* has done this for Paul's sake. Paul fervently prayed for deliverance from the thorn's pain, but God would not allow it.

Many interpreters have made various suggestions about the exact nature of the thorn. Some think that it was an oppressive spiritual force, perhaps a demon. Others suggest a psychological affliction such as anxiety or depression. Still others maintain that the thorn refers to Paul's opponents, although most agree that the thorn was a bodily ailment.

Galatians 4:13-15 describe a "physical infirmity" Paul suffered while he was in Galatia. Judging from his comments in v. 15, the affliction affected his eyes and may have caused him to write with "large letters" (Gal 6:11). Perhaps Paul had acute ophthalmia. Other suggestions for Paul's ailment include epilepsy, malaria, or a speech impediment. Paul is as cryptic about the nature of the thorn in the flesh as he is about what he saw and heard in his vision.

We can conclude only that he regarded the thorn as evil while recognizing its good purpose in God's plan for his life. Through the experience, the apostle learned that God's "power is made perfect in weakness" (2 Cor 12:9). This is the central thrust of 2 Corinthians 10–13. Paul will not glory in his personal strength or spiritual attainments. Instead, he will focus on his frailties, where the transforming grace and power of Christ is most evident. "I am content with weaknesses, insults, hardships, persecutions, and calamities for the sake of Christ; for whenever I am weak, then I am strong" (2 Cor 12:10).

Though Paul holds values opposite to his opponents, he is not comfortable with the way he has become like them and indulged in self-commendation. "I have been a fool!" he confesses to his readers. "You have forced me to it" (2 Cor 12:11). The church knows him well enough that he should not have to defend himself before them. Over the years he has patiently ministered to them as a true apostle with accompanying "signs and wonders and mighty works" (2 Cor 12:12; cf. also Rom 15:19; Gal 3:5).

To finish his boast, Paul fires two final barbs: one at his apostolic rivals and one at the church. First he insists, "I am not at all inferior to these super-apostles, even though I am nothing" (2 Cor 12:11). They, by implication, are less than nothing! Second, he asks if the Corinthians are "worse off than other churches" because he left them out of the circle that contributed to his financial support. With great irony he begs pardon for not being a burden: "Forgive me this wrong!" (2 Cor 12:13).

A Warning to the Church
(2 Cor 12:14–13:13)

Between the writing of this letter and 1 Corinthians, Paul had to make a trip to Corinth to correct degenerating attitudes in the church. He found it a disappointing visit and left with the issues unresolved (2 Cor 2:1).

This letter concludes with the threat of a third visit during which he "will not be lenient" (2 Cor 12:14; 13:2). He will come to mourn over their sin (2 Cor 12:20-21), hear their grievances against him (13:1), and exercise severe discipline (2 Cor 13:2, 10). For both their sake and his, Paul hopes what he writes now will remedy the problem so the trip can be averted.

He will not be coming to ask for personal financial support, Paul insists. Nor has he sent Titus with the letter to defraud them of it indirectly (2 Cor 12:14-17). Since this is the third time in 2 Corinthians

10–13 that Paul raises the issue, it was probably the major point of contention with Corinth (cf. also 2 Cor 11:7-11; 12:13; see also 1 Cor 9). It appears that the Corinthians trusted Titus more than they did Paul (2 Cor 12:18). The apostle acknowledges this and assures them that he shares Titus' integrity and concern for their welfare.

Because Paul cares so much for the church, he is afraid of what might happen on the third visit (2 Cor 12:19-21). If he doesn't like what he finds in them, then they will not like what they find in him, he warns. He has already been humiliated in a previous visit, and he fears that again "my God may humble me before you" (2 Cor 12:21). He may end up mourning over their unrepentant "quarreling, jealousy, anger, selfishness, slander, gossip, conceit, and disorder" (2 Cor 12:20).

Yet, the Corinthians should not think that he will cower in the face of their bold sinfulness. He will come and confront charges against him and failures on their part (2 Cor 13:1-4). To show that he will deal forthrightly, he quotes a legal text from Deuteronomy 19:15: "Any charge must be sustained by the evidence of two or three witnesses" (2 Cor 13:1).

Paul will show the power the Corinthians so eagerly want to see. Yet he warns that he will be using it to discipline them (2 Cor 13:3-4). All along Paul has boasted in his weakness. Paradoxically, by depending on the Lord, the apostle derives authority and strength. Just as Christ "was crucified in weakness, but lives by the power of God," says Paul, "we are weak in him, but in dealing with you we will live with him by the power of God" (2 Cor 13:4).

The Corinthians can avoid discipline from Paul by checking *their* Christian credentials instead of his. "Examine yourselves to see whether you are living in the faith" (2 Cor 13:5). If they want proof that Christ is speaking in Paul (2 Cor 13:3), they need only to test whether Christ is in them. After all, he brought them to faith.

Paul is confident that the church will pass the test and he will be vindicated. Still, this is not the primary reason he calls for self-examination. He simply wants the Corinthians to "do what is right" (2 Cor 13:7), and he is praying that they "may become perfect" (2 Cor 13:9). If they can amend their ways now, then he will not have to resort to stern measures when he visits (2 Cor 13:10). The choice is theirs.

Leaving his readers with this to consider, Paul bids them farewell (2 Cor 13:11-13). Compared to his other letters, the formal conclusion of 2 Corinthians is short. It has a series of six succinct exhortations, a greeting from "all the saints," and a benediction.

Because they consist of single verbs with no elaboration, two of the exhortations in v. 11 are ambiguous. With the Greek verb *chairete*, Paul could be saying "Farewell" or asking them to "Rejoice." The verb *parakaleisthe* can mean either "accept my appeal" or "encourage one another." Despite these ambiguities, the conclusion stands as a clear appeal for unity in the church.

This is the first time Paul mentions a "holy kiss" in his letters (2 Cor 13:12), but it is impossible to know whether he had previously introduced the practice in any of his churches. A kiss on the cheek was a common greeting in Paul's culture. In the church it became a liturgical symbol of love and unity among Christians (cf. Rom 16:16).

The final benediction is the fullest Paul offers in his letters: "The grace of the Lord Jesus Christ, the love of God, and the communion of the Holy Spirit be with all of you" (2 Cor 13:14). The three subjects, and their order, are important in the formulation of Trinitarian theology. This is one of the few places in the New Testament where God, Christ, and the Spirit are linked in one sentence. From our human perspective, it is through the work of Christ that we experience the love of God. In turn, we unite with others in the fellowship and ministry of the Holy Spirit.

For all the polemic in which Paul has participated, he manages to end on a high note.

Conclusion

If 2 Corinthians 10–13 is the severe letter Paul wrote before the reconciling message of chapters 1–9, then Corinth obeyed his call to repentance. If Paul wrote chapters 10–13 *after* 1–9, then the Corinthian correspondence of the New Testament ends as it began, describing rebellious divisions in the church.

In either case, it appears that a fractious attitude plagued the Corinthian church for decades. Forty years after Paul wrote, Clement of Rome wrote to the Corinthians to restore the faith and unity of that church which had split under the influence of "a few rash and self-willed individuals" (*1 Clement* 1:1).

The difficulties Paul faced in Corinth have proved to be a blessing for the church of Christ everywhere in every generation. The apostle's responses to the pastoral challenges have guided countless Christian leaders and congregations through their own crises. The letters have encouraged readers who find a little bit of Corinth in them. After all, Christ entered Corinth, founded his church there, and preserved its unstable saints. There is hope for all whom the Lord calls.

STUDY QUESTIONS

1. List four charges that Paul's critics level against him. In a sentence, summarize Paul's response to each criticism.

2. List four charges Paul makes of the "super-apostles."

3. List four examples of Paul's irony or sarcasm in 2 Corinthians 10–13.

4. Paul boasts he is a Hebrew, an Israelite, and a descendant of Abraham. Although all three claims relate to Paul's Jewishness, they each stress something different. Distinguish among them.

5. Why does Paul boast about his weaknesses?

6. What relation does Paul's thorn in the flesh have with his ecstatic vision of "the third heaven"? Do you think that Paul's thorn in the flesh was physical, emotional, or spiritual in nature? Explain your answer.

7. How did Paul cover his living expenses while he was in Corinth? How was this different from other cities? What problems arose because of his practice in Corinth?

8. List three criticisms Paul makes of the church. How does he plan to rectify the situation?

Chapter 15

READING THE LETTERS OF PAUL

Introduction

Three-quarters of the New Testament documents are letters. Through these dispatches Christians established fellowship, developed doctrine, codified ethics, and coordinated mission. In short, letter writers built the church.

Paul, in particular, worked by letter. He adapted long-standing Greek literary conventions for his unique ministry. In turn, as Christianity expanded, others preserved, copied, and distributed his letters. His style, vocabulary, and structure became models for generations of church leaders as they wrote. Today, echoes of the Christian letter reverberate in all genres of literature and speech.

Current readers run the risk of missing much in New Testament letters because first century letter structure is so familiar yet removed. We tend to skim over the standard phrases we have seen Paul use repeatedly in his introductions, transitions, and conclusions. Doing this, we miss subtle changes that mark concerns specific to each letter. Yet, since we use different protocol in our letters, we don't always understand the significance inherent in the particular forms Paul chooses.

The Greek Letter

Even more so than today, letters served a variety of functions in Paul's day. They were the only relatively accurate and reliable means of communication between two parties separated by any distance. Letters served to establish, maintain, and end relationships between friends, family members, and business associates. They reported, exhorted, advised, rebuked, consoled, mediated, and maintained dialogue. Letters substituted for the presence of the sender when he or she could not personally be with the recipient.

From the time of Augustus (27 B.C.– A.D. 14), the Roman empire employed professional letter writers and couriers for official government business. Yet the private sector did not have the benefit of the emperor's postal service. They had to rely on much more haphazard means to exchange correspondence. Wealthier households owned *grammatophoroi* ("letter carriers"), slaves whose sole responsibility was to deliver mail. Sometimes families would share their *grammatophoroi* to speed and expand communications.

Still, an informal network of merchants, sailors, and caravans carried most letters. Common people would have to pass their letters on to strangers who were passing through in the direction they wished to send the letter. A letter might change hands several times en route.

Even when the trip might normally take a matter of weeks or months, sometimes delivery could be delayed years, or the letter could be lost forever. So, people would sometimes send duplicate letters simultaneously by different means. Fortunately, the church transcended most of these difficulties. Because of their common faith and mission, Christians had a natural network of delivery that was much more reliable and widespread than all but the emperor's.

"Teachers of rhetoric" taught letter writing in the second level of education in Roman society. Few people from the lower classes, even if they had elementary schooling under a "teacher of letters," would ever have the opportunity to study with a rhetoric teacher. So, professional letter writers served government officials, wealthy families, and the uneducated public when the need to send a letter arose. The secretary or *amanuensis* could decide the actual structure and wording of a letter once the sender stipulated its general sense. As today, literate people also would sometimes dictate to a secretary.

In the early twentieth century, archeologists discovered thousands of papyrus letters in the dry sands of Egypt. Dating from the fourth century B.C. to the fourth century A.D., these Greek letters have advanced greatly our understanding of the language and form of the letters of the New Testament. Before their discovery, scholars were at a loss to explain why the Greek of the New Testament was so different from classical Greek. Some attributed it to semitic influences on the biblical writers. With the discovery of the papyri, they could see that the New Testament was written in *koine* Greek, the common language of the first century Mediterranean marketplace.

Among the papyri, archeologists found several manuals for letter writing. As well, they unearthed contracts for the training of professional letter writers and practice books for students. From these sources, we see that the skill of letter writing developed through imitation rather than through learning theory and rules. Sometimes this involved literary contests in which participants wrote under the name, and in the style, of famous authors. This is one context in which we can understand the ancient practice of pseudepigraphy, the ascriptions of false names of authors to works.

Whether letters were sent to lovers, family members, business associates, politicians, merchants, or enemies, they shared a remarkably uniform structure (see Figure 15-1). The papyri letters discovered in Egypt never exceeded one page and averaged eighty-seven words in length. The salutation consisted of two or three words, and the obligatory greeting rarely changed. The body of the letter varied according to subject matter, although writers used the same conventional expressions to introduce or change their topics. The conclusion would usually include more greetings, sometimes the date, and, always, a one-word "farewell" ("*erroso*"; cf. Acts 15:29).

Besides these short personal letters, there were also longer literary "epistles." These treatises took the form of personal letters, but were written for publication and circulation to a wider audience. They included letters to the gods, government edicts, public pleas, letter prayers, and philosophical essays set in letter form. Many philosophical essays were pseudonymous, written by disciples to perpetuate and develop the teachings of their masters.

The function of a letter or epistle dictated the specific type of structure and language it would use. For example, ancient manuals categorized different rhetorical conventions for letters of friendship, family letters, letters of praise and blame, letters of exhortation, letters of mediation, letters of accusation, and letters of rebuke. In addition, military communications and business letters such as contracts, surveys, wills, and testaments followed their specific forms.

In function and form, various letters of Paul parallel specific letter types found among the papyri. For example, the letter to Philemon is an example of the common "letter of mediation." Philippians follows the standard form of a "family letter" except for the warning against false teachers in chapter 3. Romans contains elements of the "diatribe letter," which uses hypothetical objections from opponents to advance

Letter Form in the First Century

The Greek Letter
(4th c. B.C.–A.D. 4th c.)

Opening

This section identifies the sender and recipient and relays a one-word greeting.

It often includes a health wish or prayer for deliverance from the gods.

Body

The business at hand dictates the structure of the body, so its form will vary from letter to letter.

Characteristic phrases introduce new topics and indicate whether this is new information to the readers. Also, these introductions often reveal how the writer received the information that prompts him or her to write.

Conclusion

The conclusion would usually include greetings for acquaintances, a prayer for the godly or a health wish, sometimes the date, and, always, a one-word "farewell."

The Letters of Paul
(A.D. 1st c.)

Opening

The opening identifies the sender and recipient. Compared to the typical Greek letter, Paul's openings relay a longer greeting of "Grace and peace to you from God our Father and our Lord Jesus Christ."

Thanksgiving

In place of a health wish or a prayer for deliverance from the gods, Paul substitutes a thanksgiving for what God has done in the lives of his readers and a prayer for their continued spiritual well-being. It usually ends on a note of hope in the Lord's return.

The thanksgiving often subtly announces the topics that will be dealt with in the body of the letter.

Body

The business at hand dictates the structure of the body, so its form will vary from letter to letter. Usually the body has a doctrinal section followed by ethical exhortations. Also, Paul includes elements of his "apostolic parousia" by which he makes his presence felt among the readers. This may be done by reference to the letter, travel plans, or an emissary.

Characteristic phrases introduce new topics and show whether this is new information to the readers. Also, these introductions often reveal how Paul received the information that prompts him to write.

Conclusion

The conclusion begins with a peace wish. Personal greetings follow. Then Paul will often ask his readers to greet one another with a holy kiss. A summary apostolic command is given, and Paul signs the letter in his own hand. Invariably, he ends with a benediction instead of the usual "farewell" of other Greek letters.

FIGURE 15-1

the argument. 1 Thessalonians, with its abundant praise leading to moral exhortation, follows the form of a "letter of exhortation." Galatians follows the Hellenistic "rebuke-request" pattern.

Paul's Letters

Paul's letters follow the basic form of the personal Greek letter and yet reflect certain features of the public epistle. Similar to private letters, Paul's letters are *ad hoc* documents with particular concerns for a limited audience in a specific context. Like the general epistle, Paul intended his letters to be read publicly. This was true even of his letters addressed to individuals, such as the letter to Philemon. He instructed recipients to read his letters to the assembled congregations (e.g. 1 Thes 5:27) and asked that churches exchange letters (e.g. Col 4:16).

Depending on the function of each letter, Paul adapts standard structures and expressions, creating what we can isolate as a typical Pauline form (see Figure 15-1). When we compare this form with that of other Greek letters, we can learn more about Paul's perspective on his ministry to the churches. As well, when we notice how he diverges from his pattern in each letter, the specific purpose of each document emerges.

The Opening

As in the formal opening of the private Greek letter, Paul's openings identify the sender and the recipients and offer a short greeting (see Figure 15-2). The identifications are longer in Paul's letters than they are in the papyri. Instead of simply saying "Paul to Philemon," for example, Paul will usually describe himself as an apostle and mention co-workers who are with him. In Galatians he particularly stresses his apostolic commission when he identifies himself. No doubt this is because some in Galatia have challenged his apostolic authority. The letter to the Romans contains Paul's longest self-identification since he and the church in Rome had yet to meet.

Except in the pastoral letters of 1 and 2 Timothy and Titus, the recipients are always a *group* of people, whether he calls them "the church" or "the saints" in that particular locale. 1 Corinthians has the most elaborate identification of recipients. Paul uses the opportunity to stress that the Lord has called the fractious Corinthians to unity.

The salutation of Greek letters was a single word: *"charein"* ("greetings"). Paul makes a play on the word by changing it to *"charis"*

		Greetings in Paul's Letters		
Paul's Letters	Sender	Recipients	Greeting
Romans	Paul, a servant of Jesus Christ, called to be an apostle, set apart for the gospel of God, which he promised beforehand through his prophets in the holy scriptures, the gospel concerning his Son, who was descended from David according to the spirit of holiness by resurrection through whom we have received grace and apostleship to bring about the obedience of faith among all the Gentiles for the sake of his name, including yourselves who are called to belong to Jesus Christ,	To all God's beloved in Rome, who are called to be saints:	Grace to you and peace from God our Father and the Lord Jesus Christ.
1 Corinthians	Paul, called to be an apostle of Christ Jesus by the will of God, and our brother Sosthenes,	To the church of God that is in Corinth, to those who are sanctified in Christ Jesus, called to be saints, together with all those who in every place call on the name of our Lord Jesus Christ, both their Lord and ours:	Grace to you and peace from God our Father and the Lord Jesus Christ.
2 Corinthians	Paul, an apostle of Christ Jesus by the will of God, and Timothy our brother,	To the church of God that is in Corinth, including all the saints throughout Achaia:	Grace to you and peace from God our Father and the Lord Jesus Christ.

FIGURE 15-2

Paul's Letters	Sender	Recipients	Greeting
Galatians	Paul an apostle — sent neither by human commission nor from human authorities, but through Jesus Christ and God the Father, who raised him from the dead — and all the members of God's family who are with me,	To the churches of Galatia:	Grace to you and peace from God our Father and the Lord Jesus Christ, who gave himself for our sins to set us free from the present evil age, according to the will of our God and Father, to whom be the glory forever and ever. Amen.
Ephesians	Paul, an apostle of Christ Jesus by the will of God,	To the saints who are [in Ephesus] also faithful in Christ Jesus:	Grace to you and peace from God our Father and the Lord Jesus Christ.
Philippians	Paul and Timothy, slaves of Christ Jesus,	To all the saints in Christ Jesus who are in Philippi, with the bishops and deacons:	Grace to you and peace from God our Father and the Lord Jesus Christ.
Colossians	Paul, an apostle of Christ Jesus by the will of God, and Timothy our brother,	To the saints and faithful brothers and sisters in Christ in Colossae:	Grace to you and peace from God our Father.
1 Thessalonians	Paul, Silvanus, and Timothy,	To the church of the Thessalonians in God the Father and the Lord Jesus Christ:	Grace to you and peace.

Continued on next page

FIGURE 15-2

	Greetings in Paul's Letters (cont'd)		
Paul's Letters	Sender	Recipients	Greeting
2 Thessalonians	Paul, Silvanus, and Timothy,	To the church of the Thessalonians in God our Father and the Lord Jesus Christ:	Grace to you and peace from God our Father and the Lord Jesus Christ.
1 Timothy	Paul, an apostle of Christ Jesus by the command of God our Savior and of Christ Jesus our hope,	To Timothy, my loyal child in the faith:	Grace, mercy, and peace from God the Father and Christ Jesus our Lord.
2 Timothy	Paul, an apostle of Christ Jesus by the will of God, for the sake of the promise of life that is in Christ Jesus,	To Timothy, my beloved child:	Grace, mercy, and peace from God the Father and Christ Jesus our Lord.
Titus	Paul, a servant of God and an apostle of Jesus Christ, for the sake of the faith of God's elect and the knowledge of the truth that is in accordance with godliness, in the hope of eternal life that God, who never lies, promised before the ages began — in due time he revealed his word through the proclamation with which I have been entrusted by the command of God our Savior,	To Titus, my loyal child in the faith we share:	Grace and peace from God the Father and Christ Jesus our Savior.
Philemon	Paul, a prisoner of Christ Jesus, and Timothy our brother,	To Philemon our dear friend and co-worker, to Apphia our sister, to Archippus our fellow soldier, and to the church in your house:	Grace to you and peace from God our Father and the Lord Jesus Christ.

FIGURE 15-2

("grace") and adds the Jewish greeting of "peace" ("*shalom*" in Hebrew). Then he notes "God the Father and the Lord Jesus Christ" as the source of the grace and peace. By doing this, he shows that Jew and Greek are united in the saving ministry of God through his Son. 1 and 2 Timothy add "mercy" to grace and peace.

Greek letter openings often had a health wish or a prayer for deliverance from the wrath of the gods. Paul includes neither in any of his letters. Instead, he substitutes a thanksgiving for the work of God in the lives of his readers and prays for their spiritual well-being.

The Thanksgiving

Typically, Paul begins with a reference to the past faithfulness of the congregation. He then expresses appreciation for their continued spiritual growth. The thanksgivings usually end on an eschatological note confidently predicting the completion of Christ's work in the lives of his readers (see Figure 15-3).

A close reading of Paul's thanksgivings reveals that they may function as a "table of contents" for the rest of the letter. For example, the thanksgiving of 1 Corinthians shows that Paul intends to address the issues of "speech," "knowledge," "spiritual gifts," and "the day of our Lord" (1 Cor 1:5-6; see chapter 3, Figure 3-1). 1 Thessalonians offers another clear example: its thanksgiving commends readers for their "work of faith and labor of love and steadfastness of hope" (1 Thes 1:3). In 1 Thessalonians 2:1–3:10, Paul will deal with the church's faithfulness in the past. Their love for one another is the topic of 3:11–4:12. Finally, 1 Thessalonians 4:13–5:11 discusses hope in the Lord's return.

There are at least two explanations for the absence of a thanksgiving prayer in Galatians. Angered, Paul has little for which to be thankful when he writes Galatia. Interlopers who preach a different gospel have challenged Paul's apostolic authority and drawn the church away from their faith and freedom in Christ. Perhaps Paul is so upset with the situation in Galatia that he neglects the customary thanksgiving and launches directly into his accusations.

Still, the otherwise careful structure of Galatians suggests that this letter is not some haphazard missive fired off in angry impulse. Rather, it is a carefully balanced work that follows the Greek form of a "letter of rebuke." In other words, Paul deliberately chooses a letter form that does not call for polite blessings. Instead, the letter of rebuke always opens with expressions of amazement that the recipients have behaved so shamefully (cf. Gal 1:6).

The Thanksgiving Prayers of Paul's Letters	
Paul's Letters	**The Thanksgiving**
Romans 1:8-15	First, I thank my God through Jesus Christ for all of you, because your faith is proclaimed throughout the world. For God, whom I serve with my spirit by announcing the gospel of his Son, is my witness that without ceasing I remember you always in my prayers, asking that by God's will I may somehow at last succeed in coming to you. For I am longing to see you that I may share with you some spiritual gift to strengthen you—or rather so that we may be mutually encouraged by each other's faith, both yours and mine. I want you to know, brothers and sisters, that I have often intended to come to you (but thus far have been prevented), in order that I may reap some harvest among you as I have among the rest of the Gentiles. I am a debtor both to Greeks and to barbarians, both to the wise and the foolish—hence my eagerness to proclaim the gospel to you also who are in Rome.
1 Corinthians 1:4-9	I give thanks to my God always for you because of the grace of God that has been given you in Christ Jesus, for in every way you have been enriched in him, in speech and knowledge of every kind—just as the testimony of Christ has been strengthened among you—so that you are not lacking in any spiritual gift as you wait for the revealing of our Lord Jesus Christ. He will also strengthen you to the end, so that you may be blameless on the day of our Lord Jesus Christ. God is faithful; by him you were called into the fellowship of his Son, Jesus Christ our Lord.
2 Corinthians 1:3-7	Blessed be the God and Father of our Lord Jesus Christ, the Father of mercies and the God of all consolation, who consoles us in all our affliction, so that we may be able to console those who are in any affliction with the consolation with which we ourselves are consoled by God. For just as the sufferings of Christ are abundant for us, so also our consolation is abundant through Christ. If we are being afflicted, it is for your consolation and salvation; if we are being consoled, it is for your consolation, which you experience when you patiently endure the same sufferings that we are also suffering. Our hope for you is unshaken; for we know that as you share in our sufferings, so also you share in our consolation.
Galatians	[*Because the letter to the Galatians follows the "letter of rebuke" form it has no opening blessing.*]

———————————— **FIGURE 15-3** ————————————

Paul's Letters	The Thanksgiving
Ephesians 1:15-22	I have heard of your faith in the Lord Jesus and your love toward all the saints, and for this reason I do not cease to give thanks for you as I remember you in my prayers. I pray that the God of our Lord Jesus Christ, the Father of glory, may give you a spirit of wisdom and revelation as you come to know him, so that, with the eyes of your heart enlightened, you may know what is the hope to which he has called you, what are the riches of his glorious inheritance among the saints, and what is the immeasurable greatness of his power for us who believe, according to the working of his great power. God put this power to work in Christ when he raised him from the dead and seated him at his right hand in the heavenly places, far above all rule and authority and power and dominion, and above every name that is named, not only in this age but also in the age to come. And he has put all things under his feet and has made him the head over all things for the church, which is his body, the fullness of him who fills all in all.
Philippians 1:3-11	I thank my God every time I remember you, constantly praying with joy in every one of my prayers for all of you, because of your sharing in the gospel from the first day until now. I am confident of this, that the one who began a good work among you will bring it to completion by the day of Jesus Christ. It is right for me to think this way about all of you, because you hold me in your heart, for all of you share in God's grace with me, both in my imprisonment and in the defense and confirmation of the gospel. For God is my witness how I long for all of you with the compassion of Christ Jesus. And this is my prayer, that your love may overflow more and more with knowledge and full insight to help you determine what is best, so that by the day of Christ you may be pure and blameless, having produced the harvest of righteousness that comes through Jesus Christ for the glory and praise of God.
Colossians 1:3-14	In our prayers we always thank God, the Father of our Lord Jesus Christ, for we have heard of your faith in Christ Jesus and of the love that you have for all the saints, because of the hope laid up for you in heaven. You have heard of this hope before in the word of the truth, the gospel that has come to you. Just as it is bearing fruit and growing in the whole world, so it has been bearing fruit among yourselves from the day you heard it and truly comprehended the grace of God. This you learned from Epaphras, our beloved fellow servant. He is a faithful minister of Christ on your behalf, and he has made known to us your love in the Spirit. For this reason, since the day we heard it, we have not ceased

Continued on next page

FIGURE 15-3

Paul's Letters	The Thanksgiving
	praying for you and asking that you may be filled with the knowledge of God's will in all spiritual wisdom and understanding so that you may lead lives worthy of the Lord, fully pleasing to him, as you bear fruit in every good work and as you grow in the knowledge of God. May you be made strong with all the strength that comes from his glorious power, and may you be prepared to endure everything with patience, while joyfully giving thanks to the Father, who has enabled you to share in the inheritance of the saints in the light. He has rescued us from the power of darkness and transferred us into the kingdom of his beloved Son, in whom we have redemption, the forgiveness of sins.
1 Thessalonians 1:2-10	We always give thanks to God for all of you and mention you in our prayers, constantly remembering before our God and Father your work of faith and labor of love and steadfastness of hope in our Lord Jesus Christ. For we know, brothers and sisters beloved by God, that he has chosen you, because our message of the gospel came to you not in word only, but also in power and in the Holy Spirit and with full conviction, just as you know what kind of persons we proved to be among you for your sake. And you became imitators of us and of the Lord, for in spite of persecution you received the word with joy inspired by the Holy Spirit, so that you became an example to all the believers in Macedonia and Achaia. For the word of the Lord has sounded forth from you not only in Macedonia and Achaia, but in every place your faith in God has become known so that we have no need to speak about it. For the people of those regions report to us what kind of welcome we had among you, and how you turned to God from idols, to serve a living and true God, and to wait for his Son from heaven, whom he raised from the dead—Jesus, who rescues us from the wrath that is coming.
2 Thessalonians 1:3-4	We must always give thanks to God for you, brothers and sisters, as is right, because your faith is growing abundantly, and the love of every one of you for one another is increasing. Therefore, we ourselves boast of you among the churches of God for your steadfastness and faith during all your persecutions and the afflictions that you are enduring.
1 Timothy Titus	[*1 Timothy and Titus do not have the customary thanksgiving. This may be due to the fact that they were written to individuals rather than to churches. Still, note the thanksgiving of 2 Timothy.*]

FIGURE 15-3

The Thanksgiving Prayers of Paul's Letters (cont'd)	
Paul's Letters	The Thanksgiving
2 Timothy 1:3-7	I am grateful to God—whom I worship with a clear conscience, as my ancestors did—when I remember you constantly in my prayers night and day. Recalling your tears, I long to see you so that I may be filled with joy. I am reminded of your sincere faith, a faith that lived first in your grandmother Lois and your mother Eunice and now, I am sure, lives in you. For this reason I remind you to rekindle the gift of God that is within you through the laying on of my hands; for God did not give us a spirit of cowardice, but rather a spirit of power and of love and of self-discipline.
Philemon 1:4-7	When I remember you in my prayers, I always thank my God because I hear of your love for all the saints and your faith toward the Lord Jesus. I pray that the sharing of your faith may become effective when you perceive all the good that we may do for Christ. I have indeed received much joy and encouragement from your love, because the hearts of the saints have been refreshed through you, my brother.

——————— **FIGURE 15-3** ———————

The Body

The business at hand dictates the structure of the letter's body, so its form will vary considerably from letter to letter. This is especially true of Paul's letters because most are longer and more complex than even the letter essays of classical Greek literature. Still, we can make a few generalizations about the body of the apostle's letters.

Usually, the body begins with a discussion of doctrinal matters. In this section, Paul instructs his readers and answers any questions they might have asked him in previous correspondence. The second part of the body, called the *"paranesis"* ("exhortation"), normally urges readers to conform to certain ethical standards of Christian living.

1 Corinthians and Galatians depart from this scheme. The body of 1 Corinthians *begins* with the paranesis before addressing doctrinal issues; the body of Galatians contains a rebuke for past behavior (Gal 1:6-4:11) and a request for future action to remedy the situation (cf. Gal 4:12–6:10).

As with other Greek writers, Paul used characteristic phrases to introduce topics in the body of his letters. These formulae indicate whether this is new information to the readers and often reveal how Paul received the information that prompts him to write. These phrases aid scholars in the reconstruction of the stages of communication between Paul and his churches. By them, we can interpret development in the churches and in Paul's thought.

Disclosures of New Information

1. "I don't want you to be ignorant" (*"ou thelo de humas agnoiein"* — e.g. Rom 1:13; 1 Thes 4:13; 1 Cor 10:1; 12:1; 2 Cor 1:8).

2. "I want you to know" (*"thelo de humas eidenai"* — e.g. 1 Cor 11:3; Col 2:1).

3. "I want to make known to you" (*"gnorizo gar humin"* — e.g. Gal 1:11; 1 Cor 12:3; 15:1).

Reintroduction of Familiar Material

1. "(Just as) you know" (*"[kathos] oidate"* — e.g. 1 Thes 1:5; 2:1-2; 3:3; 4:2; 5:2; 1 Cor 12:2; Gal 4:13; Phil 4:15; 2 Thes 2:6).

2. "I remind you" (*"dio mnemoneute"* — e.g. Eph 2:11; 2 Thes 2:5).

3. "You have no need to be written concerning..." (*"peri de...ou chreian echete graphein"* — e.g. 1 Thes 4:9; 2 Cor 9:1).

4. "Don't you know that...?" (*"ouk oidate oti..."* — e.g. Rom 6:16; 11:2; 1 Cor 3:16; 5:6; 6:2, 3, 15-16, 19).

Appeals Introducing the Paranesis

1. "I beseech," "I exhort," "I urge" (*"parakalo"* — e.g. Rom 12:1; 1 Cor 1:10; 4:16; 1 Thes 4:1; Eph 4:1; Phil 4:2).

2. "I ask" (*"erotao"* — e.g. Phil 4:3; 1 Thes 4:1).

The following formulae reflected the manner in which Paul received the information that prompted him to write:

1. "I rejoice greatly that..." (*"chairo"* — e.g. Rom 16:19; 1 Cor 16:17; 2 Cor 7:9).

2. "I am amazed that..." (*"thaumazo"* — e.g. Gal 1:6). This formula is used to introduce a rebuke.

3. "I hear that..." (*"akouo"* — e.g. 1 Cor 11:18; Col 1:9; 2 Thes 3:11).

4. "It has been revealed to me..." (*"delothe"* — 1 Cor 1:10; Col 1:8).

5. For response to written requests: "Now concerning..." (*"peri de"* — e.g. 1 Thes 4:9; 5:1; 1 Cor 7:1, 25; 8:1, 4; 12:1; 16:1, 12).

FIGURE 15-4

Characteristic phrases also found in the papyri letters introduce topics in the body (see Figure 15-4). They show whether this is new information to the readers and frequently reveal how Paul received the information that prompts him to write. Careful attention to these formulae aids scholars in the reconstruction of the stages of communication between Paul and his churches. By them, we can interpret development in the churches and in Paul's thought.

It is possible to discern shorter forms *within* the body of a letter. For example, scholars have isolated several early Christian creeds and hymns within Paul's letters (e.g. Phil 2:6-11; Col 1:15-20; 1 Tim 3:16). As well, Paul often uses the A-B-A structure known as a "chiasm." A chiasm is a series of assertions that move into, and then out of, a central point. The sequence of thought reverses after the central point, creating a balance and focus to the argumentation (see Figure 15-5). Another literary device Paul uses, particularly in 1 Corinthians, is the slogan. He will quote the motto of some of his readers to qualify them (cf. 1 Cor 1:12; 6:12-13; 7:1; 8:1, 4; 10:23).

An ethical exhortation, or *paranesis*, usually ends the main body. Most often, the appeal formula *"parkalo"* ("I exhort") introduces this section. Here Paul offers traditional guidance for daily life in the community of faith. The exhortations can take several traditional forms. Sometimes Paul will cluster unrelated moral maxims (e.g. Rom 12:9-13). Other times he lists virtues and vices (e.g. Gal 5:19-23). Some letters contain "house-tables" or domestic codes (e.g Col 3:18–4:1; Eph 5:22–6:9). Occasionally, he will offer prolonged exhortations on a specific topic (e.g. 1 Cor 1–4; Rom 14).

Signaling the end of the body and making a transition to the conclusion, Paul often mentions his travel plans. This is part of the "apostolic *parousia*" common to all his letters. With these sections, Paul makes his presence (i.e. *parousia*) felt among his audience. Most often Paul conveys a sense of his presence by the mention of a future visit (e.g. Rom 15:23-33; 2 Cor 13:1-2; Phil 2:24; Phlm 22). As well, Paul will refer either to an emissary (e.g. 2 Cor 8:16-24; Eph 6:21; Phil 2:19-22; Col 4:7-9) or the letter itself as his embodiment (e.g. Rom 15:15-16; Gal 6:11; Col 4:16; 1 Thes 5:27; 2 Thes 3:17; Phlm 19). Only 1 Corinthians invokes all three modes of presence (1 Cor 4:17-21; 16:2-10).

Paul does not always place elements of his apostolic parousia together in one place in the letter. Sometimes travel plans or the reference to an emissary will appear earlier. A reference to Paul's hand in writing the letter most often appears in the conclusion.

Paul often uses a common Greek literary device called a "chiasm." This is a series of assertions that move into and then out of a central point. The sequence of thought reverses after the central point, creating a balance and focus to the argumentation. The central panels of the chiasm are the points Paul wishes to stress.

2 Thessalonians 3:6-12

v. 6   A   Now we command you beloved, in the name of our Lord Jesus Christ,

        B   to keep away from believers who are living in idleness

           C   and not according to the tradition that they received from us,

v. 7   D   for you yourselves know how you ought to imitate us; we were not idle when we were with you,

v. 8   E   and we did not eat anyone's bread without paying for it.

                      F   but with toil and labor we worked night and day

                  E^1 so that we might not burden any of you.

v. 9 D^1 This was not because we do not have that right, but in order to give you an example to imitate.

v. 10 C^1 For even when we were with you we gave you this command: Anyone unwilling to work should not eat.

v. 11 B^1 For we hear that some of you are living in idleness, mere busybodies, not doing any work.

v. 12 A^1 Now such persons we command and exhort in the Lord Jesus Christ to do their work quietly and to earn their own living.

FIGURE 15-5

Philippians 1:12-18

v. 12　　A　　What has happened to me has actually helped to spread the gospel...

v. 14　　　　　B　　　Most of the brothers and sisters have been made confident

vv. 15-17　　　　　　C　　whether out of false motives or true, Christ is proclaimed

v. 18　　　　　　　　　D　　　And in that I rejoice.

　　　　　　　　　　　　D¹　　　Yes, and I will continue to rejoice,

vv. 20-24　　　　　　C¹　　whether by life or by death, Christ will be exalted

v. 25　　　　　B¹　　I am convinced of this

　　　A¹　　I will remain...for your progress in the faith.

──────────────── **FIGURE 15-5** ────────────────

The Closing

A doxology in praise of God through Christ usually marks the end of the main body of the letter. A peace wish follows in place of the concluding health wish found in other Greek personal letters. If there are any personal greetings relayed in the letter, they will be found next. By examining the names of those sending greetings, we may be able to tell where Paul is as he writes. In Romans, the secretary Tertius takes the opportunity to send his greetings (Rom 16:22).

After the greetings, Paul will ask his readers to greet one another with a holy kiss (Rom 16:16; 1 Cor 16:20; 2 Cor 13:12; 1 Thes 5:26). Then he may issue a summary apostolic command in keeping with the concerns of each particular letter. This might be expanded into some closing exhortations.

Romans	Now to God who is able to strengthen you according to my gospel and the proclamation of Jesus Christ, according to the revelation of the mystery that was kept secret for long ages but is now disclosed, and through the prophetic writings is made known to all the Gentiles, according to the command of the eternal God, to bring about the obedience of faith — to the only wise God, through Jesus Christ, to whom be the glory forever! Amen.
1 Corinthians	The grace of the Lord Jesus be with you. My love be with all of you in Christ Jesus.
2 Corinthians	The grace of the Lord Jesus Christ, the love of God, and the communion of the Holy Spirit be with all of you.
Galatians	May the grace of our Lord Jesus Christ be with your Spirit, brothers and sisters. Amen.
Ephesians	Peace be to the whole community, and love with faith, from God the Father and the Lord Jesus Christ. Grace be with all who have an undying love for our Lord Jesus Christ.
Philippians	The grace of the Lord Jesus Christ be with your spirit.
Colossians	Grace be with you.
1 Thessalonians	The grace of our Lord Jesus Christ be with you.
2 Thessalonians	The grace of our Lord Jesus Christ be with all of you.
1 Timothy	Grace be with you.
2 Timothy	The Lord be with your spirit. Grace be with you.
Titus	Grace be with all of you.
Philemon	The grace of our Lord Jesus Christ be with your spirit.

FIGURE 15-6

Because Paul regularly used a secretary to write his letters, he would often take the pen and write a personal word in his hand (e.g. 1 Cor 16:21-24; Col 4:18). In Philemon 19, his signature serves as an "I.O.U." for money a runaway slave has taken. From Galatians 6:11, we gather that his handwriting was uncharacteristically large and, judging from 2 Thessalonians 3:17, it was distinctive.

Finally, Paul invariably closes with a benediction (see Figure 15-6). This replaces the simple one-word "farewell" of other Greek letters. As his letters begin, they end with a focus on God as the source of grace for living the Christian life in the world.

Conclusion

Form conveys the message, and slight modifications in that form sharpen its thrust. If we recognize the distinctive forms of Paul's letters, we will discover unique interpretive keys that unlock fuller understanding.

There are other aspects to his letters that we must consider as well. How does each letter of Paul relate to the others? In what order did Paul write them? How do they differ? Can we see development in Paul or his churches?

Our challenge is to build a theology of Paul based on the collective witness of his letters. To do this, we must be aware of the historical contexts of the reader and writer. We must analyze the forms and language of the letter. Finally, we must read these letters in their proper sequence. Then a dynamic message emerges.

STUDY QUESTIONS

1. What are some reasons why Christians would have enjoyed more effective mail delivery than the average person of the first century?

2. What is *koine* Greek? How did we learn about it?

3. In what ways are Paul's letters similar to private Greek letters?

4. In what ways are Paul's letters similar to public epistles?

5. How do Paul's letters differ from both the private letter and the public epistle?

6. Describe at least two functions of the thanksgiving section in Paul's letters.

7. How does the general structure of 1 Corinthians differ from Paul's other letters?

8. Compare the chiasms in Figure 15-5 with that of 1 Corinthians 7:1-6 (chapter four of this book). What is the main point in each of these three chiasms?

9. List the three elements of the *apostolic parousia*. Can you find any of these in 2 Corinthians?

10. Name at least one secretary Paul used to write his letters.

Chapter 16

THEOLOGICAL THEMES IN PAUL

Introduction

When synthesizing Paul's thought, we must consider several factors relating to the nature of his letters and the circumstances of his life. The letters are *ad hoc* documents arising spontaneously to answer questions, resolve tensions, and provide direction. So, much of the time we read about *problematic* aspects of Paul's teachings, whether the problem be from the perspective of Paul or the church. Conceivably, fundamental points of Paul's preaching may be absent in his letters because people readily accepted them from the start.

The order in which the letters were written also affects their contribution to understanding the development of Pauline theology. Both the congregations and Paul developed their faith over years. As they grew in their understanding, their conversation constantly changed. It is significant, for example, that Paul's earliest letters reflect a fervent apocalyptic hope that overshadows Christian interaction with the world. Contrast this with later letters, which depict a church that has settled into a faithful, extended ministry in society as it awaits Christ's return. If we interpret the letters out of sequence, we will misrepresent the emphases of a mature theology.

Where do we begin to reconstruct Paul's theology? Because his earliest letters focus on a hope in Christ's imminent return, many scholars suggest that Paul approached life from the conviction that the end of the age loomed near. They interpret all other developments in his theology from this perspective.

Others think that we must begin with Judaism to understand Pauline Christianity. As a Pharisee, they observe, Paul began his Christian life with a focal view on God's covenant with his people and the role of the Mosaic law in that relationship. So, these interpreters argue that any understanding of Pauline theology should start by integrating Jesus Christ into a covenantal, law-centered theology.

Yet, as formative as were these factors, neither provides the starting point for Paul's theology: the person of Jesus Christ does. Most scholars speak of Paul's theology resting on a "functional christology" — his understanding of God and his will for humanity began with what the apostle had discovered about Jesus Christ. Whenever Paul confronted a theological or pastoral question, he turned to his relationship with Christ for the answer.

We can reconstruct some content of Paul's early preaching from remarks in his letters. As previously noted, certain formulaic introductions reveal whether he is giving new information or reminding his readers of something he has already taught. Judging from these phrases and other comments in the letters, whenever Paul founded the churches he proclaimed Christ crucified and resurrected. He taught that salvation came from a relationship with Christ, not from works of righteousness. He announced freedom from the law and initially did not provide much specific ethical guidance for Christian living. He instilled a hope in the imminent return of Christ, but did not mention anything about the resurrection of Christians.

In the letters, Paul expands on these basic themes, augmenting them by responding to situations arising in his life and the life of the churches. When all he wrote is considered, a full Christ-centered message unfolds. It speaks of our need of God's salvation through his Son, the nature of life in the body of Christ, and our hope for the future (see Figure 16-1).

God and Christ

Of course Paul frequently mentions God in his letters. Still, most references to God are in the context of his saving work through Christ. Paul offers the readers only the God he discovers through his relationship with Christ.

Paul rarely speaks of God in an abstract, objective, metaphysical, or ontological sense. When he does describe God, he uses relational adjectives: a God who is loving, faithful, gracious, patient, just, powerful, or angry. In other words, human beings can perceive God only in his dealings with them.

God and Christ

When Paul describes God, he uses relational adjectives that describe God's dealings with humanity through Christ. God is righteous, which means he is just and holy. He exercises his righteousness as judge and as savior through Jesus Christ.

God is also loving. He acts patiently and kindly toward us. To call him Father is to acknowledge him as our source of life. To speak of him as the Father of Jesus Christ is to stress that Christ has been sent by him with his authority.

Jesus offers the fullest embodiment of God to which we can relate. To know God, we must know his Son. To share in the life of God, we must live in Christ. Jesus is "Christ," "Son of God," and "Lord." The title "Christ" affirms his messiahship. The title "Son of God" signifies that Jesus was divinely elected for a role in salvation history. The Son's obedience to the Father's mission is emphasized. The title "Lord" identifies Jesus as *Yahweh*, the God of Israel, and places him above all other rulers and authorities.

In Paul's letters, Jesus Christ is described as pre-existent and active in the creation of the world. He was incarnated as a human being to save the world from the power of sin and death. The resurrected Christ is now exalted in the presence of his heavenly Father.

The Law and the Gospel

The apparently inconsistent statements that Paul makes about the Mosaic law can be understood when we realize Paul's view of the limited and temporary function of the law. Before Christ, the law was the highest expression of God's standards. However, the law was *never* a means to gain righteousness in God's sight. It gave people a way in which to respond to God because of the saving covenant he established with them.

With the coming of Christ, the high standards of the law served to expose the extent of humanity's sinfulness and lead people to Christ for grace and forgiveness. The law is like a disciplinarian who guards and supervises people until they come to faith in Christ. Once they do, they are no longer under the law of Moses. Instead, they are to live by the "law of Christ."

Humanity, Fallen and Redeemed

When Paul describes human beings, he uses many different words: body, flesh, soul, spirit, mind, and heart. In doing so, he is *not* referring to component parts that make up a person. Rather, he uses each of these terms to refer to the whole person from differing perspectives.

While Paul affirms that human existence reflects the creative hand of God, he also insists that everyone has fallen short of God's standards. Before Christ came, all people were under the power of sin and its ultimate consequence — death. This is due to our corporate identity with Adam *and* our individual choice to sin.

Sin is an objective reality that exists independent of human participation in it. Human beings enter sin whenever they put themselves at the center of their lives

Continued on next page

FIGURE 16-1

instead of God. Sin breaks human relationships with God, each other, and creation. We are saved from sin when we recognize that Christ has faithfully done what only he could do to save us. To be freed from the power of sin and enter new life, we must put our trust in him.

The Church and Ministry

Being in Christ means being a member of his body, the church. As with a physical body, the church is a single living organism of diverse members joined in the mutually dependent life. Christ, as head of the church, is its original member, its source of life and growth, and its ruler or director.

Most often, Paul uses the word "church" or "churches" to refer to local congregations. However, in a few places he speaks of the church in a universal sense to include all Christians in every place. Each congregation functions as the body of Christ in its particular location, possessing the complete spectrum of gifts for ministry through the Spirit. At the same time, the local church exists in solidarity with Christ and the universal church.

The Lord's supper and baptism facilitate participation in Christ's body. Baptism marks union with Christ in his death, burial, and resurrection. The Lord's supper allows believers to covenant together through Christ. By partaking of the common loaf and cup, they declare the gospel in unity as they await Christ's return.

Ethics

Rather than impose a legalistic code of ethics, Paul taught that "all things were lawful" but not all things edified the body of Christ. Individuals were free to decide how they would live, but they were to live in such a way so that they did not cause someone else to act contrary to their faith or convictions. Christians were not to judge others or allow themselves to be judged on opinions regarding personal lifestyle. Yet they were to put the welfare of others before themselves. Most importantly, believers were to realize that they were accountable to the Lord for their lifestyle. No longer were Christians to "walk in the flesh"—instead they were to "walk in the Spirit."

The apostle gave ethical direction for the life of the *community* as well as the individual. In Christ, the social barriers that divide races, classes, and genders are transcended. Paul refused to allow these factors to determine a person's role or status in the believing community.

The End Times

Just as Paul believed new life *began* with the coming of Christ, he also saw Christ's second coming as the *consummation* of all things. This event marked the completion of God's saving ministry in the world. Christ will come to resurrect those who have died and transform the faithful who are alive. He will overcome all powers and authorities, subject them to his judgment, and bring them before the heavenly Father. All creation will be liberated from the bonds of sin and death.

--- **FIGURE 16-1** ---

Above all, God is righteous. This attribute involves both the concepts of justice and holiness. In some contexts, when Paul says that God is righteous, he is using legal language to imply that God is just or fair (Rom 2:5; 3:5, 25; 2 Thes 1:5). In other contexts, righteousness conveys the ethical character of uprightness, purity, or faithfulness (Rom 10:3; 2 Cor 5:21; 6:14; Eph 4:24; Phil 3:9).

God exercises his righteousness as judge and as savior. As judge, he reacts against sin and evil with *wrath* (Rom 1:18–2:11; 1 Thes 2:16). As savior, God reveals the saving way by his wrath (Rom 9:19-29). Those who turn to him through faith in Christ will be spared from condemnation (Rom 5:6-11; Eph 2:1-10; 1 Thes 1:10; 5:9).

God is also loving. "God's love has been poured into our hearts," says Paul (Rom 5:5). Paul goes on to say, "God proves his love for us in that while we still were sinners Christ died for us" (Rom 5:8). In other words, God's love for humanity motivates his saving actions through Christ.

Paul's classic description of love in 1 Corinthians 13, especially vv. 4-7, can help us understand God's love for us. Because he loves us, he waits patiently and acts kindly. He never seeks his own advantage. He cannot be quickly irritated and harbors no grudges. He does not enjoy wickedness but celebrates the truth. He always supports, trusts, hopes, and perseveres.

The idea of God's fatherhood pervades Paul's theology. The greeting of every letter contains a reference to God as Father, and the body of every letter except 2 Timothy and Titus repeats the theme. The image of fatherhood suggests that Paul is presenting God as the head of a family unit. He is progenitor, provider, and authority. To speak of him as the father of Jesus Christ is to stress that Christ has been sent by him with his authority.

Paul's God is proactive. He takes the initiative in all his dealings with us. He touches all arenas of life; he is creator, redeemer, sustainer, and judge. To fallen humanity, God is transcendent, invisible, and unapproachable. By contrast, redeemed people live in him alone (Rom 6:11, 13, 22; 9:8; 12:1; 14:18).

Romans 11:33-36 presents what may be Paul's loftiest description of God. After three chapters of trying to describe God's plan of salvation, Paul stops in wonder, unable to plumb the mystery of God any deeper:

O the depth of the riches and wisdom and knowledge of God!
How unsearchable are his judgments and how inscrutable his ways!

> "For who has known the mind of the Lord?
> Or who has been his counselor?"
> "Or who has given a gift to him, to receive a
>   gift in return?"

For from him and through him and to him are all things. To him
be the glory forever. Amen.

According to Paul, Jesus Christ offers the fullest embodiment of
God to which we can relate. To know God, we must know his Son. To
share in the life of God, we must live in Christ. Paul communicates
his understanding of the person and work of Christ in the titles he
gives to Jesus, the many ways he relates the Son to the Father, and
the even more frequent occasions when he describes Christ's work in
the world.

Three titles in particular emerge from Paul's presentation of Jesus:
"Christ," "Son of God," and "Lord." Of these, Paul uses "Christ" so frequently in association with Jesus that we can regard it practically as a
second proper name for Jesus. For Paul, as for all Jews, the term
"Christ" (Hebrew: *"Masiah"*) meant "Anointed One" and referred to
the messiah appointed by God to deliver his people. Paul's view of
Jesus as God's messiah was so fundamental to his thinking that he
affirmed it automatically almost every time he spoke of Jesus.

"Son of God" was also a messianic title, but it was not limited to the
messiah. Contrary to what many modern readers assume, to call Jesus
the Son of God does not necessarily imply anything about his divinity.
Attributing success to blessings from the gods, Greeks and Romans
could call a public benefactor, military conqueror, or political leader a
son of god. In Judaism, the nation of Israel as a whole, the progeny of
David, the coming messiah, righteous people, miracle workers, and
charismatic figures all received the honor of this title. Generally "Son of
God" signified the divine election for a role in salvation history.

Paul calls Jesus the Son of God in contexts that imply Christ was
sent on a mission on behalf of his Father (Rom 8:3; Gal 4:4). The obedience of the Son to the Father and the Son's dedication to the task are
emphasized (cf. esp. 1 Cor 15:24-28; Phil 2:5-8).

Although non-Jewish readers might not immediately catch it,
"Lord" is the most significant title Paul uses for Jesus. In Greek society,
as in English, "Lord" (Greek: *Kurios*) signified respect and could be
used to address anyone of a higher social status. In the Old Testament,
however, the title was used almost exclusively as a substitute for *Yahweh*, the sacred name of God.

With this background, the early church in Palestine developed the Aramaic (Hebrew) confession "Jesus is Lord" to affirm its faith in Christ. This profound confession is absolute: it equates Jesus with God and places him above all other rulers and authorities.

As Romans 10:9, 1 Corinthians 12:3, and Philippians 2:11 attest, Paul received and passed on the foundational creed "Jesus is Lord." Note also 1 Corinthians 16:22, where Paul calls Jesus "Lord" (*Mar*) in the Aramaic prayer *"Maranatha"* ("Our Lord, come!"). Paul's frequent references to Jesus as Lord teach that the apostle regarded the exalted Christ worthy to be worshiped in the same manner as Yahweh was. It also affirms that the risen Christ has the right and power to exercise dominion over all creation.

Literary critics have isolated what they suggest are early Christian hymns in Paul's letters (Phil 2:6-11; Col 1:15-20; 1 Tim 3:16). Notably, these passages present a pre-existent Christ, most explicit in Colossians 1:15-20, which states that he was active in creation and now "in him all things hold together" (Col 1:17).

These passages also affirm Christ's incarnation. He became human to save the world. Throughout his letters, Paul describes Christ's saving work in many ways. It is a work of faithfulness or obedience to God the Father and his law (Rom 5:19; Phil 2:8). Using legal language, Paul says that Christ justifies or exonerates us (Rom 3:24; 4:25; 5:9, 16-18; 1 Cor 6:11). His life and death was a sacrifice for the forgiveness of sins (Rom 3:25). Christ "redeems" or buys our freedom by offering his life in exchange (Rom 3:24; 1 Cor 1:30; Gal 3:13; 4:5; Eph 1:7; Col 1:14; Tit 2:14). He exercises a ministry of reconciliation — restoring broken relationships between God and his people and among his people (Rom 5:10-11; 2 Cor 5:18-20; Eph 2:16; Col 1:20-21). Christ sanctifies us (1 Cor 1:2, 30; 6:11): he makes us holy or sets us apart from the world for God. He becomes our source of power, grace, and peace. His earthly life serves as our example.

Christ's resurrection, as the ultimate sign of God's redemptive power, is crucial to Paul's faith (Rom 1:4; 6:5; and esp. 1 Cor 15). The risen Christ has broken sin's deadly stranglehold over creation. Because Jesus was resurrected, those who are united with him in faith will also be resurrected (Phil 3:10-11).

Christ is now exalted in the presence of his heavenly Father (Phil 2:9-11; Eph 1:19-23; 1 Tim 3:16). He will abolish all evil, suffering, pain, deceit, ignorance, and oppression that mark earthly life. Christ will conquer death, the last enemy of God. Brought before God by the reigning Son, all creation will bow down and worship him.

God's Revelation to Humanity—The Law and the Gospel

How does Paul relate God's revelation of Jesus Christ to God's earlier revelation in the Torah? What is the relationship between the old and new covenants? This highly controversial issue of Paul's ministry continues to divide biblical scholarship today.

On a surface reading, Paul seems inconsistent in his attitude toward the law. Sometimes Paul recognizes value of the law. He declares "the law is holy, and the commandment is holy and just and good" (Rom 7:12; cf. 7:16). The apostle says "I delight in the law in my inmost self" (Rom 7:22) and he acknowledges the law to be an "embodiment of truth and knowledge" (Rom 2:20).

At other times, he condemns it as "the law of sin and death" (Rom 8:2; cf. 1 Cor 15:56). Christ is the end of the law (Rom 7:4-6; 10:4; Gal 3:23-26), having "abolished the law with its commandments and ordinances, that he might create in himself one new humanity" (Eph 2:15).

These apparently contradictory statements about the law can stand together when we realize Paul's view of the limited and temporary function of the law. Before Christ, the law was the highest expression of God's standards. However, in itself the law was *never* a means to gain righteousness in God's sight. It gave God's people a way in which to respond to God because of the saving covenant he established with them.

With the coming of Christ, the high standards of the law served to expose the extent of humanity's sinfulness and lead people to Christ for grace and forgiveness (Rom 3:19-20). The law is like a disciplinarian who guards and supervises people until they come to faith in Christ (Gal 3:24-25). Once they do, they are no longer under the law of Moses. Instead, they are to live by the "law of Christ" (Gal 6:2; 1 Cor 9:21) or "law of the Spirit" (Rom 8:2).

Paul's life is an excellent case study of the place of the law in the Christian life (1 Cor 9:19-23). If following the religious laws of Judaism will open the doors to the synagogue community, Paul will follow them (1 Cor 9:20). If those same laws are a barrier to faith in Christ among Gentiles, he will discard them (1 Cor 9:21). He regards himself as neither "under the law" nor "lawless"—always he lives by "Christ's law" (1 Cor 9:21).

Humanity, Fallen and Redeemed

Echoing Genesis, Paul teaches that God created humanity in his image (Rom 8:29; 1 Cor 11:7; 15:49; cf. Gen 1:27). When he speaks of human beings, the apostle uses many different words, including body (*soma*), flesh (*sarx*), soul (*psuche*), spirit (*pneuma*), mind (*nous*), and heart (*kardia*). In doing so, he is *not* referring to component parts that make up a person. Rather, he uses each of these terms to refer to the whole person from differing perspectives.

As well, in different contexts these words mean different things. For example, "body" and "flesh" are sometimes synonymous, referring to our physical existence (1 Cor 6:16; 15:37-39; 2 Cor 4:10-11; Phil 1:20-22). Other times, "flesh" refers to our sinful nature set in rebellion against God (1 Cor 3:1-3; Gal 5:16-26; Rom 8:1-14).

While Paul affirms that human existence reflects the creative hand of God, he also insists that everyone has fallen short of God's standards (Rom 3:23). Prior to Christ, all people were under the power of sin and its ultimate consequence — death. Paul teaches that this human dilemma has arisen due to our corporate solidarity with Adam *and* our individual choice to sin.

Romans 5:12 is foundational to Paul's understanding of sin and death: "Sin came into the world through one man, and death came through sin, and so death spread to all *because* (or '*in whom*') all have sinned." We may take this statement to mean that all have sinned in Adam's sin, or all have sinned in the same way Adam sinned. In either case, Paul's main point in clear: we are all in Adam, and so we share in the condemnation he incurred (see also 1 Cor 15:21-22).

Still, Paul does not release the individual from personal responsibility. All have made the choice to sin (Rom 3:23). In Romans 7:14-23, Paul describes the universal human experience of bondage to sin. He puts himself in the place of every person who has yet to be delivered by faith in Christ:

> I am of the flesh, sold into slavery under sin. I do not understand my own actions. For I do not do what I want, but I do the very thing I hate...in fact it is no longer I that do it, but sin that dwells within me. For I know that nothing good dwells within me, that is, in my flesh. I can will what is right, but I cannot do it (Rom 7:14-18).

Sin exists as an objective reality whether or not we recognize it. It is a power that conquers an individual's will, entering lives and taking control. Human beings express sin in many ways, as the "vice lists" of Paul's letters show (Rom 1:29-32; 1 Cor 6:9-10; Gal 5:19-21). Yet sin is more than a specific action; it is a wrong posture or attitude toward God. It is the placement of self at the center of life, where only God should be.

Romans 1:18-32 is probably Paul's most basic description of the nature of sin and evil. God has revealed himself to all people through many ways. Though they knew him through his revelation, people "did not honor him as God or give thanks to him" (Rom 1:21). Instead, they have elevated themselves to the place of God. People have "exchanged the truth about God for a lie and worshiped and served the creature rather the creator" (Rom 1:25). Consequently, God "gave them up" (Rom 1:24, 26, 28) to their self-centered desires.

Sin corrupts and breaks human relationships with God, each other, and creation. It results in the ultimate separation from life and its source, God. Sin has unleashed the power of evil in the world and has spread suffering throughout creation. There is no escape from its hold except through Christ.

Humanity is freed from sin and enters a new order of life by the "faith of Christ" (Rom 3:22, 26; Gal 2:16; 3:22; Eph 3:12; Phil 3:9). This phrase can be understood in two ways. *"Pistis,"* the Greek word for "faith," can mean either "faithfulness" or "trust." Christ can be either the subject who exercises faithfulness *or* the object of our trust. In other words, Paul may be affirming that we are saved because Christ has been faithful, or we are saved when we entrust ourselves to Christ.

Most versions translate the phrase "faith of Christ" as "faith *in* Christ," but in so doing they may be neglecting the initiative and role of Christ in salvation. Both his faithfulness and our trust in that faithfulness are essential elements of the process. In other ways, Paul teaches that Christ's obedience brought salvation (Rom 5:19; Phil 2:5-8; 2 Thes 3:5). Also, in each of his letters the apostle makes it clear that we must trust or believe in Christ if we are to experience the deliverance he provides.

To be saved is to be "in Christ." Under this concept of incorporation Paul subsumes all other images of salvation. Sometimes he speaks of being physically transformed (1 Cor 15:50-54; 2 Cor 3:18) or dying and rising (Rom 6:3-11; Col 3:1-4). At other times he uses language from society: we are freed from slavery (Rom 8:21; 1 Cor 7:22; Gal 5:1), made slaves to the Lord (Rom 6:18-22; 1 Cor 7:22), declared not guilty (Rom 5:9, 16-18), reconciled (Rom 5:10-11; 2 Cor 5:18-20; Eph 2:16; Col 1:20-21), bought (1 Cor 6:20; 7:23) or redeemed (Gal 3:13; 4:5; Eph 1:7; Col 1:14; Tit 2:14).

The Church and Ministry

Being in Christ means being a member of his body, the church. Paul also calls the church a field (1 Cor 3:9), a building (1 Cor 3:9), a temple (1 Cor 3:16-17; 2 Cor 6:16; Eph 2:21), and a bride (2 Cor 11:2). Each of these metaphors illuminates a facet of the nature of the church, but Paul develops most thoroughly the image of a body.

In Romans and 1 Corinthians, Paul compares the church to a physical body. Saying we are all parts of one body, Paul likens the individual to a foot, hand, ear, or eye to emphasize both the diversity and the unity within the local church (1 Cor 12:12-27; cf. Rom 12:4-5). The church is a single living organism of diverse members joined in a mutually dependent life. Health comes from wholeness and, most importantly, union with *Christ*.

Other Greek writers used the metaphor of the body to describe social or political organizations. Yet Paul pushes the imagery beyond all other comparisons when he equates the body of the church with Christ's body. "Just as the body is one and has many members, so it is with *Christ* . . . you are the body of *Christ*" (1 Cor 12:12, 27).

When Paul writes his later letters, his "body language" is no longer illustrative, it is descriptive. In reality, the church is Christ's body. What is more, the head is not just one among many congregational members. *Christ* himself is the head. Ephesians 4:15-16 puts it graphically:

> We must grow up in every way into him who is the head, into Christ, from whom the whole body, joined and knit together by every ligament with which it is equipped, as each part is working properly, promotes the body's growth in building itself up in love (cf. also Col 2:19).

What does it mean for Christ to be *head* of the church? Figuratively, the Greek word for "head" (*kephale*) can mean "source," "origin," "first in sequence," "furthest extremity," or "authoritative leader." Depending on where he calls Christ the head (1 Cor 11:3; Eph 1:22; 5:23; Col 1:18; 2:10, 19), Paul implies that, as head of the church, Christ is its original member, its source of life and growth, and its ruler or director.

Most often, Paul uses the word "church" or "churches" to refer to local congregations. However, in a few places he speaks of the church in a universal sense to include all Christians in every place (1 Cor 15:19; Gal 1:13; Phil 3:6; Eph 1:22; 3:10; Col 1:18, 24). Each congregation functions as the body of Christ in its particular location, possessing the complete spectrum of gifts for ministry through the Spirit. At the same time, the local church exists in solidarity with Christ and the universal church.

All who are in Christ receive gifts from the Holy Spirit to accomplish distinctive and varying tasks in the life of the church. In several places Paul lists some of these gifts (1 Cor 12:7-11, 28-31; Rom 12:6-8; Eph 4:11). A comparison of these lists shows that Paul never created an exhaustive list, nor did he set up a static priority of order or office. All the gifts are to be practiced in relation to others to build up the body.

Paul's views of baptism and the Lord's supper relate to his concept of the body of Christ. "For in the one Spirit we were all baptized into one body—Jews or Greeks, slaves or free—and we were made to drink of one Spirit" (1 Cor 12:13). Baptism marks union with Christ in his death, burial, and resurrection (Rom 6:3-5; Gal 3:27; Eph 4:5; Col 2:12).

The Lord's supper also facilitates participation in Christ's body. 1 Corinthians, the only letter to refer to this sacrament, teaches that the cup is "a sharing in the blood of Christ" and the bread "is a sharing in the body of Christ" (1 Cor 10:16). In 1 Corinthians 11:17-24, Paul instructs the Corinthians to remember Jesus' death for them whenever they gather to eat and drink. By doing so, they are covenanting together through Christ and declaring the gospel as they await his return.

Because of the unity that exists between all Christians and Jesus, taking the Lord's supper with no consideration for fellow believers displays disrespect for "the body and blood of the Lord" (1 Cor 11:27). Believers must not "eat and drink without discerning the body" (1 Cor 11:29). In other words, they must decide whether they are living in unity with their brothers and sisters in the church before they partake of another expression of Christ's body, the eucharist.

Ethics

Judging from the way Paul introduces ethical matters in his earlier letters, he offered little moral direction when he first founded the churches. As behavior in certain congregations degenerated in one way or another after Paul moved on, he would have to respond with ethical exhortations in his letters.

The exhortations sometimes take the form of a cluster of unrelated moral maxims (Rom 12:9-13). Other times, Paul lists virtues and vices (Rom 1:29-31; 1 Cor 5:10-11; 6:9-10; 2 Cor 6:6-7; Gal 5:19-23; Col 3:5-8, 12-14; Eph 5:3-5). Some letters contain "house-tables" or domestic codes for conduct in the Christian home (Col 3:18-41; Eph 5:22–6:9; 1 Tim 2:8-15; Tit 2:1-10). Occasionally, Paul delivers prolonged exhortations on a specific topic (1 Cor 1–4, 8–10; Rom 14).

Because Paul's audience was predominantly Gentile, he did not present the Mosaic law as the ethical system by which to live. In 1

Corinthians 8–10 and Romans 14 he develops a "weaker Christian" ethic that was neither legalistic nor *laissez-faire*: all things were lawful, but not all things edified the body of Christ. Individuals were free to decide how they would live, but they were to live so that they did not cause someone else to act contrary to his or her convictions.

In other words, Christians were not to judge others or allow themselves to be judged on opinions regarding personal lifestyle (Rom 14:1-4). Yet they were to put the welfare of others before themselves (Rom 14:13-16). Most important, believers were to realize that they were accountable to the Lord for their lifestyle (1 Cor 8:12; 10:31; Rom 14:7-8, 12, 22-23).

Paul's ethic is Christ-centered. It is based on the new creation in Christ (2 Cor 5:17; Gal 6:15; Eph 2:15). It is directed by the "law of Christ" (Rom 8:2; 1 Cor 9:21; Gal 6:2) and the "mind of Christ" (1 Cor 2:16; Phil 2:5). The Christian's lifestyle is motivated by the "love of Christ" (1 Cor 16:22; 2 Cor 5:14; Eph 3:19; 5:2) and enabled by the "Spirit of Christ" (Rom 8:2, 9; 2 Cor 3:18; Gal 4:6). No longer were believers to "walk in the flesh"—instead they were to "walk in the Spirit" (Rom 8:4-13; Gal 5:16-26). The result is a dynamic ethic that is responsive to both spiritual and circumstantial realities.

The apostle gave ethical direction for the life of the *community* as well as the individual. He summarizes his social ethic in Galatians 3:28: "There is no longer Jew or Greek, there is no longer slave or free, there is no longer male and female; for all of you are one in Christ Jesus." In Christ, the social barriers that divide races, classes, and genders are transcended.

While Paul did not seek to eradicate these distinguishing factors, he refused to allow them to determine a person's role or status in the believing community. His agenda for change began in the heart of individuals. If Jews and Gentiles, slaves and masters, or men and women treated each other as equal brothers and sisters engaged in a mutual ministry, these outward distinctions would eventually lose their divisive power.

The End Times

Just as Paul believed new life *began* with the coming of Christ, he also saw Christ's second coming as the *consummation* of all things. The end of the age revolved around the personal return of the glorified Christ. This event would mark the completion of God's saving ministry in the world.

Christ will come to resurrect those who have died and transform the faithful who are alive (1 Thes 4:13–5:11; 1 Cor 15:20-58; 2 Cor 4:16–5:10). Christ will overcome all other powers and authorities, subject them to his judgment, and bring them before the heavenly Father (1 Cor 15:24-28). All creation will be liberated from the bonds of sin and death (Rom 8:18-25; 1 Cor 15:54-58).

Paul's earliest letters glow with a dominant apocalyptic hope (2 Thes 2:1-12; 1 Thes 4:13–5:11; 1 Cor 7:26, 29; 15:50-58). His later letters, however, do not. This has led many scholars to suggest that Paul's eschatology began as a fervent hope in the imminent end of the present world. They argue, however, that with time Paul adopted a more mystical view, focusing on the spiritual transition that was already being realized in the hearts of believers. In technical terms, they see Paul change from an apocalyptic to a realized eschatology.

Certainly Paul's eschatological perspective developed over the years of his ministry. Take, for example, his teaching on the resurrection of believers. After reflecting on the resurrection of Christ in light of a pastoral problem in Thessalonica, Paul began to preach that Christians will also be resurrected (cf. 1 Thes 4:13-18). A short while later, in response to questions from Corinth, he developed the doctrine more fully (1 Cor 15). In 2 Corinthians 4:16–5:10, he pushes further to say that the Christian's life straddles the present physical existence and the future spiritual one. Later, in Colossians 3:1, he says we already "have been raised with Christ."

Still, nothing Paul says in his later letters is incompatible with the message of earlier writing. There are elements of realized eschatology in his early letters (1 Cor 4:8; 2 Cor 4:16–5:10) and an imminent, future hope still exists in the later documents (Rom 8:18-25; 13:11; 14:10-11; Phil 1:6, 10; 2:16; 3:20-21; 4:5; Col 3:4). Paul's eschatological perspective always looked to Christ's future return, but as time went on he taught more about how that hope affected Christian life and ministry in the present age.

Conclusion

Paul centered his theology on Christ, presenting him as the Lord of creation. As in Adam all died, so in Christ all could live. Christ alone was victorious over the powers of sin and death. The function of the Mosaic law was to lead to faith in Christ. By faith people were incorporated into Christ; he was the head of a spiritual body that transcended geographical, racial, social, and sexual barriers. Those in Christ now lived by the law of Christ written in their hearts. Christ, the resurrected one, would be the resurrecter for those who died in him. That hope, and all others, would be realized when Jesus the messiah returned in glory to establish completely his reign.

STUDY QUESTIONS

1. According to Paul's letters, what does it mean to say that God is righteous?...holy?...loving?

2. Which are the three most prominent titles Paul uses of Jesus? Which main idea does each convey?

3. Read Romans 3:21-26. What are at least three terms Paul uses to describe the process of salvation through Christ? What does each expression mean?

4. Is the Mosaic law good or bad in the eyes of Paul? According to Paul, what function is it to have in relation to the Christian life?

5. Read Romans 5:12-21 and 1 Corinthians 15:20-22, 45-49. How does Paul compare Adam and Christ?

6. Paul teaches that the "faith of Christ" saves us. What are two ways of interpreting this phrase?

7. Outline how Paul develops his idea of the church as the "body of Christ." Relate his view of baptism and the Lord's supper to this concept.

8. In the area of Christian ethics, Paul taught that "all things are lawful" (1 Cor 6:12; 10:23; cf. Rom 14:14, 20). How does he qualify this statement?

9. Read Galatians 3:28. Can you find examples in Paul's letters where he modeled this principle of equality between race, class, and gender?

10. How did Paul's teaching about this present life and our future hope develop?

FOR FURTHER READING

The following bibliography is not exhaustive, nor does it contain all
the resources used for this book. It does offer, however, a list of major
works on Paul's life and thought, particularly as they relate to his
Corinthian ministry. While many of these are technical works and pre-
suppose a knowledge of Greek, they will be useful for anyone who
wishes to delve deeper.

The bibliography is divided into five sections: (1) Introduction and
Background (*for biographical, historical, and sociological introductions
to Paul and the Corinthians*); (2) Commentaries (*on 1 and 2 Corinthians*); (3) Books and Articles on 1 and 2 Corinthians (*dealing with
specific topics or passages from the two letters*); (4) Letter Structure
(*dealing with the epistolary form and function of New Testament
letters*); (5) Pauline Theology (*providing syntheses of Paul's theology
based on all his letters*).

INTRODUCTION AND BACKGROUND

Barrett, C.K. "Cephas and Corinth." In *Abraham unser Vater: Juden
und Christen im Gespräch über die Bibel*, pp. 1-12. Edited by O.
Betz. Leiden: E.J. Brill, 1963.

Broneer, Oscar. "The Apostle Paul and the Isthmian Games." *Biblical
Archaeologist* 25 (1962):2-31.

——. "Corinth: Center of St. Paul's Missionary Work in Greece." *Biblical Archaeologist* 14 (1951):78-96.

——. "Hero Cults in the Corinthian Agora." *Hesperia* 11 (1942):128-61.

——. "Paul and Pagan Cults at Isthmia." *Harvard Theological Review* 64 (1971):169-87.

Bruce, F.F. *Paul: Apostle of the Heart Set Free*. Grand Rapids: Wm. B. Eerdmans, 1977.

——. *The Pauline Circle*. Grand Rapids: Eerdmans, 1985.

Ellis, E. Earle. "Paul and His Co-Workers." *New Testament Studies* 17 (1971):437-53.

Gasque, W. Ward. "Images of Paul in the History of Biblical Interpretation." *Crux* 16 (1980):7-16.

Hammond, Mason. *The City in the Ancient World*. Cambridge: Harvard University Press, 1972.

Harrison, Percy N. "Erastus and His Pavement." In *Paulines and Pastorals*, pp. 100-05. London: Villiers, 1964.

Hermann, Ingo. "Apollos." *Revue des sciences religieuses* 50 (1976): 330-36.

Hill, Andrew. "The Temple of Asclepius: An Alternative Source for Paul's Body Theology?" *Journal of Biblical Literature* 99 (1980): 437-39.

Hock, Ronald F. *The Social Context of Paul's Ministry: Tentmaking and Apostleship*. Philadelphia: Fortress Press, 1980.

Jewett, Robert. *A Chronology of Paul's Life*. Philadelphia: Fortress Press, 1979.

Jones, Arnold H.M. *The Cities of the Eastern Roman Provinces*. 2d ed. Oxford: Clarendon Press, 1971.

Keck, Leander. *Paul and His Letters*. Philadelphia: Fortress Press, 1973.

Longenecker, Richard N. *The Ministry and Message of Paul*. Grand Rapids: Zondervan, 1971.

Mattusch, Carol C. "Bronze and Iron-Working in the Area of the Athenian Agora." *Hesperia* 46 (1977):340-89.

Meeks, Wayne A. *The First Urban Christians: The Social World of the Apostle Paul*. New Haven: Yale University Press, 1983.

——, ed. *The Writings of St. Paul*. New York: Norton, 1972.

Murphy-O'Connor, Jerome. "Paul and Gallio." *Journal of Biblical Literature* 112 (1993):315-17.

——. *St. Paul's Corinth. Texts and Archeology*. Good News Studies, no. 6. Wilmington: Glazier, 1983.

Neyrey, Jerome H. *Paul, In Other Words: A Cultural Reading of His Letters*. Louisville: Westminster/John Knox, 1991.

Ogg, George. *The Chronology of the Life of Paul*. London: Epworth Press, 1968.

Plevnik, Joseph. *What Are They Saying About Paul?* New York: Paulist Press, 1986.

Ralston, Timothy J. "The Theological Significance of Paul's Conversion." *Bibliotheca Sacra* 147 (1990):198-215.

Robinson, Henry S. *The Urban Development of Ancient Corinth.* Athens: American School of Classical Studies in Athens, 1965.

Sanders, E.P. *Paul, the Law and the Jewish People.* Philadelphia: Fortress, 1983.

————. *Paul and Palestinian Judaism.* Philadelphia: Fortress Press, 1977.

Scranton, Robert L. "The Corinth of the Apostle Paul." *The Emory University Quarterly* 5 (1949):72-83.

Slingerland, Dixon. "Acts 18:1-18, The Gallio Inscription, and Absolute Pauline Chronology." *Journal of Biblical Literature* 110 (1991):439-49.

Stambaugh, John E. and David L. Blach. *The New Testament in Its Social Environment.* Philadelphia: Westminster Press, 1986.

Tambasco, Anthony J. *In the Days of Paul: The Social World and Teaching of the Apostle.* Mahwah: Paulist Press, 1991.

Taylor, J. "The Ethnarch of King Aretas at Damascus: A Note on 2 Cor 11:32-33." *Revue Biblique* 99 (1992):719-28.

Theissen, Gerd. *The Social Setting of Pauline Christianity: Essays on Corinth.* Philadelphia: Fortress, 1982.

Thompson, C.L. "Hairstyles and Headcoverings, and St. Paul: Portraits from Roman Corinth." *Biblical Archaeologist* 51 (1988):99-115.

Wiseman, James R. *The Land of the Ancient Corinthians.* Studies in Mediterranean Archaeology, no. 50. Göteborg: Aströms, 1978.

COMMENTARIES

Balthasar, Hans Urs von. *Paul Struggles with His Congregation: The Pastoral Message of the Letters to the Corinthians.* San Francisco: Ignatius Press, 1992.

Barclay, William. *The Letters to the Corinthians.* Philadelphia: Westminster Press, 1975.

Barrett, C.K. *A Commentary on the First Epistle to the Corinthians.* Black's New Testament Commentaries. London: Black, 1971.

————. *A Commentary on the Second Epistle to the Corinthians.* New York: Harper and Row, 1973.

Beasley-Murray, George R. *2 Corinthians.* The Broadman Bible Commentary, no. 11. Nashville: Broadman Press, 1971.

Best, Ernest. *Second Corinthians*. Atlanta: John Knox Press, 1987.

Betz, Hans Dieter. *2 Corinthians 8 and 9*. Hermeneia. Philadelphia: Fortress Press, 1985.

Boyer, James L. *For a World Like Ours: Studies in I Corinthians*. Grand Rapids: Baker Book House, 1971.

Brown, Ernest Faulkner. *The First Epistle of Paul the Apostle to the Corinthians*. London: S.P.C.K., 1923.

Bruce, F.F. *1 and 2 Corinthians*. New Century Bible. Grand Rapids: Wm. B. Eerdmans, 1971.

Bultmann, Rudolf. *The Second Letter to the Corinthians*. Minneapolis: Augsburg Publishing House, 1985.

Chafin, Kenneth L. *1, 2 Corinthians*. Waco: Word Books, 1985.

Clarke, Andrew D. *Secular and Christian Leadership in Corinth: A Socio-Historical and Exegetical Study of 1 Corinthians*. Arbeiten zur Geschichte des antiken Judentums und des Urchristentums, no. 18. Leiden: E.J. Brill, 1993.

Conzelmann, Hans. *1 Corinthians*. Hermeneia. Philadelphia: Fortress Press, 1975.

Craig, C.T. *The First Epistle to the Corinthians*. Interpreter's Bible. New York: Abingdon, 1953.

Danker, Frederick W. *II Corinthians*. Augsburg Commentary on the New Testament. Minneapolis: Augsburg Publishing House, 1989.

Denney, James. *The Second Epistle to the Corinthians*. London: Hodder & Stoughton, 1894.

Dods, Marcus. *The First Epistle to the Corinthians*. 6th ed. London: Hodder and Stoughton, 1900.

Evans, Ernest. *The Epistles of Paul the Apostle to the Corinthians in the Revised Version: With Introduction and Commentary*. The Clarendon Bible. Oxford: Clarendon Press, 1930.

Fallon, F.T. *2 Corinthians*. New Testament Message, no. 11. Wilmington: Glazier, 1980.

Fee, Gordon D. *The First Epistle to the Corinthians*. The New International Commentary on the New Testament. Grand Rapids: Wm B. Eerdmans, 1987.

Fisher, Fred L. *Commentary on 1 & 2 Corinthians*. Waco: Word Books, 1975.

Furnish, Victor Paul. *II Corinthians*. The Anchor Bible, no. 32 A. New York: Doubleday, 1984.

Getty, Mary Ann. *First Corinthians, Second Corinthians*. Collegeville: Liturgical Press, 1983.

Goudge, H.L. *The First Epistle to the Corinthians*. Westminster Commentaries. London: Methuen & Co., 1903.

Gromacki, R.G. *Called To Be Saints. An Exposition of 1 Corinthians.* Grand Rapids: Baker Book House, 1977.

Grosheide, F.W. *Commentary on the First Epistle to the Corinthians.* New International Commentary on the New Testament. Grand Rapids: Wm. B. Eerdmans, 1953.

Hanson, R.P.C. *II Corinthians.* London: SCM Press, 1954.

Hargreaves, John Henry Monsarrat. *A Guide to I Corinthians.* London: SPCK, 1978.

Harris, Murray J. *2 Corinthians.* The Expositor's Bible Commentary. Grand Rapids: Zondervan, 1976.

Harrisville, Roy A. *1 Corinthians.* Minneapolis: Augsburg Publishing House, 1987.

Héring, Jean. *The Second Epistle of Saint Paul to the Corinthians.* Translated by A.W. Heathcote and P.J. Allcock. London: Epworth Press, 1967.

——. *The First Epistle of Saint Paul to the Corinthians.* New York: Hodder & Stoughton, 1974.

Hughes, P.E. *Paul's Second Epistle to the Corinthians.* New International Commentary on the New Testament, no. 47. Grand Rapids: Wm. B. Eerdmans, 1962.

Kent, Homer A. *A Heart Opened Wide: Studies in II Corinthians.* Grand Rapids: Baker Book House, 1982.

Kilgallen, John J. *First Corinthians: An Introduction and Study Guide.* New York: Paulist Press, 1987.

Kruse, Colin. *2 Corinthians.* Tyndale New Testament Commentary. Grand Rapids: Wm. B. Eerdmans, 1987.

Kugelman, R. "The First Letter to the Corinthians." In *The Jerome Biblical Commentary.* Englewood Cliffs: Prentice-Hall, 1968.

Lenski, R.C. *The Interpretation of St. Paul's First and Second Epistle to the Corinthians.* Columbus: Wartburg Press, 1937.

MacArthur, John F. *I Corinthians.* Chicago: Moody Press, 1984.

Mare, W.H. *1 Corinthians.* The Expositor's Bible Commentary. Grand Rapids: Baker Book House, 1976.

Martin, Ralph P. *2 Corinthians.* Word Biblical Commentary, no. 40. Waco: Word Books, 1986.

Menzies, Allan. *The Second Epistle of Paul to the Corinthians.* London: Macmillan, 1912.

Moffat, James. *The First Epistle of Paul to the Corinthians.* Moffat New Testament Commentary. New York: Harper and Brothers, 1938.

Morgan, G. Campbell. *The Corinthian Letters of Paul: An Exposition of I and II Corinthians.* New York: Fleming H. Revell, 1946.

Morris, Leon. *The First Epistle of Paul to the Corinthians*. Tyndale New Testament Commentary. 2d ed. Leicester: InterVarsity Press, 1985.

Murphy-O'Connor, Jerome. *1 Corinthians*. The New Testament Message. Wilmington: Glazier, 1979.

Orr, William F. and James Arthur Walther. *1 Corinthians*. Anchor Bible, no. 32. New York: Doubleday, 1976.

Patterson, Paige. *The Troubled, Triumphant Church: An Exposition of First Corinthians*. Nashville: Nelson, 1983.

Plummer, Alfred. *A Critical and Exegetical Commentary on the Second Edition of Paul to the Corinthians*. International Critical Commentary, no. 47. Edinburgh: T & T Clark, 1915.

Prior, David. *The Message of 1 Corinthians*. The Bible Speaks Today. Downers Grove: InterVarsity Press, 1985.

Robertson, Edwin H. *Corinthians 1 and 2*. J.B. Phillips' New Testament Commentaries. New York: Macmillan, 1973.

Robinson, William Gordon. *The Gospel and the Church in a Pagan World: A Study in I Corinthians*. London: Independent Press, 1958.

Ruef, John Samuel. *Paul's First Letter to Corinth*. Westminster Pelican Commentaries. Philadelphia: Penguin Books, 1971.

Schelkle, Karl H. *The Second Epistle to the Corinthians*. Translated by K. Smyth. New York: Crossroad, 1981.

Simon, William Glyn Hughes. *The First Epistle to the Corinthians: Introduction and Commentary*. London: SCM Press, 1959.

Snyder, Graydon F. *First Corinthians: A Faith Community Commentary*. Macon: Mercer University Press, 1992.

Strachan, Robert Harvey. *The Second Epistle of Paul to the Corinthians*. Moffat New Testament Commentary, no. 7. New York: Harper and Brothers, 1935.

Talbert, Charles H. *Reading Corinthians: A Literary and Theological Commentary on 1 and 2 Corinthians*. New York: Crossroad, 1989.

Tasker, R.V.G. *The Second Epistle to the Corinthians*. Tyndale New Testament Commentaries, no. 8. Grand Rapids: Wm. B. Eerdmans, 1958.

Thrall, M.E. *The First and Second Letter of Paul to the Corinthians*. The Cambridge Bible Commentary, no. 1965. Cambridge: Cambridge University Press, 1965.

Walter, Eugen. *The First Epistle to the Corinthians*. London: Sheed & Ward, 1971.

Wcela, Emil A. *Paul the Pastor: His Teaching in the First Letter to the Corinthians*. New York: Pueblo Publishing, 1976.

BOOKS AND ARTICLES ON 1 AND 2 CORINTHIANS

Allison, R.W. "Let the Women Be Silent in the Church (1 Cor 14.33b-36): What Did Paul Really Say and What Did It Mean?" *Journal for the Study of the New Testament* 32 (1988):32-34.

Baird, William R. "Letters of Recommendation: A Study of 2 Cor 3:1-3." *Journal of Biblical Literature* 87 (1961):27-41.

Balch, David L. "Backgrounds of 1 Cor VII: Sayings of the Lord in Q; Moses as an Ascetic *theios aner* in II Cor III." *New Testament Studies* 18 (1972):351-64.

Barré, Michael L. "Paul as an 'Eschatologic Person': A New Look at 2 Cor 11:29." *Catholic Biblical Quarterly* 37 (1975):500-26.

———. "To Marry or To Burn: *Pyrousthai* in 1 Cor 7:9." *Catholic Biblical Quarterly* 36 (1974):193-202.

Barrett, C.K. "Paul's Opponents in II Corinthians." *New Testament Studies* 17 (1971):233-54.

Bartchy, S.S. *MALLON CHRESAI: First Century Slavery and the Interpretation of 1 Corinthians 7:21.* Society of Biblical Literature Dissertation Series, no. 11. Missoula: Scholars Press, 1973.

Bates, W.H. "The Integrity of II Corinthians." *New Testament Studies* 12 (1965):56-59.

Batey, Richard. "Paul's Interaction with the Corinthians." *Journal of Biblical Literature* 84 (1965):139-46.

Belleville, Linda. *Reflections of Glory: Paul's Polemical Use of the Moses-Doxa Tradition in 2 Corinthians 3:1-18.* Journal for the Study of the New Testament Supplement Series, no. 52. Sheffield: Sheffield Academic Press, 1991.

Betz, Hans Dieter. "2 Cor 6:14–7:1: An Anti-Pauline Fragment?" *Journal of Biblical Literature* 92 (1973):88-108.

Bornkamm, Günther. "The History of the Origin of the So-called Second Letter to the Corinthians." *New Testament Studies* 8 (1962): 258-64.

Bryden, W.W. *The Spirit of Jesus in St. Paul: A Study in the Soul of St. Paul Based upon the Corinthian Letters.* London: Clarke, 1925.

Buck, Charles H., Jr. "The Collection for the Saints." *Harvard Theological Review* 43 (1950):1-29.

Campbell, R. Alastair. "Does Paul Acquiesce in Divisions at the Lord's Supper?" *Novum Testamentum* 33, 1 (1991):61-70.

Carson, D.A. *From Triumphalism to Maturity: An Exposition of 2 Corinthians 10–13.* Grand Rapids: Baker Book House, 1984.

———. *Showing the Spirit: A Theological Exposition of 1 Corinthians 12–14.* Grand Rapids: Baker Book House, 1987.

Chenderlin, Fritz. *"Do this as my memorial": The Sematic and Conceptual Background and Value of 'Anamnesis' in 1 Corinthians.* Analecta Biblica, no. 99. Rome: Biblical Institute Press, 1982.

Craddock, Fred B. "The Poverty of Christ. An Investigation of II Corinthians 8:9." *Interpretation* 22 (1968):158-70.

Crafton, Jeffrey A. *The Agency of the Apostle: A Dramatistic Analysis of Paul's Responses to Conflict in 2 Corinthians.* Journal for the Study of the New Testament Supplement Series, no. 51. Sheffield: Sheffield Academic Press, 1991.

Dahl, M.E. *The Resurrection of the Body. A Study of 1 Corinthians 15.* Studies in Biblical Theology. London: SCM Press, 1962.

Dahl, Nils. "Paul and the Church at Corinth according to I Corinthians 1–4." In *Christian History and Interpretation*, pp. 313-15. Edited by W.R. Farmer. Cambridge: Cambridge University Press, 1967.

Danker, Frederick W. "Consolation in 2 Cor 5:1-10." *Concordia Theological Monthly* 39 (1968):552-56.

Davis, James A. *Wisdom and the Spirit: An Investigation of 1 Corinthians 1.18–3.20 Against the Background of Jewish Sapiential Traditions in the Greco-Roman Period.* Lanham: University Press of America, 1985.

De Boer, M. *The Defeat of Death: Apocalpytic Eschatology in 1 Corinthians 15 and Romans 5.* Journal for the Study of the New Testament, no. 22. Sheffield: Sheffield Academic Press, 1988.

Derret, J. Duncan M. "2 Cor 6,14ff a Midrash on Dt 22,10." *Biblica* 59 (1978):231-50.

Duff, Paul B. "Metaphor, Motif, and Meaning." *The Catholic Biblical Quarterly* 53, 1 (1991).

Dunn, James D.G. "2 Corinthians III.17 — 'The Lord Is the Spirit.'" *Journal of Theological Studies* 21 (1970):309-20.

Ellis, E. Earle. "II Cor v.1-10 in Pauline Eschatology." *New Testament Studies* 6 (1960):211-24.

———. "Traditions in 1 Corinthians." *New Testament Studies* 32 (1986): 481-502.

Engberg-Pedersen, T. "1 Corinthians 11:16 and the Character of Pauline Exhortation." *Journal of Biblical Literature* 110 (1991): 679-89.

Fahy, Thomas. "St. Paul's 'Boasting' and 'Weakness.'" *Irish Theological Quarterly* 17 (1964):214-27.

Fee, Gordon D. "CHARIS in II Corinthians 1.15: Apostolic Parousia and Paul — Corinth Chronology." *New Testament Studies* 24 (1978):533-38.

Fitzmyer, Joseph A. "Another Look at KEPHALE in 1 Corinthians 11.3." *New Testament Studies* 35 (1989):503-11.

——. "Glory Reflected on the Face of Christ (2 Cor 3:7–4:6) and a Palestinian Jewish Motif." *Theological Studies* 42 (1981):630-44.

Garrison, Roman. "Paul's Use of the Athlete Metaphor in 1 Corinthians 9." *Studies in Religion* 22, 2 (1993):209-17.

Georgi, Dieter. *The Opponents of Paul in Second Corinthians.* Philadelphia: Fortress Press, 1986.

Gettys, Joseph Miller. *How To Study 1 Corinthians.* Richmond: John Knox Press, 1968.

Gill, D. "The Importance of Roman Portraiture for Head-Coverings in 1 Corinthians 11:2-16." *Tyndale Bulletin* 41 (1990):245-60.

Glen, John Stanley. *Pastoral Problems in First Corinthians.* Philadelphia: Westminster Press, 1964.

Goldingay, John. *The Church and the Gifts of the Spirit: A Practical Exposition of 1 Corinthians 12–14.* Bramcote: Grove Books, 1972.

Greenwood, David. "The Lord Is the Spirit: Some Considerations of 2 Cor 3:17." *Catholic Biblical Quarterly* 34 (1972):467-72.

Grudem, Wayne A. *The Gift of Prophecy in 1 Corinthians.* Washington: University Press of America, 1982.

Hafemann, Scott J. *Suffering and Ministry in the Spirit: Paul's Defense of His Ministry in II Corinthians 2:14–3:3.* Grand Rapids: Wm. B. Eerdmans, 1990.

Hanson, A.T. "The Midrash in II Corinthians 3: A Reconsideration." *Journal for the Study of the New Testament* 9 (1980):2-28.

Harris, Murray J. "Paul's View of Death in 2 Corinthians 5:1-10." In *New Dimensions in New Testament Study*, pp. 317-28. Edited by M.C. Tenney and R.N. Longenecker. Grand Rapids: Zondervan, 1974.

Hemer, Colin J. "A Note on 2 Corinthians 1:9." *Tyndale Bulletin* 23 (1972): 103-07.

Hickling, Colin J.A. "The Sequence of Thought in II Corinthians, Chapter Three." *New Testament Studies* 21 (1975):380-95.

Hisey, Alan. "Paul's 'Thorn in the Flesh': A Paragnosis." *Journal of Bible and Religion* 29 (1961):125-29.

Hooker, Morna D. "Authority on Her Head: An Examination of 1 Cor XI.10." *New Testament Studies* 10 (1964):410-20.

Horsley, R.A. "'How can some of you say there is no resurrection of the dead?' Spiritual Elitism in Corinth." *Novum Testamentum* 20 (1978):203-31.

——. "The Background of the Confessional Formula in 1 Cor 8:6." *Zeitschrift für die Neutestamentiche Wissenschaft* 69 (1978):130-35.

——. "Consciousness and Freedom Among the Corinthians: 1 Corinthians 8–10." *Catholic Biblical Quarterly* 40 (1978):203-31.

——. "Gnosis in Corinth: 1 Corinthians 8:1-6." *New Testament Studies* 27 (1980):32-51.

——. "Pneumatikos vs. Psychikos: Distinctions of Spiritual Status Among the Corinthians." *Harvard Theological Review* 69 (1976): 269-88.

——. "Spiritual Marriage with Sophia." *Vigilae Christianae* 33 (1979): 30-54.

——. "Wisdom of Word and Words of Wisdom in Corinth." *Catholic Biblical Quarterly* 39 (1977):224-39.

House, Wayne. "Should a Woman Prophesy or Preach before Men?" *Bibliotheca Sacra* 145 (1988):141-61.

Hurd, John Coolidge, Jr. *The Origin of 1 Corinthians*. Macon: Mercer University Press, 1983.

Jervis, L. Ann. "'But I Want You to Know...' Paul's Midrashic Intertextual Response to the Corinthian Worshippers (1 Cor 11:2-16)." *Journal of Biblical Literature* 112 (1993):231-46.

Jewett, Robert. "The Redaction of I Corinthians and the Trajectory of the Pauline School." *Journal of the American Academy of Religion Supplements* 44 (1978):389-444.

Kee, Doyle. "Who Were the 'Super-Apostles' of 2 Corinthians 10–13?" *Restoration Quarterly* 23 (1980):65-76.

Kijne, J.J. "We, Us, and Our in I and II Corinthians." *Novum Testamentum* 8 (1966):171-79.

Kuck, David W. *Judgment and Community Conflict: Paul's Use of Apocalyptic Judgment Language in 1 Corinthians 3:5–4:5*. Leiden: E.J. Brill, 1992.

Lambrecht, Jan. "The Fragment 2 Cor vi 14–vii 1. A Plea for Its Authenticity." In *Miscellanea Neotestamentica*, pp. 143-61. Edited by T. Baarda. Leiden: E.J. Brill, 1978.

Lampe, Geoffrey W.H. "Church Discipline and the Interpretation of the Epistles to the Corinthians." In *Christian History and Interpretation*, pp. 337-61. Edited by W. Farmer. Cambridge: Cambridge University Press, 1967.

Lampe, Peter. "Theological Wisdom and the 'Word About the Cross': The Rhetorical Scheme in 1 Corinthians 1–4." *Interpretation* 44, 2 (April 1990):117-31.

Lewis, Jack P., ed. *Interpreting 2 Corinthians 5.14-21: An Exercise in Hermeneutics*. Studies in Bible and Early Christianity, no. 17. New York: Edwin Mellen Press, 1989.

Lincoln, Andrew T. "'Paul the Visionary': The Setting and Significance of the Rapture to Paradise in II Corinthians XII.1-10." *New Testament Studies* 25 (1979):204-20.

Madros, Pierre. *The Pride and Humility of Saint Paul in His Second Letter to the Corinthians.* Jerusalem: Franciscan Printing Press, 1981.

Marshall, Peter. *Enmity in Corinth: Social Conventions in Paul's Relations with the Corinthians.* Wissenschaftliche Untersuchungen zum Neuen Testament, no. 23. Tübingen: J.C.B. Mohr (Paul Siebeck), 1987.

Martin, Ralph P. *The Spirit and the Congregation: Studies in 1 Corinthians 12–15.* Grand Rapids: Wm. B. Eerdmans, 1984.

Mealand, David L. "'As having nothing yet possessing everything.' 2 Cor 6:10c." *Zeitschrift für die Neutestamentliche Wissenschaft* 67 (1976):277-79.

Menoud, Philippe H. "The Thorn in the Flesh and Satan's Angel (2 Cor 12:7)." In *Jesus Christ and the Faith: A Collection of Studies*, pp. 19-30. Pittsburgh: Pickwick, 1978.

Milligan, William. *The Resurrection of the Dead: An Exposition of I Corinthians XV.* Edinburgh: Clark, 1895.

Minear, Paul S. "Some Pauline Thoughts on Dying: A Study of 2 Corinthians." In *From Faith to Faith*, pp. 91-106. Edited by D.Y. Hadidian. Pittsburgh: Pickwick, 1979.

Minn, Herbert R. *The Thorn That Remained: Materials for the Study of St. Paul's Thorn in the Flesh: 2 Corinthians XII. vv. 7-9.* Auckland: G.W. Moore, 1972.

Mitchell, Margaret Mary. *Paul and the Rhetoric of Reconciliation: An Exegetical Investigation of the Language and Composition of 1 Corinthians.* Tübingen: J.C.B. Mohr, 1991.

Morgan-Wynne, John E. "2 Corinthians VIII.18f. and the Question of *Traditionsgrundlage* for Acts." *Journal of Theological Studies* 30 (1979):172-73.

Morton, Andrew Queen. *A Critical Concordance to I and II Corinthians.* Wooster: Biblical Research Association, 1979.

Moule, C.F.D. "2 Cor 3, 18b." In *Neues Testamentliche und Geschichte*, pp. 231-38. Edited by H. Baltensweiler and B. Reicke. Zürich: Theologischer Verlag, 1972.

Mullins, Terence Y. "Paul's Thorn in the Flesh." *Journal of Biblical Literature* 76 (1957):299-303.

Murphy-O'Connor, Jerome. "'Baptized for the Dead' (I Cor XV,29). A Corinthian Slogan?" *Revue Biblique* 88 (1981):532-43.

———. "1 Corinthians 11:2-16 Once Again." *Catholic Biblical Quarterly* 50 (1988):265-74.

———. "I Cor VIII,6: Cosmology or Soteriology?" *Revue Biblique* 85 (1978):253-67.

———. "Corinthian Slogans in 1 Cor 6:12-20." *Catholic Biblical Quarterly* 40 (1978):391-96.

———. "I Corinthians V.3-5." *Revue Biblique* 84 (1977):239-45.

———. "The Divorced Woman in 1 Cor 7:10-11." *Journal of Biblical Literature* 100 (1981):601-06.

———. "Eucharist and Community in First Corinthians." *Worship* 51 (1977):56-69.

———. "Food and Spiritual Gifts in 1 Cor 8:8." *Catholic Biblical Quarterly* 41 (1979):292-98.

———. "Freedom or the Ghetto (1 Cor. VIII,1-13; X,23–XI,1)." *Revue Biblique* 85 (1978):543-74.

———. "Interpolations in 1 Corinthians." *Catholic Biblical Quarterly* 48 (1986):81-84.

———. "The Non-Pauline Character of 1 Corinthians 11:2-16?" *Journal of Biblical Literature* 95 (1976):615-21.

———. "Sex and Logic in 1 Corinthians 11:2-16." *Catholic Biblical Quarterly* 42 (1980):482-500.

———. *The Theology of the Second Letter to the Corinthians*. Cambridge: Cambridge University Press, 1991.

———. "Tradition and Redaction in 1 Cor 15:3-7." *Catholic Biblical Quarterly* 43 (1981):582-89.

———. "Works Without Faith in I Cor VII,14." *Revue Biblique* 84 (1977): 349-61.

Nickle, Keith Fullerton. *The Collection: A Study in Paul's Strategy*. Studies in Biblical Theology. London: SCM Press, 1966.

Nisbet, Patricia. "The Thorn in the Flesh." *Expository Times* 80 (1969):126.

Noack, Bent. "A Note on 2 Cor 4:15." *Studia Theologica* 17 (1963): 129-32.

O'Collins, Gerald G. "Power Made Perfect in Weakness: 2 Cor 12: 9-10." *Catholic Biblical Quarterly* 33 (1971):528-37.

O'Day, Gail R. "Jeremiah 9:22-23 and 1 Corinthians 1:26-31: A Study in Intertextuality." *Journal of Biblical Literature* 109 (1990):259-67.

Oostendorp, Derk William. *Another Jesus: A Gospel of Jewish-Christian Superiority in II Corinthians*. Kampen: Kok, 1976.

Paige, Terence. "1 Corinthians 12.2: A Pagan *Pompe*?" *Journal for the Study of the New Testament* 44, 1 (December 1991):57-65.

Park, David M. "Paul's *skolops te sarki*: Thorn or Stake? (2 Cor xii:7)." *Novum Testamentum* 22 (1980):179-83.

Pearson, B.A. *The Pneumatikos-Psychikos Terminology in 1 Corinthians: A Study in the Theology of the Corinthian Opponents of Paul and Its Relation to Gnosticism.* Society of Biblical Literature Dissertation Series. Missoula: Scholars Press, 1973.

Pherigo, Lindsey P. "Paul and the Corinthian Church." *Journal of Biblical Literature* 68 (1949):341-50.

Pogoloff, Stephen M. *Logos and Sophia: The Rhetorical Situation of 1 Corinthians.* Atlanta: Scholars Press, 1992.

Price, Robert M. "Punished in Paradise (An Exegetical Theory on II Corinthians 12:1-10)." *Journal for the Study of the New Testament* 7 (1980):33-40.

Provence, Thomas E. "'Who Is Sufficient for These Things?' An Exegesis of 2 Corinthians ii:15–iii:18." *Novum Testamentum* 24 (1982): 54-81.

Richard, Earl. "Polemics, Old Testament, and Theology. A Study of II Cor III:1–IV:6." *Revue Biblique* 88 (1981):340-67.

Schmithals, W. *Gnosticism in Corinth: An Investigation of the Letters to the Corinthians.* New York: Abingdon, 1971.

Schneider, Bernardin. "HE KOINONIA TOU HAGIOU PNEU-MATOS (II Cor 13, 13)." In *Studies Honouring Ignatius Charles Brady, Friar Minor*, pp. 421-47. Edited by R.S. Almagno and C.L. Harkins. St. Bonaventure: Franciscan Institute Publications, 1976.

Schüssler-Fiorenza, Elisabeth. "Rhetorical Situation and Historical Reconstruction in 1 Corinthians." *New Testament Studies* 33 (1987):386-403.

Scroggs, Robin. "Paul and the Eschatological Woman." *Journal of the American Academy of Religion* 40 (1972):298.

Sevenster, Jan N. "Some Remarks on the *gumnos* of 2 Cor 5:3." In *Studia Paulina*. Haarlem: Bohn, 1953.

Smedes, Lewis B. *Love Within Limits: A Realist's View of 1 Corinthians 13.* Grand Rapids: Wm. B. Eerdmans, 1978.

Spencer, Aida Besançon. *Paul's Literary Style: A Stylistic and Historical Comparison of II Corinthians 11:16–12:13.* Jackson: Evangelical Theological Society, 1986.

———. "The Wise Fool (and the Foolish Wise): A Study of Irony in Paul." *Novum Testamentum* 23 (1981):349-60.

Spittler, Russell P. "The Limits of Ecstasy: An Exegesis of 2 Corinthians 12:1-10." In *Current Issues in Biblical and Patristic Interpretation*, pp. 259-66. Edited by G.F. Hawthorne. Grand Rapids: Wm. B. Eerdmans, 1975.

Stephenson, Alan M.G. "A Defence of the Integrity of 2 Corinthians."
    In *The Authorship and Integrity of the New Testament*, pp. 82-97.
    London: S.P.C.K., 1965.
——. "Partition Theories on II Corinthians." In *Studia Evangelica: The
    New Testament Scriptures*, pp. 639-46. Edited by F.L. Cross.
    Berlin: Akademie-Verlag, 1964.
Sumney, J.L. *Identifying Paul's Opponents: The Question of Method in
    2 Corinthians*. Journal for the Study of the New Testament Supple-
    ment Series, no. 40. Sheffield: Sheffield Academic Press, 1990.
Taylor, N.H. "The Composition and Chronology of Second Corinthi-
    ans." *Journal for the Study of the New Testament* 44, 1 (December
    1991):67-87.
Thiselton, Anthony C. "Realized Eschatology at Corinth." *New Testa-
    ment Studies* 24 (1978):510-26.
Thrall, M.E. "The Problem of II Cor. vi.15–vii.1 in Some Recent Dis-
    cussion." *New Testament Studies* 24 (1977):132-48.
——. "Super-Apostles, Servants of Christ, and Servants of Satan." *Jour-
    nal for the Study of the New Testament* 6 (1980):42-57.
Travis, Stephen H. "Paul's Boasting in 2 Corinthians 10–12." In *Studia
    Evangelica*, vol. 112, pp. 527-32. Edited by E.A. Livingstone.
    Berlin: Akademie-Verlag, 1973.
Trompf, G. "On Attitudes Toward Women in Paul and Paulinist Litera-
    ture: 1 Corinthians 11:3-16 and Its Context." *Catholic Biblical
    Quarterly* 42 (1980):196-215.
Unnik, Willem C. van. "'With Unveiled Face,' an Exegesis of 2 Co-
    rinthians iii 12-18." *Novum Testamentum* 6 (1964):153-69.
Wagner, Guy. "The Tabernacle and Life 'in Christ,' Exegesis of 2
    Corinthians 4:1-10." *Irish Biblical Studies* 3 (1981):145-65.
Walker, W.O. "1 Corinthians 11:2-16 and Paul's View Regarding
    Women." *Journal of Biblical Literature* 94 (1975):94-110.
Webb, William J. *Returning Home: New Covenant and Second Exodus
    as the Context for 2 Corinthians 6.14–7.1*. Journal for the Study of
    the New Testament Supplement Series, no. 85. Sheffield: Sheffield
    Academic Press, 1993.
Williamson, Jr. "Led in Triumph. Paul's Use of *Thriambeuo*." *Interpre-
    tation* 22 (1968):317-32.
Willis, Wendell Lee. *Idol Meat in Corinth. The Pauline Argument in 1
    Corinthians 8 and 10*. Society for Biblical Literature Dissertation
    Series, no. 68. Chico: Scholars Press, 1985.
Wilson, R.M. "How Gnostic Were the Corinthians?" *New Testament
    Studies* 19 (1973):65-74.

Wimbush, Vincent L. *Paul, the Worldly Ascetic: Response to the World and Self-Understanding According to 1 Corinthians 7.* Macon: Mercer University Press, 1987.

Wire, Antoinette Clark. *The Corinthian Women Prophets: A Reconstruction through Paul's Rhetoric.* Minneapolis: Fortress Press, 1990.

Young, Frances Margaret. *Meaning and Truth in 2 Corinthians.* Grand Rapids: Wm. B. Eerdmans, 1987.

Zodhiates, Spiros. *Conquering the Fear of Death: An Exposition of I Corinthians 15, Based Upon the Original Greek Text.* Grand Rapids: Wm. B. Eerdmans, 1970.

LETTER STRUCTURE

Aune, David Edward. *The New Testament in Its Literary Environment.* Philadelphia: Westminster Press, 1987.

Deismann, Adolf. *Paul — A Study in Social and Religious History.* New York: Harper and Brothers, 1957.

Mullins, Terence Y. "Benediction as a NT Form." *Andrews University Seminary Studies* 15 (1977):59-64.

——. "Disclosure: A Literary Form in the New Testament." *Novum Testamentum* 7 (1964):44-50.

——. "Formulas in New Testament Epistles." *Journal of Biblical Literature* 91 (1972):380-90.

——. "Greeting as a New Testament Form." *Journal of Biblical Literature* 87 (1968):418-26.

——. "Petition as a Literary Form." *Novum Testamentum* 5 (1962): 46-54.

O'Brien, Peter T. *Introductory Thanksgivings in the Letters of Paul.* Novum Testamentum Supplements, no. 49. Leiden: E.J. Brill, 1977.

Roetzel, Calvin J. *The Letters of Paul: Conversations in Context.* 3d. ed. Louisville: Westminster/John Knox Press, 1990.

Sanders, Jack T. "The Transition from Opening Epistolary Thanksgiving to Body in the Letters of the Pauline Corpus." *Journal of Biblical Literature* 81 (1962):348-62.

Schubert, Paul. *Form and Function in Pauline Thanksgivings.* Beihefte zur Zeischrfit für die neutestamentliche Wissenschaft, no. 20. Berlin: Töpelmann, 1939.

Thrall, M.E. "A Second Thanksgiving Period in II Corinthians." *Journal for the Study of the New Testament* 16 (1982):101-24.

White, John L. *The Body of the Greek Letter.* Society of Biblical Literature Dissertation Series, no. 2. Missoula: Scholars Press, 1972.

Wiles, Gordon P. *Paul's Intercessory Prayers.* Society for New Testament Studies Monograph Series, no. 24. Cambridge: Cambridge University Press, 1974.

PAULINE THEOLOGY

Banks, Robert. *Paul's Idea of Community.* Grand Rapids: Wm. B. Eerdmans, 1980.

Beker, J. Christiaan. *Paul the Apostle.* Philadelphia: Fortress Press, 1980.

———. "Paul the Theologian." *Interpretation* 43 (1989):352-65.

Bowers, Paul. "Church and Mission in Paul." *Journal for the Study of the New Testament* 44, 1 (December 1991):89-111.

Doohan, Helen. *Paul's Vision of Church.* Good News Studies, no. 32. Wilmington: Michael Glazier, 1989.

Ellis, E. Earle. *Pauline Theology: Ministry and Society.* Grand Rapids: Wm. B. Eerdmans, 1989.

———. "Soma in First Corinthians." *Interpretation* 44, 2 (April 1990): 132-44.

Fitzmyer, Joseph A. *Paul and His Theology: A Brief Sketch.* 2d. ed. Englewood Cliffs: Prentice-Hall, 1989.

Furnish, Victor Paul. "Belonging to Christ: A Paradigm for Ethics in First Corinthians." *Interpretation* 44, 2 (April 1990):145-57.

———. *The Moral Teaching of Paul.* New York: Abingdon, 1979.

———. *Theology and Ethics in Paul.* New York: Abingdon, 1968.

Gaston, Lloyd. *Paul and Torah.* Vancouver: UBC Press, 1987.

Gundry, Robert H. *SOMA in Biblical Theology with Emphasis on Pauline Anthropology.* Society for New Testament Studies Monograph Series, no. 29. Cambridge: Cambridge University Press, 1976.

Hanson, A.T. *Studies in Paul's Technique and Theology.* Grand Rapids: Wm. B. Eerdmans, 1974.

Hooker, Morna D. *Pauline Pieces.* London: Epworth Press, 1979.

———. and S.G. Wilson. *Paul and Paulinism.* London: SPCK, 1982.

Hunter, A.M. *The Gospel According to St. Paul.* London: SCM Press, 1966.

Jewett, Robert. *Paul's Anthropological Terms: A Study of Their Use in Conflict Settings*. Leiden: E.J. Brill, 1979.

Käsemann, Ernst. *Perspectives on Paul*. Philadelphia: Fortress Press, 1969.

Kim, S. *The Origin of Paul's Gospel*. Grand Rapids: Wm. B. Eerdmans, 1981.

Longenecker, Richard N. *New Testament Social Ethics for Today*. Grand Rapids: Wm. B. Eerdmans, 1984.

———. *Paul, Apostle of Liberty*. Grand Rapids: Baker, 1971.

Maccoby, Hyam. "Paul and the Eucharist." *New Testament Studies* 37, 2 (1991):247-67.

MacDonald, Margaret. *The Pauline Churches: A Socio-Historical Study of Institutionalization in the Pauline and Deutero-Pauline Writings*. Society for New Testament Studies Monograph Series. Cambridge: Cambridge University Press, 1988.

Martin, Ralph P. *Reconciliation: A Study in Paul's Theology*. Atlanta: John Knox Press, 1981.

Proudfoot, C. Merrill. "Imitation or Realistic Participation? A Study of Paul's Concept of 'Suffering ʷ .ih Christ.'" *Interpretation* 17 (1963): 140-60.

Richardson, Peter. *Paul's Ethic of Freedom*. Philadelphia: Westminster Press, 1979.

Ridderbos, Herman. *Paul: An Outline of His Theology*. Grand Rapids: Wm. B. Eerdmans, 1975.

Robinson, John A.T. *The Body. A Study in Pauline Theology*. Studies in Biblical Theology, no. 5. Naperville: Allenson, 1952.

Scroggs, Robin. *Paul for a New Day*. Philadelphia: Fortress Press, 1977.

Sloan, Robert B. "Paul and the Law: Why the Law Cannot Save." *Novum Testamentum* 33, 1 (1991):35-60.

Stanley, D.M. *Boasting in the Lord*. New York: Paulist Press, 1973.

Westerholm, Stephen. *Israel's Law and the Church's Faith: Paul and His Recent Interpreters*. Grand Rapids: Wm. B. Eerdmans, 1988.

Whiteley, D.E.H. *The Theology of St. Paul*. Oxford: Basil Blackwell, 1964.

SUBJECT INDEX